Instructor's Manual

to accompany

Statistical Techniques in Business and Economics

Tenth Edition

Robert D. Mason
late of The University of Toledo

Douglas A. Lind
The University of Toledo

William G. Marchal
The University of Toledo

Prepared by
Denise Heban

Irwin McGraw-Hill

Boston   Burr Ridge, IL   Dubuque, IA   Madison, WI   New York   San Francisco   St. Louis
Bangkok   Bogotá   Caracas   Lisbon   London   Madrid
Mexico City   Milan   New Delhi   Seoul   Singapore   Sydney   Taipei   Toronto

Irwin/McGraw-Hill

A Division of The McGraw·Hill Companies

Instructor's Manual to accompany
STATISTICAL TECHNIQUES IN BUSINESS AND ECONOMICS

3 4 5 6 7 8 9 0 BKM/BKM 9 3 2 1 0 9

ISBN 0-07-303929-2

http://www.mhhe.com

TABLE OF CONTENTS

Statistical Techniques for Business and Economics is designed to provide a sound coverage of the basic techniques of statistics whether the text is used on the quarter of semester system. Beginning with Chapter 16, the chapters are independent of each other, so instructors may chooses not to cover various chapters or topics without concern for the loss of continuity.

In fact, some chapters such as 10 and 11 could be omitted and other chapters— say chapter 16 on quality control could be substituted.

Instructors are urged to require the use of at least one of the many statistical software systems available. The authors have used MINITAB for many years. Solutions too many examples in the text are provided using MINITAB. In recent years, Excel, provided by the Microsoft Corporation, has become popular. It has available many of the statistical tools. Examples using the Excel system are also provided in the text. Computer example are given in most chapters, but Chapter 4 (Measures of Dispersion), Chapter 11 (Analysis of Variance), and Chapter 13 (Multiple Regression) are particularly applicable.

I. A ONE-SEMESTER COURSE

A. The following outline is suggested for a one-semester course with three one-hour meetings per week for 15 weeks. Four examinations are given during the semester.

Chapter	Topic	Meetings	
1	Introduction	1	
2	Summarizing Data	3	
3	Central Tendency	4	(omit geometric mean)
4	Dispersion	4	
	EXAM	1	
5	Probability	4	
6	Probability Distributions	3	(omit hypergeometric)
7	Normal Distribution	2	
	EXAM	1	
8	Sampling Methods	4	
9	Large Sample Tests	3	(omit Type II error)
10	Small Sample Tests	3	
	EXAM	1	
12	Regression and Correlation	5	
14	Chi-Square tests	3	
	EXAM	1	
	TOTAL	45	

B. The following outline is suggested for a one-semester course with four one-hour meetings per week for 15 weeks. Five examinations are given during the semester.

Chapter	Topic	Meetings	
1	Introduction	1	
2	Summarizing Data	3	
3	Central Tendency	4	(omit geometric mean)
4	Dispersion	4	
	EXAM	1	
5	Probability	4	
6	Probability Distributions	3	(omit hypergeometric)
7	Normal Distribution	3	
	EXAM	1	
8	Sampling Methods	4	
9	Large Sample Tests	4	(omit Type II error)
10	Small Sample Tests	3	
	EXAM	1	
11	ANOVA	3	(omit two-way)
12	Regression and Correlation	5	
13	Multiple Regression	2	
	EXAM	1	
14	Chi-Square tests	3	
15	Nonparametric Tests	3	(omit Kruskal-Wallis)
16 or 19	QC or Decision Making	2	
17	Index Numbers	1	
18	Time Series and Forecasting	3	
	EXAM	1	
	TOTAL	60	

II. A TWO-SEMESTER COURSE

The following outline is suggested for a two-semester course that meets 3 times a week for 30 weeks. A total of six examinations are given during the period.

Chapter	Topic	Meetings
1	Introduction	1
2	Summarizing Data	3
3	Central Tendency	5
4	Dispersion	5
	EXAM	1
5	Probability	4
6	Probability Distributions	4
7	Normal Distribution	4
	EXAM	1
8	Sampling Methods	4
9	Large Sample Tests	5
10	Small Sample Tests	3
	EXAM	1
11	ANOVA	6
12	Regression and Correlation	6
13	Multiple Regression	5
	EXAM	1
14	Chi-Square tests	4
15	Nonparametric Tests	5
16	Quality Control	4
	EXAM	1
17	Index Numbers	2
18	Time Series and Forecasting	5
19	Decision Making	4
	Catch-up	1
	EXAM	1
	TOTAL	90

PART II

1. a. Interval
    b. Ratio
    c. Interval
    d. Nominal
    e. Ordinal
    f. Ratio

2. a. Ratio
    b. Nominal
    c. Ratio
    d. Ratio

3. Answers will vary

4. a. Sample
    b. Population
    c. Population
    d. Sample

5. Qualitative data is not numerical, whereas quantitative data is numerical. Examples will vary by student.

6. A population is the entire group, which you are studying. A sample is a subset taken from a population.

7. Nominal, ordinal, interval, and ratio. Examples will vary.

8. Categories are mutually exclusive if an object is included in only one class.

9. A categorization is exhaustive if every object appears in some category.

10. Answers will vary

11. Based on these sample findings, we can infer that 270/300 or 90 percent of the executives would move.

12. An overwhelming number of consumers tested (400/500, or 80%) believe this toothpaste is excellent. Based on these findings, we can expect a similar proportion of all consumers to feel the same way.

13. Discrete variables can assume only certain values, but continuous variable can assume any values within some range. Examples will vary.

14. Consumer satisfaction in the economy in June 1997 (50.6) fell below the lowest level recorded since 1988.

15.   a.   Township is qualitative variable, the others are quantitative.

       b.   Township is nominal level variable, the others are ratio level variables.

16.   a.   Team is a qualitative variable, the others are quantitative.

       b.   Team is a nominal level variable, the others are ratio level variables.

17.   a.   The name of the magazine is a qualitative variable, the others are quantitative.

       b.   The name of the magazine is a nominal level variable, the others are ratio level variables.

18.   a.   The name of the school district is a qualitative variable, the others are quantitative.

       b.   The name of the school district is a nominal level variable, the others are ratio level variables.

CHAPTER 2
DESCRIBING DATA: FREQUENCY DISTRIBUTIONS AND GRAPHIC PRESENTATION

1. $2^5 = 32, 2^6 = 64$ therefore 6 classes

2. $\dfrac{\$29 - \$0}{1 + 3.322(\log 45)} = 4.47$ suggest interval of 5

3. $\dfrac{\$567 - \$235}{1 + 3.322(\log 230)} = \dfrac{\$332}{8.846} = \$37.53$ suggests an interval of 40

4.   a. $\dfrac{129 - 42}{1 + 3.322(\log 53)} = 12.9$ suggests an interval of 15 starting at 40.

     b. $2^6 = 64$

5.   a.   Using the formula $2^k \geq n$, we suggest 4 classes (although a minimum of 5 classes is usually preferred.)
     b.   Using formula 2-1, the suggested class interval would be 1.5, found by $(31 - 25)4$. For ease of computations 2.0 would be better.
     c.   24
     d.

	f	Relative frequency
24 up to 26	2	0.125
26 up to 28	8	0.500
28 up to 30	4	0.250
30 up to 32	2	0.125
Total	16	1.000

     e.   The largest concentration of scores is in the 26 up to 28 class (8).

6.   a.   Using the formula $2^k \geq n$, would result in 5 classes.
     b.   Using formula 2-1, the suggested class interval would be 9.40, found by $(98 - 51)5$. A class interval of 10 would be better.
     c.   50
     d.

	f	Relative frequency
50 up to 60	4	0.20
60 up to 70	5	0.25
70 up to 80	6	0.30
80 up to 90	2	0.10
90 up to 100	3	0.15
Total	20	1.00

     e.   The fewest number of oil changes is about 50, the highest number about 100. The greatest concentration of oil changes is between 60 and 80 per day.

7.	a.	Shoppers	f
		0 up to 3	9
		3 up to 6	21
		6 up to 9	13
		9 up to 12	4
		12 up to 15	3
		15 up to 18	1
		Total	51

b. The largest group of shopper's (21) shop at Food Queen 3, 4 or 5 times during a two week period. Some customers visit the store only 1 time during the two weeks, but others shop as many as 15 times.

c.

Number of Shoppers	Percent of Total
0 up to 3	17.65
3 up to 6	41.18
6 up to 9	25.49
9 up to 12	7.84
12 up to 15	5.88
15 up to 18	1.96
Total	100.00

8. a. Using formula 2-1, the suggested class interval is 9.43 found by $(18 - 84)/7$
An interval of 10 is more convenient to work with. The distribution using 10 is:

	f
15 up to 25	1
25 up to 35	2
35 up to 45	5
45 up to 55	10
55 up to 65	15
65 up to 75	4
75 up to 85	3
Total	40

b. Data tends to cluster between 45 and 65.

c. Based on the distribution, the youngest person taking the Caribbean cruise is 15 years (actually 18 from the raw data). The oldest person was less than 85 years. The largest concentration of ages is between 45 up to 65 years.

d.

Ages	Percent of Total
15 up to 25	2.5
25 up to 35	5.0
35 up to 45	12.5
45 up to 55	25.0
55 up to 65	37.5
65 up to 75	10.0
75 up to 85	7.5
Total	100.0

9. a. 620 to 629
b. 5
c. 621, 623, 623, 627, 629

10.   a.   210 to 219
      b.   6
      c.   210, 211, 213, 215, 217, 219

11.   a.   25
      b.   one
      c.   38, 106
      d.   60, 61, 63, 63, 65, 65, 69
      e.   No values
      f.   9
      g.   9
      h.   76
      i.   16

12.   a.   50
      b.   one
      c.   126, 270
      d.   155, 158, 159
      e.   No values
      f.   13
      g.   12
      h.   193 or 194
      i.   19

13.   Stem   Leaves
      0   5
      1   28
      2
      3   0024789
      4   12366
      5   2
      There were a total of 16 calls studied. The number of calls ranged from 5 to 52 received. Seven of the 16 subscribers received between 30 and 39 calls.

14.   Stem   Leaves
      3   6
      4   7
      5   22499
      6   0113458
      7   035678
      8   0344447
      9   055
      The daily usage ranged from 36 to 95. In a typical day the ATM is used about 70 times.

15.   a.   Histogram
      b.   100
      c.   5
      d.   28
      e.   0.28
      f.   12.5
      g.   13

16. a. 3
     b. about 26
     c. 76
     d. 2
     e. frequency polygon

17. a. 50
     b. 1.5 days
     c. Using lower limits on the X-axis

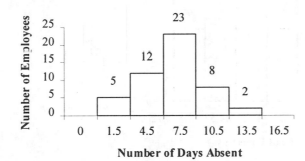

     d. X = 1.5, Y = 5
     e.

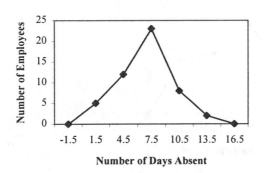

     f. For the 50 employees about half are absent between 6 and 8 days. Five were absent less
         than 3 days, and two were absent 12 or more days.

18. a. 40
     b. 2.5
     c. 2.5, 6 assuming we plan to draw a frequency polygon using the midpoints
     d.

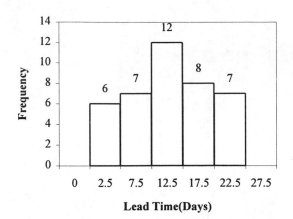

     e.

     f. Based on the charts, the shortest lead time is 2 days, the longest 22 days. The
         concentration of lead times is 10-15 days.

19. a. 40
     b. 5
     c. 11 or 12
     d. about $18 per hour
     e. about $9 per hour
     f. about 75%

20. a. 200
     b. about 50 or $50,000
     c. about $180,000
     d. about $240,000
     e. about 60 homes
     f. about 130 homes

21. a. 5, 17

b.
Days absent	f	CF
0 up to 3	5	5
3 up to 6	12	17
6 up to 9	23	40
9 up to 12	8	48
12 up to 15	2	50

c.

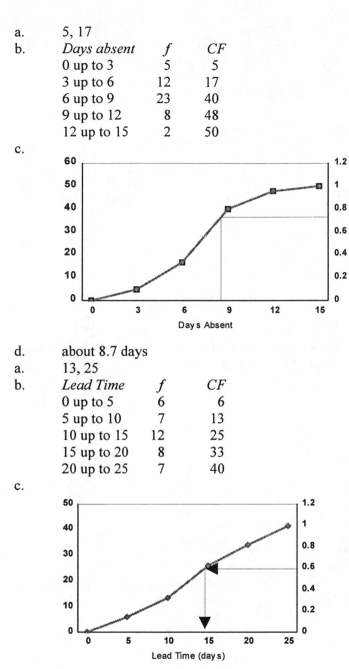

d. about 8.7 days

22. a. 13, 25

b.
Lead Time	f	CF
0 up to 5	6	6
5 up to 10	7	13
10 up to 15	12	25
15 up to 20	8	33
20 up to 25	7	40

c.

d. 14

23.

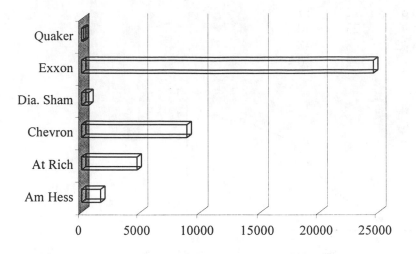

Exxon far exceeds the other corporations in sales. Quaker State and Diamond Shamrock are the two corporations with the least amount of fourth quarter sales.

24.

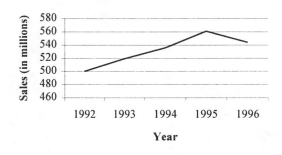

b.   In 1995 the Blair Corporation had their best year for sales. Sales increased from 1992 to 1995. The sales decreased between 1995 and 1996.

25.

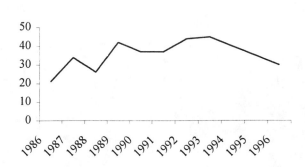

Homicides reached the highest number in 1993. They decreased from 1993 to 1996.

26. Tax Revenue 1964-1996

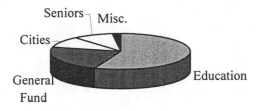

27. Population Growth in the USA

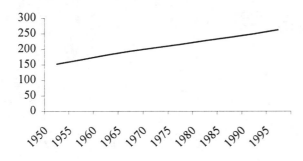

Population in the United States has increased steadily since 1950.

28 Military & Civilian Expenditures

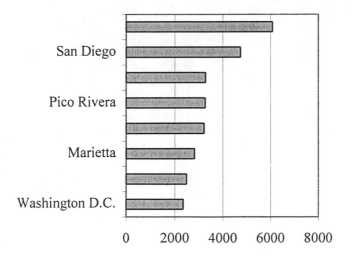

29. $2^6 = 64$ and $2^7 = 128$ suggest 7 classes

30. $i = \dfrac{490 - 56}{1 + 3.322(\log 145)} = 53.06$ suggests an interval of 50

31. a. 5 because $2^4 = 16 < 25 \text{ and } 2^5 = 32 > 25$

     b. 6, found by $\dfrac{48 - 16}{1 + 3.322(\log 25)}$ or 7, found by $\dfrac{48 - 16}{5}$

     c. 15

     d.
Class	Frequency
15 up to 22	3
22 up to 29	8
29 up to 36	7
36 up to 43	5
43 up to 50	2
	25

     e. It is fairly symmetric with most of the values between 22 and 36.

32. a. 6 because $2^5 = 32 < 45 \text{ and } 2^6 = 64 > 45$

     b. 100, found by $\dfrac{570 - 41}{1 + 3.322(\log 45)} = 81.5$

     c. 0

     d.
Class	Frequency
0 up to 100	3
100 up to 200	12
200 up to 300	16
300 up to 400	10
400 up to 500	3
500 up to 600	1
	45

33. a. 70
     b. one
     c. 0, 145
     d. 30, 30, 32, 39
     e. 24
     f. 21
     g. 77
     h. 25

34. a. 55
     b. two
     c. 91, 237
     d. 141, 143, 145
     e. 8
     f. 12
     g. three
     h. 180

35.   a.   56
        b.   10 (found by 60 – 50)
        c.   55
        d.   17

36.   a.   Less-than-cumulative frequency polygon
        b.   250
        c.   50 (found by 100 – 50)
        d. $240,000
        e. $230,000

37.   a. $36.60, (found by 265 – 82)/5
        b. $40
        c.

$80 up to $120	8
120 up to 160	19
160 up to 200	10
200 up to 240	6
240 up to 280	1
Total	44

        d.   The purchases ranged from a low of about $80 to a high of about $280. The concentration is in the $120 up to $160 class.

38.   a.   Class interval is 19, found by (266 – 133)/7. We selected 20.

Stockholders (000)	Number of companies	Less than CF
130 up to 150	4	4
150 up to 170	9	13
170 up to 190	4	17
190 up to 210	6	23
210 up to 230	3	26
230 up to 250	2	28
250 up to 270	4	32
Total	32	

        b.

c.

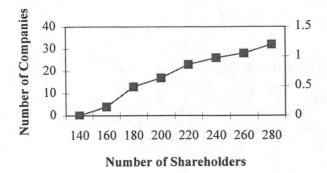

Number of Shareholders

d.   About 220 thousand, found by ¾ of 32 = 24. The 24th company has about 220 thousand shareholders found by drawing a line to the curve from 24 and down to the X-axis.

e.   The largest number of companies (9) have 150 up to 170 thousand shareholders. The smallest number is about 130 thousand, the largest number is about 270 thousand.

39.

Expenditures (vertical axis)

Depreciation

Repairs

Fuel

0   200   400   600   800   1000

Amount

40.   a.

Balance	f	CF
0 up to 100	9	9
100 up to 200	6	15
200 up to 300	6	21
300 up to 400	6	27
400 up to 500	5	32
500 up to 600	2	34
600 up to 700	1	35
700 up to 800	3	38
800 up to 900	1	39
900 up to 1000	1	40
Total	40	

Probably a class interval of $200 would be better.

b.

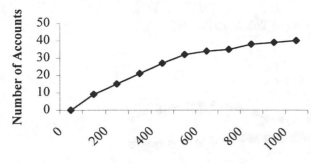

Balances

c. About 67% have less than a $400 balance. Therefore, about 33% would be considered "preferred."

d. Less than $50 would be a convenient cutoff point.

41. a. unit = 0.10

3	76	149
3	77	
4	78	1
2	79	77
6	80	14
4	81	04
2	82	77

The lowest percent of on time is 76.1%, the largest is 82.7%. The typical airline is on time 79.7% of the time.

42. Class interval of 3

Number of Raisins	f
190 up to 193	1
193 up to 196	5
196 up to 199	11
199 up to 202	20
202 up to 205	13
205 up to 208	<u>10</u>
Total	60

About one third of the boxes have between 199 and 202 raisins. The number of raisins ranges from 190 up to 208.

43.

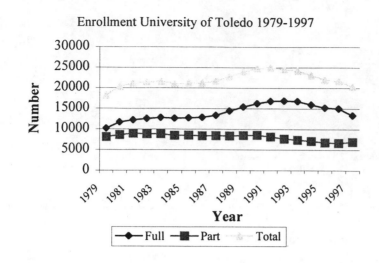

Enrollment University of Toledo 1979-1997

Enrollment increased up to 1992. From 1995 to 1997 there is a decrease due mostly to a decline in full time students.

44.

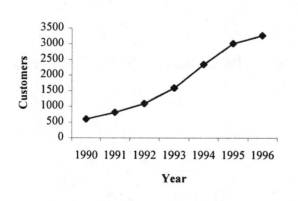

Number of GTE subscribers has increased from 1990.

45.

Sales tax and income tax dominate the total revenues for the state of Georgia.

46.

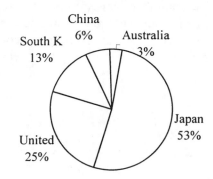

47. There are 50 observations so the recommended number of classes is 6. However, there are several states that have many more farms than the others, so it may be useful to have an open ended class.
One possible frequency distribution is.

Farms in USA	Frequency
0 up to 20	16
20 up to 40	13
40 up to 60	8
60 up to 80	6
80 up to 100	4
100 or more	3
Total	50

Twenty-nine of the 50 states, or 58 percent, have fewer than 40,000 farms. There are three states that have more than 100,000 farms. Most states have around 40,000 farms.

48. The following pie chart shows the breakdown of the six colors. About 75% of the candies are either brown, yellow or red. Each of these colors represents about 25% of the total. The percent of orange and blue is less than 10 percent each. About 4 percent of the candies are green.

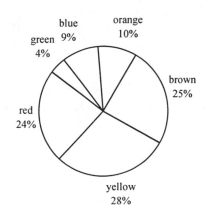

49.   In 1990 the price for a Toyota Camry and a Ford Taurus was about the same, a little more than
        $11,000 each. Since that time the price of both cars has increased but the rate of increase of the
        Camry has been larger than the Taurus. The difference in the selling price between the two cars
        was the largest in 1996, about $6500. From 1996 to 1997 the selling price of the Camry
        decreased about $500, the only price decrease for either car during the 9 year period.

50. | Sales | f |
        |---|---|
        | 0 up to 1000 | 22 |
        | 1000 up to 2000 | 21 |
        | 2000 up to 3000 | 8 |
        | 3000 up to 4000 | 4 |
        | 4000 up to 5000 | 6 |
        | 5000 up to 6000 | 4 |
        | 6000 up to 7000 | 3 |
        | 7000 or more | 11 |
        | Total | 79 |

        Fifty-four percent of the companies had sales of less than $2000 (million). Eleven companies, or
        14 percent had sales of $7000 (million or more).

51.   Stem and Leaf of run-up

1	-1	1
3	-0	96
14	-0	33332211000
45	0	000111112222223333333333333444444
(26)	0	5555566666777778888889999
24	1	0000011122334
11	1	5666799
4	2	24
2	2	
2	3	
2	3	
2	4	2
1	4	
1	5	
1	5	
1	6	
1	6	
1	7	0

        The percentage of waste, or run-up, ranged from −11.0 percent to 70.0 percent. The middle value
        is 0.5 percent. Fifty-seven of the 95 observations are between 0 and 9 percent.

52.   a. $n = 105$ $2^k = 2^7 = 128$

$$i = \frac{345.33 - 125.01}{1 + 3.322 \log 105} = \frac{220.32}{7.71} = 28.6 \text{ suggests an interval of 30.}$$

Selling Price	f	CF
120 up to 150	4	4
150 up to 180	18	22
180 up to 210	30	52
210 up to 240	19	71
240 up to 270	17	88
270 up to 300	10	98
300 up to 330	6	104
330 up to 360	1	105

1.   The 180 up to 210 class includes 28.6 percent ((30/105)100) of the observations.
2.   The smallest selling price is about $120 (000) and the largest is about $360 (000).
3.   From the frequency distribution we would estimate that 1 of the homes sold for less than $125. So the percent is less than one percent.

b.

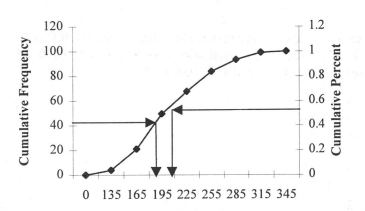

1.   About 42
2.   About 56 percent of the homes sold for less than $220,000, so 44 percent sold for more than $220,000.
3.   About 1 percent

c.   The selling price ranged from about $120,000 up to about $360,000. A typical home sold for about $210,000.

53.   a. $2^5 = 32$

$$i = \frac{64.9896 - 12.1742}{1 + 3.322 \log(28)} = \frac{52.8154}{5.8075} = 9.09 \text{ suggests an interval of 10.}$$

Team Salary	f	CF
10 up to 20	4	4
20 up to 30	1	5
30 up to 40	9	14
40 up to 50	9	23
50 up to 60	3	26
60 up to 70	2	28

1. The salaries ranged from about $10,000,000 per team to nearly $70,000,000 per team. Ten of the 28 teams or 36% had team salaries between $40,000,000 and $50,000,000.
2. There is a very large difference in the salaries, $60,000,000, but no team seems to be really out of line to all the others.

b.

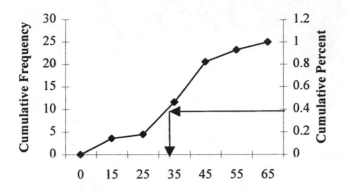

1. Forty-percent of the teams have salaries less than about $38,000,000.
2. Twenty-three of the teams have total salaries of less than $50,000,000.
3. The five lowest teams pay less than $30,000,000

54. a.

Circulation	f
0 up to 1000	15
1000 up to 2000	13
2000 up to 3000	6
3000 up to 4000	2
4000 up to 5000	2
5000 up to 6000	3
6000 or more	7
Total	48

1. Twenty-eight , or 58% of the magazines have circulation less than 2000 (actually 2,000,000). Note the use of the open-ended class.
2 & 3. The circulation ranged from $450,000 up to 17,900,000. Note that the circulation for Reader's Digest and TV Guide is much larger than the rest. The best way to handle this is to use an open-ended upper class.

b. Because of the open-ended class we cannot determine a less-than cumulative frequency distribution.
1. About 75% of the magazines have a circulation of less than 4,000,000.
2. About 79% of the magazines have a circulation of less than 5,000,000.

55. a. The salaries are in $000.

I	26	1
4	27	146
11	28	1449999
14	29	059
29	30	122344677889999
40	31	11222335889
(12)	32	112234677889
42	33	112446889
33	34	22446789
25	35	05567889
17	36	001
14	37	0179
10	38	0
9	39	13456
4	40	3
3	41	6
2	42	7
1	43	2

a. The lowest salary($00) is $26.1 and the largest is $43.2

b. A typical salary is about $32.6

c. Fourteen districts have salaries of less than #30, so 80 have salaries of 30.0 or more.

d. The teacher salaries in ($000) ranged from a low of $26.1 to a high of $43.2. The typical salary is about $32,000. There were 14 districts where the average salary was less than $30,000 and four where the salary was more than $40,000.

DESCRIBING DATA: MEASURES OF LOCATION

1. $\mu = 5.4$ found by 27/5

2. $\mu = 5.5$ found by 33/6

3.   a.   Mean = 7.0, found by 28/4
      b. $(5-7)+(9-7)+(4-7)+(10-7)=0$

4.   a.   4.2 found by 21/5
      b. $(1.3-4.2)+(7.0-4.2)+(3.6-4.2)+(4.1-4.2)+(5.0-4.2)=0$

5.   14.58, found by 43.74/3

6. $20.95, found by $125.68/6

7.   a.   15.4, found by 154/10
      b.   Population parameter since it includes all the salespersons at Midtown Ford.

8.   a.   23.9, found by 167/7
      b.   Population parameter since it includes all the calls during a seven-day period.

9.   a. $54.55, found by $1091/20
      b.   A sample statistic, assuming that the power company serves more than 20 customers.

10.   a.   10.73, found by 161/15
       b.   Sample of RN's

11. $0.775, found by ($10 + $37.50 + $30)/100

12. $1.50 found by ($40 + $35)/50

13. $11.50, found by ($400 + $500 + $1400)/200

14. $143.75, found by ($1000 +$750 + $4000)/40

15.   a.   no mode
       b.   The given value would be the mode
       c.   3 and 4, bimodal

16.   Median = 33,   Mode = 15

17.   Median = 5   Mode = 5

18.   Median = 10.5   Mode = 8

19.   a.   Median = 2.9
       b.   Mode = 2.9

20. Median = 9.2 Modes are 8.2, 8.5, and 10.3

21. 11.18 found by $\sqrt[5]{8(12)(14)(26)(5)}$

22. 5.4 found by $\sqrt[8]{2(8)(6)(4)(10)(6)(8)(4)}$

23. 0.284 or 2.84% found by $\sqrt[46]{\dfrac{185}{51}} - 1.00$

24. 12.16 found by $\sqrt[5]{(9.4)(13.8)(11.7)(11.9)(14.7)}$

25. $GM = \sqrt[12]{\dfrac{14.0}{3.9}} - 1 = 1.112 - 1 = 0.112$ or 11.2%

26. $GM = \sqrt[10]{\dfrac{54.87}{9.19}} - 1 = 0.1956$

27. Because the exact values in a frequency distribution are not known, the computed mean is an estimate.

28.

Class	f	X	fX
0 up to 5	2	2.5	5.00
5 up to 10	7	7.5	52.50
10 up to 15	12	12.5	150.00
15 up to 20	6	17.5	105.00
20 up to 25	3	22.5	67.50
Total	30		380.00

$\overline{X} = \dfrac{380}{30} = 12.67$

29.

Class	f	X	fX
20 up to 30	7	25	175
30 up to 40	12	35	420
40 up to 50	21	45	945
50 up to 60	18	55	990
60 up to 70	12	65	780
Total	70		3310

$\overline{X} = \dfrac{3310}{70} = 47.2857$

30.

Selling Price	f	X	fX
70 up to 80	3	75	225
80 up to 90	7	85	595
90 up to 100	18	95	1710
100 up to 110	20	105	2100
110 up to 120	12	115	1380
Total	60		6010

$$\overline{X} = \frac{\$6010}{60} = \$100.17$$

31.

Age	f	X	CF
20 up to 30	1	25	25
30 up to 40	15	35	525
40 up to 50	22	45	990
50 up to 60	8	55	440
60 up to 70	4	65	260
Total	50		2240

$$\overline{X} = \frac{2240}{50} = 44.8$$

32.

Advertising	f	X	CF
25 up to 35	5	30	150
35 up to 45	10	40	400
45 up to 55	21	50	1050
55 up to 65	16	60	960
65 up to 75	8	70	560
Total	60		3120

$$\overline{X} = \frac{3120}{60} = 52$$

33.

Class	f	CF
0 up to 5	2	2
5 up to 10	7	9
10 up to 15	12	21
15 up to 20	6	27
20 up to 25	3	30

$$\text{Median} = 10 + \frac{\frac{30}{2} - 9}{12}(5) = 12.5 \qquad \text{Mode} = 12.5$$

34.

Class	f	CF
20 up to 30	7	7
30 up to 40	12	19
40 up to 50	21	40
50 up to 60	18	58
60 up to 70	12	70

$$\text{Median} = 40 + \frac{\frac{70}{2} - 19}{21}(10) = 47.62 \qquad \text{Mode} = 45$$

35.

Amount	f	CF
0 up to 2000	4	4
2000 up to 4000	15	19
4000 up to 6000	18	37
6000 up to 8000	10	47
8000 up to 10,000	4	51
10,000 up to 12,000	3	54

a. $\text{Median} = \$4000 + \dfrac{\dfrac{54}{2} - 19}{18}(\$2000) = \$4889$

b. Mode = $5000

36.

Age	f	CF
up to 20	15	15
20 up to 25	33	48
25 up to 30	19	67
30 up to 35	17	84
35 up to 40	11	95
40 up to 45	4	99
45 up to 50	1	100

$\text{Median} = 25 + \dfrac{\dfrac{100}{2} - 48}{19}(5) = 25.53 \text{ years}$ Mode = 22.5 years

37. a. Mean = 5, found by $(6 + 4 + 3 + 7 + 5)/5$
Median is 5, found by rearranging the values and selecting the middle value.
b. Population because all partners were included.
c. $\Sigma(X - \mu) = (6-5) + (4-5) + (3-5) + (7-5) + (5-5) = 0$

38. a. Mean = 21.71, Median = 22.00
b. $(23 - 21.7) + (19 - 21.7) + ... + (22 - 21.7) = 0$

39. $\overline{X} = \dfrac{545}{16} = 34.06$ Median = 37.50

40. $\overline{X} = \dfrac{2116}{30} = 70.5333$

41. 370.08, found by 18,504/50

42. a. 4.84, found by 121/25
b. Median = 4.0
c. On half the days she made at least 4 appointments. The arithmetic mean number of appointments per day is 4.84.

43. $\overline{X}_w = \dfrac{\$5.00(270) + \$6.50(300) + \$8.00(100)}{270 + 300 + 100} = \$6.12$

44. $\overline{X}_w = \dfrac{3(4) + 3(4) + 5(3) + 2(3) + 1(4)}{3 + 3 + 5 + 2 + 1} = 3.50$

45. $$\overline{X}_w = \frac{[15,300(4.5) + 10,400(3.0) + 150,600(10.2)]}{176,300} = 9.28$$

46. $59.1 million

47. 3.38%, found by (3.25 + 3.51)/2

48.
   a. $1.238 found by 18.57/15
   b. $1.24
   c. $1.29

49. Earthquake Mean Size = 7.0 found by 168.2/24   Median Size = 7.05
   Earthquake Deaths Mean = 5607.79   Median = 1100
   Mean for the size and the median for the deaths because of all the extreme values listed.

50. $$GM = \sqrt[21]{\frac{6,286,800}{5,164,900}} - 1 = 1.0094, \text{ so about } 0.94\%$$

51. 61.68%

52. $$GM = \sqrt[10]{\frac{33,598}{25,000}} - 1 = 1.0300 - 1 = 0.03 \text{ or } 3.0 \text{ percent}$$

   $$GM = \sqrt[10]{\frac{44,771}{25,000}} - 1 = 1.0599995 - 1 = 0.06 \text{ or } 6.0 \text{ percent}$$

53. 83.215

54. $\overline{X} = 60.14\%$ GM = 55.209%

55.

Weights	f	X	fX	CF
130 up to 140	2	135	270	2
140 up to 150	8	145	1160	10
150 up to 160	20	155	3100	30
160 up to 170	15	165	2475	45
170 up to 180	9	175	1575	54
180 up to 190	7	185	1295	61
190 up to 200	3	195	585	64
200 up to 210	2	205	410	66
Total	66		10,870	

   a. $$\overline{X} = \frac{10,870}{66} = 164.697$$

   b. $$\text{Median} = 60 + \frac{33 - 30}{15}(10) = 162.0$$

56.
   a. 2, because that number appears most frequently. More families have two income earners than any other number.

   b. $$\text{Median} = .5 + \frac{28,224 - 25,704}{22,414}(1) = 1.61$$

   c. Mean cannot be computed because of open end (4 or more).

57.

Income	Percent	CF
Less than $20,000	18.3	18.3
$20,000 up to $30,000	21.2	39.5
30,000 up to 40,000	18.4	57.9
40,000 up to 50,000	15.1	73.0
50,000 up to 60,000	11.3	84.3
60,000 or greater	15.7	100.0

$$\text{Median} = \$30,000 + \frac{50.0 - 39.5}{18.4}(\$10,000) = \$35,706.52 \qquad \text{Mode} = \$25,000$$

58.

Calls	f	X	fX	CF
3 up to 6	5	4	20	5
6 up to 9	19	7	133	24
9 up to 12	20	10	200	44
12 up to 15	20	13	260	64
15 up to 18	4	16	64	68
18 up to 21	2	19	38	70
Total	70		715	

a. $\overline{X} = \dfrac{715}{70} = 10.21$

b. $\text{Median} = 9.0 + \dfrac{\frac{70}{2} - 24}{20}(3) = 10.65$

59.

Mortgage	f	X	fX	CF
$100 up to $500	1	300	300	1
500 up to 900	9	700	6300	10
900 up to 1300	11	1100	12,100	21
1300 up to 1700	23	1500	34,500	44
1700 up to 2100	11	1900	20,900	55
2100 up to 2500	4	2300	9200	59
2500 up to 2900	1	2700	2700	60
Total	60		86,000	

a. $\overline{X} = \dfrac{\$86,000}{60} = \$1433$

b. $\text{Median} = \$1300 + \dfrac{30 - 21}{23}(\$400) = \$1456.52$

60.

Sales	f	X	fX	CF
100 up to 120	5	110	550	5
120 up to 140	7	130	910	12
140 up to 160	9	150	1350	21
160 up to 180	16	170	2720	37
180 up to 200	10	190	1900	47
200 up to 220	3	210	630	50
Total	50		8060	

a. $\overline{X} = \dfrac{8060}{50} = 161.20$

b. Median $= 60 + \dfrac{\dfrac{50}{2} - 21}{16}(20) = 165$

c. Mode = 170, the midpoint of the class with the most observations.

61. Answer will vary. The paragraph should discuss issues such as:
The average is higher for part time nurses compared to full time nurses. This may be due to the fact that there are not as many part time nurses. Therefore, when you calculate the mean it will be higher. Also, as the number of beds increases the average hourly wage increases. Again this could be due to the fact that there are not too many hospitals with 500 or more beds. On the other hand the lowest average is the hospital located in the rural setting. The type of hospital dictates the average. The private, non-profit hospital has a greater hourly wage compared to the public hospital.

62. Answers will vary. Discussion should include the following: For first time buyers the average age from 1995 to 1996 remained the same at 31.6 years. In regards to the average cost of a home it decreased in 1996 compared to 1995. A factor for this event could be that in 1996 more homes were sold, and the price of a home remained the same from 1995 to 1996. First time buyers visited about the same number of homes, and had approximately the same average monthly payments.

Repeat buyers on the average spent more money for a house in comparison to the first time they purchased a home. The typical age of a first time buyer in 1995 and 1996 is about the same at 41.0. Along with remaining constant is the number of homes visited between 1995 and 1996. Interesting to note that the average home cost increased in 1996 in comparison to 1995. This is reversed from the first time homebuyers average cost for a home.

63. Johnson & Johnson
$$\bar{X}_w = \frac{1(6) + 2(10) + 3(7)}{23} = \frac{47}{23} = 2.04$$

PepsiCo
$$\bar{X}_w = \frac{1(10) + 2(7) + 3(6)}{23} = \frac{42}{23} = 1.83 \qquad \text{The PepsiCo stock has the better rating.}$$

64. A stock split can cause the total stock price of the 30 Dow Companies to decrease, which would mean a lower Dow. So the keepers of the Dow lower the number divided into the total Dow stock. This keeps stock splits from dragging it down. Thus the reported figure for the Dow is nothing more than a trend. It is a line on a graph-indicated change over time.
The mean of the 30 stocks is $67.26

65. a. $\bar{X} = \$221.1$ and the median is $213.57 (answers in 000). Either measure is acceptable.
b. $\bar{X} = 3.8$, median = 4
c. $\bar{X} = 2.08$, median = 2
d. $\bar{X} = 14.6$ miles, and the median is 15.0 miles

66.   a. $\overline{X} = 38.58$ (million), Median = 39.62. The distribution is negatively skewed. The median is a better value.

       b.   The mean attendance per team is 2.26 million. The median is 2.07 million. Either value is representative.

       c. $GM = \sqrt[8]{\dfrac{1,383,578}{512,804}} - 1 = 1.132 - 1.0 = 0.132$

       Average salary increased at a rate of 13.2 percent per year.

67.   a. $\overline{X} = 3,048,000$ and the median is 1,600,000. The median is more representative. The two large values distort the mean.

       b. $\overline{X} = 26,622,000$ and the median is 17,625,000. Again, the median is more representative.

       c. $\overline{X} = 36,629,000$ and the median is 26,722. The median is more representative.

68.   a. $\overline{X} = 33.181$ and the median is 32.708 (both in 000). Either representative

       b. $\overline{X} = 2134$ and the median is 1227. Median is better because of the large values.

       c. $\overline{X} = 24,069$ and the median is 23,689. Either representative

1.   a.   7, found by 10 – 3
       b.   6, found by 30/5
       c.   2.4, found by 12/5
       d.   The difference between the highest number sold (10) and the smallest number sold (3) is 7. On the average the number of service reps on duty deviates by 2.4 from the mean of 6.

2.   a.   24, found by 52 – 28
       b.   38
       c.   6.25, found by 50/8
       d.   The difference between 28 and 52 is 24. On the average the number of students enrolled deviates 6.25 from the mean of 38.

3.   a.   30, found by 54 – 24
       b.   38, found by 380/10
       c.   7.2, found by 72/10
       d.   The difference between 54 and 24 is 30. On the average the number of minutes required to install a door deviates 7.2 minutes from the mean of 38 minutes.

4.   a.   7.6%, found by 18.2 – 10.6
       b.   13.85%
       c.   2%, found by 16/8
       d.   The difference between 18.2 and 10.6 is 7.6%. On the average the return on investment deviates two percent from the mean of 13.85%.

5.   a.   15, found by 41 – 26
       b.   33.9, found by 339/10
       c.   4.12, found by 41.2/10
       d.   The ratings deviate 4.12 from the mean of 33.9 on the average.

6.   a.   10 days, found by 10 – 0
       b.   3.5 days found by 28/8
       c.   2.375 days, found by 19/8
       d.   Days lost to illness deviates 2.375 days on average from the mean. The difference of 10 and 0 is 10.

7.   a.   5

       b.   4.4 found by $\dfrac{(8-5)^2+(3-5)^2+(7-5)^2+(3-5)^2+(4-5)^2}{5}$

8.   a.   8

       b.   9.66 found by $\dfrac{(13-8)^2+(3-8)^2+(8-8)^2+(10-8)^2+(8-8)^2+(6-8)^2}{6}$

9.   a. $2.77

       b. $\sigma^2 = \dfrac{(2.68 - 2.77)^2 + ... + (4.30 - 2.77)^2 + (3.58 - 2.77)^2}{5} = 1.26$

10.   a.   11.76%, found by 58.8/5
       b.   16.89%, found by 84.452/5

11.   a.   Range = 7.3, found by 11.6 – 4.3
             Arithmetic mean = 6.94, found by 34.7/5
             Variance = 6.5944, found by 32.972/5   Standard Deviation = 2.568
       b.   Dennis has a higher mean return (11.76 > 6.94). However, Dennis has greater spread in their returns on equity (16.89 > 6.59).

12.   a.   18, found by 90 – 72
       b. $79.6, found by 398/5
       c.   Variance = 40.24, found by 201.2/5   Standard Deviation = 6.3435
       d.   Means about the same, but less dispersion in salary for TMV vice presidents.

13.   a. $\overline{X} = 4$ $s^2 = \dfrac{(7-4)^2 + ... + (3-4)^2}{5-1} = 5.5$

       b. $s^2 = \dfrac{102 - \dfrac{(20)^2}{5}}{5-1} = 5.50$

       c. $s = 2.3452$

14.   a. $\overline{X} = 8$ $s^2 = \dfrac{(11-8)^2 + ... + (7-8)^2}{5-1} = 5.5$

       b. $s^2 = \dfrac{342 - \dfrac{(40)^2}{5}}{5-1} = 5.50$

       c. $s = 2.3452$

15.   a. $\overline{X} = 38$ $s^2 = \dfrac{(28-38)^2 + ... + (42-38)^2}{10-1} = 82.6667$

       b. $s^2 = \dfrac{15,184 - \dfrac{(380)^2}{10}}{10-1} = 82.6667$

       c. $s = 9.0921$

16.   a. $\overline{X} = 13.85$ $s^2 = \dfrac{(10.6-13.85)^2 + ... + (15.6-13.85)^2}{8-1} = 6.0086$

       b. $s^2 = \dfrac{1576.64 - \dfrac{(110.8)^2}{8}}{8-1} = 6.0086$

       c. $s = 2.4512$

17. a. $\bar{X} = 124$ $\qquad$ $s^2 = \dfrac{(124-124)^2 + \ldots + (121-124)^2}{10-1} = 4.6667$

    b. $s^2 = \dfrac{153{,}802 - \dfrac{(1240)^2}{10}}{10-1} = 4.6667$

    c. $s = 2.1602$

18. AB4 yields a higher mean weight with less spread.

19. a. 25, found by $25 - 0$

    b. 5.331 found by $\sqrt{\dfrac{5637.50 - \dfrac{(380)^2}{30}}{30-1}}$

    c. 28.42 found by 5.331^2

20. a. 50, found by $70 - 20$

    b. 12.178 found by $\sqrt{\dfrac{166{,}750 - \dfrac{(3310)^2}{70}}{70-1}}$

    c. 148.30 found by 12.178^2

21. a. 12 minutes, found by $14 - 2$

    b. 2.5959 found by $\sqrt{\dfrac{2594 - \dfrac{(312)^2}{42}}{42-1}}$

    c. 6.7387 found by 2.5959^2

22. a. \$2.00 found by $2.50 - 0.50$

    b. 0.3641 found by $\sqrt{\dfrac{171.50 - \dfrac{(113.50)^2}{80}}{80-1}}$

    c. 0.1326 found by 0.3641^2

23. About 69%, found by $1 - \dfrac{1}{(1.8)^2}$

24. About 84%, each income levels lie 2.5 standard deviations from the mean. Then $-\dfrac{1}{(2.5)^2} = 0.84$

25. a. About 95%
    b. 47.5%, 2.5%

26. a. 85, halfway between the endpoints of 140 and 30
    b. About 18, found by $(140 - 30)/6$
    c. 103 and 67, found by $85 \pm (1)18$
    d. 121 and 49, found by $85 \pm (2)18$

27. 8.06%, found by $(0.25/3.10)(100)$

28. Domestic 21.28%, found by (10/47)(100)   Overseas 19.23
There is slightly less relative dispersion in the weights of luggage for domestic passengers.

29. a. Because the two series are in different units of measurement.
    b. P.E. ratio = 16.51%   ROI 20.8%, less spread in the P.E. ratios

30. The relative dispersion in stocks under \$10 is 28.95%. For stocks over \$60, 5.71%. Less relative dispersion in stocks over \$60.

31. Symmetrical because mean, median and mode are equal. The coefficient of skewness is zero.

32. 0.95, found by $\dfrac{3(542 - 400)}{448.5}$, positively skewed

33. a. Positively skewed
    b. 2.949

34. a. Negatively skewed
    b. -1.8, found by $\dfrac{3(2.1 - 2.4)}{0.5}$

35. Median = 53 found by $(11 + 1)(1/2)$ therefore 6th value in from lowest.
    $Q_1 = 49$ found by $(11 + 1)(1/4)$ therefore 3rd value in from lowest
    $Q_3 = 55$ found by $(11 + 1)(3/4)$ therefore 9th value in from lowest

36. Median = 9.53, found by $(9.45 + 9.61)/2$
    $Q_1 = 7.69$ found by $7.59 + (7.99 - 7.59)\, 1/4$
    $Q_3 = 12.59$ found by $12.22 + (12.71 - 12.22)3/4$

37. a. $Q_1 = 33.25$ $Q_3 = 50.25$
    b. $D_2 = 27.8$ $D_8 = 52.6$
    c. $P_{67} = 47$

38. a. Median = 58
    b. $Q_1 = 51.25$ $Q_3 = 66.0$
    c. $D_1 = 45.3$ $D_9 = 76.4$
    d. $P_{33} = 53.53$

39. a. 350
    b. $Q_1 = 175$ $Q_3 = 930$
    c. 755, found by $930 - 175$
    d. Less than zero, or more than about 2060
    e. There are no outliers
    f. The distribution is positively skewed

40. a. 450
    b. $Q_1 = 300$ $Q_3 = 700$
    c. 400, found by $700 - 300$
    d. Less than zero or more than 1300
    e. One outlier at about 1500
    f. Distribution is positively skewed

41. The distribution is somewhat positively skewed. Note that dashed line above 35 is longer than below 18.

```
                    ---------------------
       --------|          +          |---------------------
                    ---------------------
    ---+-------+-------+-------+-------+-------+---
       14      21      28      35      42      49
```

42. The median is $253, the smallest value is $116 to $353. About 25% of the semi-private rooms are less than $214 and 25% above $304. The distribution is negatively skewed.

```
                               -----------------
          ------------------ |         +        |--------
                               -----------------
    ---|---------|---------|---------|---------|---------|--
    100        150       200       250       300       350
```

43. Line 2

44. Line 3, it has the largest standard deviation

45. 239.2 and 240.8

46. Line 3

47. 239.9 and 240.1

48. $242.9 \pm 3(3.9) = 231.2$ up to 254.6

49. 1.6 found by 3.9/242.9(100)

50. -1.9 found by $\dfrac{3(238.1 - 240)}{3.0}$

51. 9 found by 3^2

52. The amount of commission earned has 10% more relative dispersion than the number of years with the company.

53. Negatively skewed. The mean is smaller than the median. The longer tail is to the left.

54. a. 4, found by $12 - 8$
    b. 1.0, found by 8/8
    c. 1.31, found by $\sqrt{\dfrac{12}{8-1}}$
    d. 1.3093, found by $\sqrt{\dfrac{734 - \dfrac{(76)^2}{8}}{7}}$

55. a. 55, found by $72 - 17$
    b. 14.4, found by $144/10$ where $\bar{X} = 43.2$
    c. 17.6245

56. a. 9, found by $12 - 3$
    b. 2.72, found by $13.6/5$ where mean $= 7.6$
    c. 3.5071

57. a. population
    b. 183.47
    c. 94.92%

58. a. 30, found by $110 - 80$
    b. $s = \sqrt{\dfrac{1,029,937.5 - \dfrac{(10,620)^2}{110}}{109}} = 6.514$

59. Range is $25 - 0 = 25$
    $s = \sqrt{\dfrac{13,637.50 - \dfrac{(910)^2}{70}}{69}} = 5.118$

60. a. 30 found by $30 - 0$
    b. 6.09 found by $\sqrt{\dfrac{34,758 - \dfrac{(2094)^2}{150}}{149}}$

61. The following results were found using MINITAB
    $Q_1 = 44.25$ $Q_3 = 68.50$ Median $= 55.50$
    The distribution is approximately symmetric. The box plot is as follows.

```
                              --------------------
      -----------------------|          +          |------------
                              --------------------
    -----|----------|----------|----------|----------|----------|---
    24            36         48         60         72         84
```

62. a.
```
                    -----------------
      -----------                  +                -------------
                    -----------------
    -----|-----|-----|-----|-----|-----|-----|-----|-----|
         10    15    20    25    30    35    40    45
```
    b. No outliers
    c. The distribution is positively skewed. The median time to change a muffler is 23.50 minutes. The first quartile is 15.75 minutes and the third quartile is 29.25 minutes. The range of time is 10 minutes to 44 minutes.

63. The distribution is positively skewed. The first quartile is approximately $20 and the third quartile is approximately $90. There is one outlier located at $255. The median is about 50.

64. The distribution is positively skewed. With the first quartile equal to 10 and the third quartile is equal to 40. There are four outliers located at 85, 86, 95 and 99. The median is about 25.

65. a. $-18.6434, 78.76104$ found by $30.05882 \pm 2(24.35111)$
    b. 81% found by $24.35111/30.05882(100)$ The standard deviation is 81% of the mean.
    c. Positive skewness because the mean is greater than the median.

66. a. 1017 found by $1019 - 2$
    b. 99.5 found by $138.2 - 38.7$
    c. 127% found by $162/7/128.1(100)$
    d. 0.86 found by $3(128.1 - 81)/162.7$
    e.
```
                   ------------------------------
        ---------|             +              |-----------
                   ------------------------------
    -----|-----|-----|-----|-----|-----|-----+-----+-----+-----
        20    40    60    80   100   120   140   160   1019
```

67. a. $\overline{X} = \dfrac{857.90}{50} = 17.158$ Median = 16.35

    b. $s = \sqrt{\dfrac{20{,}206.73 - \dfrac{(857.90)^2}{50}}{50-1}} = 10.58$

    c. $7.158 \pm (1.5)(10.58) = 1.288$ up to 33.028
    d. $7.158 \pm (2)(10.58) = -4.002$ and 38.318
    e. $CV = \dfrac{10.58}{17.158}(100) = 61.66$
    f. $sk = \dfrac{3(17.158 - 16.35)}{10.58} = 0.23$
    g. $L_p = (50+1)\dfrac{25}{100} = 12.75$ $L_p = (50+1)\dfrac{75}{100} = 38.25$
       $Q_1 = 7.825$ $Q_3 = 27.400$
```
                        ----------------------
        ------------|          +           |---------
                        ----------------------
    -----+----------+----------+----------+----------+-----
        0          10         20         30         40
```

    h. The distribution is nearly symmetrical. The mean is 17.158, the median is 16.35 and the standard deviation is 10.58. About 75 percent of the companies have a value less than 27.4 and 25 percent have a value less than 7.825.

68. $\overline{X} = \dfrac{1291.82}{50} = 25.8364$ Median = 20.73

    $s = \sqrt{\dfrac{46{,}161.5736 - \dfrac{(1291.82)^2}{50}}{50-1}} = 16.15$

    $sk = \dfrac{3(25.8634 - 20.73)}{16.15} = 0.95$

The distribution is positively skewed with several outliers increasing the value of the mean.

```
                    -----------------
    -------|          +            |---------              **  *
                    ----------------

    -----+----------+----------+----------+----------+-----
         12         24         36         48         60
```

69. a. $\bar{X} = \$67.26$ Median $= \$63.62$, $s = \$21.46$ $Q_1 = \$49.72$ $Q_3 = \$78.28$

$sk = \dfrac{3(67.26 - 63.62)}{21.46} = 0.51$

There is some positive skewness and one outlier. This is the stock price of JP Morgan.

```
                    -----------------
    -------|            +        |--------------              *
                    -----------------

    -----+----------+----------+----------+----------+-----
         48         64         80         96         112
```

b. The standard deviation is $21.46. The coefficient of variation is 31%.

c. Answers will vary

70. a. From MINITAB
```
Variable   N     Mean    Median   Tr Mean   StDev    SE Mean
Price      105   221.10  213.57   220.00    47.11    4.60

Variable   Min     Max      Q1      Q3
Price      125.01  345.33   186.86  251.84
```

1. $\bar{X} = \$221.10$ Median $= \$213.57$ $s = \$47.11$

2. $sk = \dfrac{3(\$221.10 - \$213.57)}{\$47.11} = 0.48$ slight positive skewness

3. See MINITAB above: $Q_1 = \$186.86$, $Q_3 = \$251.84$, the smallest selling price is $125.01 and the largest is $345.33.

```
                         ----------
        ----------|          +      |---------
                         ----------

    ------+------+------+------+------+------+----
         100    150    200    250    300    350
```

4. The mean selling price is $221,100 and the median is $213,570. Fifty percent of the selling prices are between $186,860 and $251,840. The smallest selling price is $125,010 and the largest is $345,330.

b. From MINITAB
```
Variable   N     Mean    Median   Tr Mean   StDev    SE Mean
Size       105   2231.4  2217.0   2226.3    249.3    24.3

Variable   Min      Max      Q1       Q3
Size       1593.0   2908.4   2076.5   2373.9
```

1. $\bar{X} = 2231.4$ Median $= 2217.0$ $s = 249.3$

2. $sk = \dfrac{3(2231.4 - 2217.0)}{249.3} = 0.17$ very near a symmetrical distribution

3.   See MINITAB above: $Q_1 = 2076.5$, $Q_3 = 2373.9$, the smallest value is 1593 and the largest is 2908.4. There are two outliers on the large side of the distribution and done on the small side.

```
                           - - - - - - - - - -
*          - - - - - - - -|     +     |- - - - - - - -       **
                           - - - - - - - - - -

- - - - - -+- - - - - -+- - - - - -+- - - - - -+- - - - - -+- - - - - - - -
        1750      2000      2250      2500      2750
```

4.   The mean home size is 2231.4 and the median is 2217.0. The standard deviation is 249.3. The smallest house is 1593.0 and the largest 2908.4.

71.   a.   1. $\bar{X} = 38.58$($million)   Median $= 39.62$($million) $s = 13.74$

        2. $sk = \dfrac{3(38.58 - 39.62)}{13.74} = -0.23$

        3.   Minimum team salary is 12.17 and the maximum is 64.99. $Q_1 - 31.04$ and $Q_3 = 47.60$

```
                                - - - - - - - - - -
- - - - - - - - - - - - - - - - - -|        +     |- - - - - - - - -  **
                                - - - - - - - - - -

- - - - - -+- - - - - -+- - - - - -+- - - - - -+- - - - - -+- - - - - -+- - - -
        10        20        30        40        50        60
```

        4.   A typical team salary is about 40 million dollars. The distribution is symmetrical and the team salaries range from 12.17 million dollars to 64.99 million dollars.

    b.   1. $\bar{X} = 2.26$(million)   Median $= 2.07$ (million)$s = 0.79$

        2. $sk = \dfrac{3(2.26 - 2.07)}{0.79} = -0.72$ The distribution is negatively skewed.

        3.   The largest attendance is 3.89 million and the smallest is 1.26 million. $Q_1 = 1.55$ and $Q_3 = 2.87$

```
                - - - - - - - - - - - - - - - - - -
- - - - - - -|         +            |- - - - - - - - -
                - - - - - - - - - - - - - - - - - -

- - - - - -+- - - - - -+- - - - - -+- - - - - -+- - - - - -+- - - - - -
        1.5       2.0       2.5       3.0       3.5
```

        4.   A typical attendance was a little more than 2.0 million. The attendance ranged from 1.26 million up to almost 6.5 million spectators. The standard deviation was 0.79 million.

72.   a.   1. $\bar{X} = 3048$ Median $= 1600$ $s = 3756$

        2. $sk = \dfrac{3(3048 - 1600)}{3756} = 1.16$ The distribution is positively skewed.

        3.   The smallest circulation is 450 and the largest is 17,900, $Q_1 = 811$ and $Q_3 = 4250$

```
            - - - - - - - - -
          -|    +     |- - - - - - - - -                    00
            - - - - - - - - -

- - - - - -+- - - - - -+- - - - - -+- - - - - -+- - - - - -+- - - - - -+- - - - - - -
        0        3500      7000     10500     14000     17500
```

        4.   The distribution is positively skewed with two extreme outliers.

b. 1. $\overline{X} = 36{,}629$ Median $= 26{,}727$ $s = 22{,}973$

2. $sk = \dfrac{3(36{,}629 - 26{,}727)}{22{,}973} = 1.29$ The distribution is positively skewed.

3. The minimum color advertising cost is 7220 and the maximum is 97,700. $Q_1 = 20{,}638$ and $Q_3 = 55{,}324$

```
                        - - - - - - - - -
              - - -|      +            |- - - - - - - -
                        - - - - - - - - -
        - - - - - -+- - - - - -+- - - - - -+- - - - - -+- - - - - -+- - - -
                0      20000   40000   60000   80000
```

4. The median color advertising cost is \$26,727. The distribution is positively skewed .

73. a. 1. $\overline{X} = \$33{,}181$ Median $= \$32{,}708$ $s = 3549$

2. $sk = \dfrac{3(33{,}181 - 32{,}708)}{3549} = 0.40$

3. The largest salary is \$43,256 and the smallest is \$26,125. $Q_1 = 30{,}816$ and $Q_3 = 35{,}519$

```
                         - - - - - - - - - - - - -
          - - - - - - - - - -|     +     |- - - - - - - - - - - - - - -  *  *
                         - - - - - - - - - - - -
        +- - - - - - - -+- - - - - - - -+- - - - - - - -+- - - - - - - -+- - - - - - - -+- - - - - -
      24500       28000      31500      35000      38500      42000
```

4. The typical teacher salary is about \$33,000. The salaries range from \$26,125 up to \$43,256. There are two outliers on the positive side.

b. 1. $\overline{X} = 2134$ Median $= 1227$ $s = 3895$

2. $sk = \dfrac{3(2134 - 1227)}{3895} = 0.70$

3. The range of students is quite large. The smallest number of students in a distribution is 20 and the largest is 36,790. The box plot shows several outliers and extreme outliers. $Q_1 = 794$ and $Q_3 = 2282$

```
            - - -
        -|+ |- - -***00                                              0
            - - -
      - -+- - - - - - - -+- - - - - - - -+- - - - - - - -+- - - - - - - -+- - - - - - - -+- - - - -
        0       7000       14000      21000      28000      35000
```

4. There is a wide range in the data. The number of students in the Toledo system is much larger than the others. This has the effect of increasing the standard deviation.

1. | Outcome | 1 | 2 |
    | --- | --- | --- |
    | 1 | A | A |
    | 2 | A | F |
    | 3 | F | A |
    | 4 | F | F |

2. | Outcome | 1 | 2 |
    | --- | --- | --- |
    | 1 | A | A |
    | 2 | A | R |
    | 3 | A | S |
    | 4 | R | A |
    | 5 | R | R |
    | 6 | R | S |
    | 7 | S | A |
    | 8 | S | R |
    | 9 | S | S |

3. a. 0.176 found by 6/34
    b. Empirical

4. a. 0.40, found by 2/5
    b. Classical

5. a. The experiment is asking the 500 citizens whether they favor or oppose widening Indiana Avenue to three lanes.
    b. Possible outcomes include 321 favor the widening, 387 favor the widening, 444 favor the widening and so on.
    c. Answers will vary, but two possibilities are: a majority favors the widening, which would be 251 or more, and more than 300 favor the widening.

6   a. The experiment is counting the number of stockholders who favor the merger.
    b. The possible outcomes include one through six favoring the merger.
    c. Two possible evens would include: more than half favor the merger or all oppose the merger.

7. a. Empirical
    b. Classical
    c. Classical
    d. Subjective, because this is someone's opinion

8. a. | Outcome | 1st | 2nd |
        | --- | --- | --- |
        | 1 | M | M |
        | 2 | M | F |
        | 3 | F | F |
        | 4 | F | M |
    b. Classical

9. a. 0.25 found by 13/52
    b. 0.019 found by 1/52
    c. Classical

10. a. 0.167, found by 1/6
    b. Classical
    c. Yes, the events are equally likely. The probability that a 1, 2, 3, 4, 5 or 6 spot will occur is the same. The events are mutually exclusive, because, for example, a two-spot and a five-spot cannot occur at the same time.

11. a. The survey of 40 people about abortion
    b. 26 or more, respond yes for example
    c. 0.25 found by 10/40
    d. Empirical
    e. The events are not equally likely but they are mutually exclusive

12. a. Recording the number of violations
    b. at least one violation, for example
    c. 0.009, found by 18/2000
    d. Empirical

13. a. Answers will vary, here are some possibilities: 123, 124, 125, 999
    b. $\left(\dfrac{1}{10}\right)^3$
    c. Classical

14. a. Answers will vary, value goes up 1/16, goes up 1/8, goes down 1
    b. 0.01, 0.02, 0.01
    c. Subjective

15. $P(A \text{ or } B) = P(A) + P(B)$
    $= 0.30 + 0.20$
    $= 0.50$
    $P(\text{neither}) = 1 - 0.50 = 0.50$

16. $P(X \text{ or } Y) = P(X) + P(Y)$
    $= 0.05 + 0.02$
    $= 0.07$
    $P(\text{neither}) = 1 - 0.07 = 0.93$

17. a. 0.51 found by 102/200
    b. 0.49 found by $61/200 + 37/200 = 0.305 + 0.185$ Special rule of addition

18. a. Recording the opinions of the designers with respect to the color.
    b. Any color but red, for example
    c. 0.4575, found by $92/400 + 91/400$
    d. 0.885, found by $1 - 46/400$

19.   a.   80%, found by 50% + 30%
        b.   80%, found by 100% − 20%

20.   0.75, found by 0.25 + 0.50

21.   Events A and C, B and C are mutually exclusive, Events B and C are complements

22.   yes, no

23. $P(A \text{ or } B) = P(A) + P(B) - P(A \text{ and } B)$
$$= 0.30 + 0.20 - 0.15$$
$$= 0.35$$

24. $P(X \text{ or } Y) = P(X) + P(Y) - P(X \text{ and } Y)$
$$= 0.55 + 0.35 - 0.20$$
$$= 0.70$$

25.   When two events are mutually exclusive it means that if one occurs the other event cannot not occur, Therefore, the probability of their joint occurrence is zero.

26. $P(H \text{ or } M) = P(H) + P(M) - P(H \text{ and } M)$
$$= 0.60 + 0.70 - 0.50$$
$$= 0.80$$

27.   a.   0.65, found by 0.35 + 0.40 − 0.10
        b.   A joint probability
        c.   No, an executive might read more than one magazine

28.   a.   0.55, found by 0.50 + 0.40 − 0.35
        b.   Joint probability
        c.   No, a vacationer can visit both attractions

29. $P(A \text{ and } B) = P(A) \times P(B|A)$
$$= 0.40 \times 0.30.$$
$$= 0.12$$

30. $P(X_1 \text{ and } Y_2) = P(X_1) \times P(Y_2|X_1)$
$$= 0.75 \times 0.40$$
$$= 0.30$$

31.   0.90, found by (0.80 + 0.60) − 0.50
       0.10, found by (1 − 0.90)

32.   5%, found by (1 − 0.95)

33.   a. $P(A_1) = 3/10 = 0.30$
        b. $P(B_1|A_2) = 1/3 = 0.33$
        c. $P(B_2 \text{ and } A_2) = 1/10 = 0.10$

34.   a.   6/380 or 0.01579, found by 3/20 x 2/19

        b.   272/380 or 0.7158, found by 17/20 x 16/19

35.   a.   A contingency table

        b.   0.27, found by 300/500 x 135 x 300

        c.   A tree diagram would appear as:

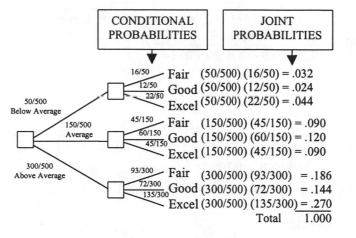

36.

Outcome	A	B	C	Outcome	A	B	C	Outcome	A	B	C
1	U	U	U✓	10	D	U	U✓	19	S	U	U✓
2	U	U	D✓	11	D	U	D	20	S	U	D
3	U	U	S✓	12	D	U	S	21	S	U	S
4	U	D	U✓	13	D	D	U	22	S	D	U
5	U	D	D	14	D	D	D	23	S	D	D
6	U	D	S	15	D	D	S	24	S	D	S
7	U	S	U✓	16	D	S	U	25	S	S	U
8	U	S	D	17	D	S	D	26	S	S	D
9	U	S	S	18	D	S	S	27	S	S	S

U = Stock is up   D = Stock is down   S = Stock is same

✓indicates the criteria that two stocks went up is met.

37.   2 of the stocks went up on seven of the 27 outcomes. P(A) = 7/27 = 0.259

      Probability the 1st presentation wins 3/5 = 0.60

      Probability the 2nd presentation wins 2/5(3/4) = 0.30

      Probability the 3rd presentation wins (2/5)(1/4)(3/3) = 0.10

38.   a. $\left(\dfrac{1}{7}\right)^3 = 0.0029$

        b. $\left(\dfrac{7}{7}\right)\left(\dfrac{6}{7}\right)\left(\dfrac{5}{7}\right) = 0.612$

        c. $\left(\dfrac{6}{7}\right)^3 = 0.630$

40. 0.3636, found by: $P(A_3|B_1) = \dfrac{0.40 \times 0.10}{(0.20 \times 0.25) + (0.40 \times 0.05) + (0.40 \times 0.10)}$

41. 0.5645, found by: $P(\text{night}|\text{win}) = \dfrac{P(\text{night}) \times P(\text{win}|\text{night})}{P(\text{night}) \times P(\text{win}|\text{night}) + P(\text{day}) \times P(\text{win}|\text{day})}$

$$= \dfrac{0.70 \times 0.50}{[(0.70 \times 0.50)] + [(0.30 \times 0.90)]}$$

42. 0.8571, found by: $\dfrac{0.80 \times 0.90}{(0.80 \times 0.90) + (0.20 \times 0.60)}$

43. 0.1053, found by:

$$P(\text{cash}|> \$50) = \dfrac{P(\text{cash}) \times P(> \$50|\text{cash})}{P(\text{cash}) \times P(> \$50|\text{cash}) + P(\text{check}) \times P(> \$50|\text{check}) + P(\text{charge}) \times P(> \$50|\text{charge})}$$

$$= \dfrac{0.20 \times 0.30}{[(0.30 \times 0.20)] + [(0.30 \times 0.90)] + [(0.40)(0.60)]}$$

44.   a. $P(\text{rural}/c) = 0.10$
     b. $P(c)P(\text{rural}/c) = (0.10)(0.10) = 0.01$
     c. $P(c|\text{rural}) = \dfrac{0.10 \times 0.10}{[(0.60 \times 0.20)] + [(0.30 \times 0.20)] + [(0.10)(0.10)]} = 0.0526$

45.   a. $78{,}960{,}960$
     b. 840, found by $(7)(6)(5)(4)$. That is $7!/3!$
     c. 10, found by $5!/3!2!$

46.   a. $6{,}840$
     b. 504
     c. 21

47. 210, found by $(10)(9)(8)(7)/(4)(3)(2)$

48. $10{,}000$, found by $(10)^4$

49. 120, found by $5!$

50. 3003, found by $_{15}C_{10} = \dfrac{15 \times 14 \times 13 \times 12 \times 11}{5 \times 4 \times 3 \times 2}$

51. $10{,}897{,}286{,}400$ found by $_{15}P_{10} = 15 \times 14 \times 13 \times 12 \times 11 \times 10 \times 9 \times 8 \times 7 \times 6$

52. 210

53.   a.   Asking teenagers their reactions to a newly developed soft drink.
     b.   Answers will vary, one possibility is more than half of the respondents like it.

54. Empirical

55.   Subjective

56.   No, probability would be 0.00

57.   3/6 or ½, found by 1/6 + 1/6 + 1/6, classical

58.   a.   0.10, found by 50/500
       b.   Yes, mutually exclusive, because at the same time an envelope cannot contain, for example, a total offering of $2 and a total offering of $56.
       c.   1.00
       d.   0.60, found by 300/500
       e.   0.90, found by 450/500 or 1 – (50/500)

59.   a.   The likelihood an event will occur, assuming that another event has already occurred.
       b.   The collection of one or more outcomes of an experiment.
       c.   A measure of the likelihood that two or more events will happen concurrently.

60.   a.   4/52, or 0.077
       b.   3/51, or 0.059
       c.   0.0045, found by (4/52)(3/51)

61.   a.   0.8145, found by $(0.95)^4$
       b.   Special rule of multiplication
       c.   P(A and B and C and D) = P(A) x P(B) x P(C) x P(D)

62.   a.   Venn diagram
       b.   Complement rule
       c.   1

63.   a.   0.08, found by 0.80 x 0.10
       b.

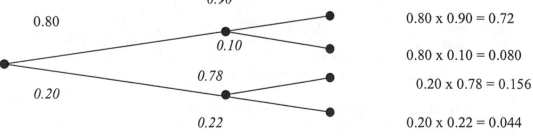

       c.   Yes, because all the possible outcomes are shown on the tree diagram.

64.   a.   1/16 or 0.0625, found by $(1/2)^4$
       b.   P(A and B and C and D) = P(A)P(B)P(C)P(D)
       c.   ½ or 0.50

65.   0.99, found by 57/100 + 40/100 + 2/100

66. a. 0.0459 found by $(0.358)^3$
    b. 0.2646 found by $(1 - 0.358)^3$

67. All hit = 0.4096, found by $(0.80)^4$. None hit = 0.0016, found by $(0.20)^4$

68. 0.3059, found by (50/90)(49/89)

69. a. 0.3818, found by (9/12)(8/11)(7/10)
    b. 0.6182, found by 1 − 0.3818

70. a. 0.40, found by 200/500
    b. 0.60, found by 100/500 + 200/500
    c. 0.60, found by (200/500) + (200/500) − (100/500)
    d. 0.33, found by 100/300
    e. 0.1595, found by (200/500)(199/499)

71. a. 0.5467, found by 82/150
    b. 0.76, found by (39/150) + (75/150)
    c. 0.6267, found by 82/150 + 39/150 − 27/150
    d. 0.3293, found by 27/82
    e. 0.2972, found by (82/150)(81/149)

72. a. 0.42
    b. 0.70(0.40) = 0.28
    c. 0.88

73. $P(\text{poor}|\text{profit}) = \dfrac{(0.10)(0.20)}{[(0.10)(0.20)] + (0.60)(0.80)] + [0.30)(0.60)]} = 0.0294$

74. a. 0.625, found by 250/400
    b. 0.250, found by 100/400
    c.
Smokes	Male	Female	Total
Yes	75	25	100
No	175	125	300
Total	250	150	400

       0.1875, found by 75/400
    d. 0.6875, found by 250/400 + 100/400 − 75/400

75. a. P(P or D) =(1/50)(9/10) + (49/50)(1/10) = 0.116
    b. P(No) = (49/50)(9/10) = 0.882
    c. P(No on 3) = $(0.882)^3$ = 0.686
    d. P(at least one prize) = 1 − 0.686 = 0.314

76. a. (10)(9)(8) = 720
    b. 0.00139, found by 1/720
    c. 0.99583, found by 1 − 3/720

77. 24, found by 4!

78. 0.70, found by $= P(A) + P(B) - P(A \text{ and } B)$

$$= 0.60 + 0.40 - 0.30$$

$$= 0.70$$

79. 0.4545, found by $\dfrac{(0.50)(0.625)}{(0.50)(0.625) + (0.50)(0.75)} = \dfrac{0.3125}{0.6875}$

80. 4320 different meals, found by 4 x 3 x 12 x 6 x 5
4104 early bird different meals found by (12 x 4 x 3 x 6) + (12 x 4 x 3 x 5) + (12 x 4 x 6 x 5) + (12 x 3 x 6 x 5)

81. Yes, 256 is found by 2^8

82. 15, found by 5 x 3

83. 2520, found by $_7P_5 = \dfrac{7!}{(7-5)!}$

84. 45, found by $_nC_r = \dfrac{10!}{2!(10-2)!}$

85. 0.9744, found by $1 - (0.40)^4$

86. 17,576,000 found by (26)(26)(26)(10)(10)(10)

87. a. 0.185, found by (0.15)(0.95) + (0.05)(0.85)
    b. 0.0075, found by (0.15)(0.05)

88. a. 0.333, found by (6/10)(5/9)
    b. 0.9286, found by $1 - [(6/10)(5/9)(4/8)(3/7)]$
    c. dependent

89. a. P(F and > 60) = 0.25, found by solving with the general rule of multiplication:
    $1 = P(F) \cdot P(>60|F) = (0.50)(0.50)$
    b. 0
    c. 0.3333, found by 1/3

90. a. 2024, found by $_{24}C_3 = \dfrac{24!}{3!(24-3)!}$
    b. 0.125, found by $1 - [(23/24)(22/23)(21/22)]$

91. a. 0.3034, found by 18.9/62.3
    b. 0.7047, found by (5.8/62.3) + (43.4/62.3) − (5.3/62.3)

c. 0.3346, found by $\dfrac{4.3 + 2.6 + 1.7}{12.5 + 8.0 + 5.2}$

d. First time $\dfrac{8.2 + 5.4 + 3.5}{43.4} = 0.3940$ Repeat $\dfrac{4.3 + 2.6 + 1.7}{18.9} = 0.4550$

e. 0.4853, found by $\left(\dfrac{42,400}{62,300}\right)\left(\dfrac{43,399}{62,299}\right)$

92. a. The overall percent defective is 5.175,
   found by $(0.20)(0.03) + (0.30)(0.04) + (0.25)(0.07) + (0.25)(0.065)$

   b. Using Bayes Rule:

   $$P(Tyson|Defective) = \dfrac{0.20(0.03)}{(0.20)(0.03) + (0.30)(0.04) + (0.25)(0.07) + (0.25)(0.065)} = 0.1159$$

   c.
Supplier	Joint	Revised
Tyson	0.00600	0.1159
Fuji	0.01200	0.2319
Kirkpatricks	0.01750	0.3382
Parts	0.01625	0.3140
Total	0.05175	1.0000

93. For the system to operate both components in the series must work. The probability they both work is 0.81, found by $(0.90)(0.90)$

94. 0.99, found by $1 - [((0.90)(0.90) + (0.90)(0.10) + (0.10)(0.90)]$

95. 1/3, 628,800

96. The following tree diagram lists the probabilities

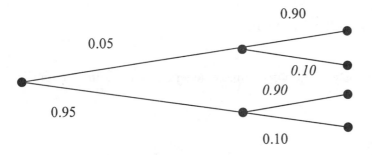

P(G) = Probability of guilty = 0.05
P(NG) = Probability of not guilty = 0.95
P(C/G) = Probability of correct assessment if guilty = 0.90
P(C/NG) = Probability of correct assessment if *not* guilty = 0.90

   a. George will not fire all those that fail the lie detector test, whether they are guilty or not.
   P(fire) = $(0.05)(0.90) + (0.95)(0.10) = 0.14$

   b. $P(G/F) = \dfrac{0.05(0.90)}{0.05(0.90) + 0.95(0.10)} = 0.3214$

c. $P(G/N) = \dfrac{0.05(0.10)}{0.05(0.10)+0.95(0.90)} = 0.0058$

d. George's policy is not very effective. About 2/3 of the time innocent people are fired. (The complement of part b)

97. See diagram below:

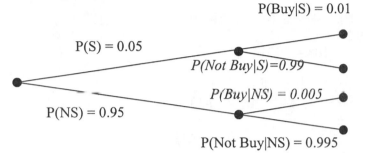

$$P(Buy|S) = 0.01$$
$$P(S) = 0.05$$
$$P(Not\ Buy|S)=0.99$$
$$P(Buy|NS) = 0.005$$
$$P(NS) = 0.95$$
$$P(Not\ Buy|NS) = 0.995$$

a. $P(Buys) = (0.05)(0.01) + (0.95)(0.005) = 0.00525$

b. $P(S/Buy) = \dfrac{0.05(0.01)}{0.05(0.01)+0.95(0.005)} = 0.0952$

c. $P(S/Not\ buy) = \dfrac{0.05(0.99)}{0.05(0.99)+0.95(0.995)} = 0.0498$

98. a. $P(G/A) = \dfrac{0.30(0.01)}{0.30(0.01)+0.50(0.03)+0.20(0.10)} = \dfrac{0.003}{0.038} = 0.0789$

b. $P(M/A) = \dfrac{0.50(0.03)}{0.30(0.01)+0.50(0.03)+0.20(0.10)} = \dfrac{0.015}{0.038} = 0.3947$

c. $P(P/A) = \dfrac{0.20(0.10)}{0.30(0.01)+0.50(0.03)+0.20(0.10)} = \dfrac{0.020}{0.038} = 0.5263$

99. a. P(male) = 140/182 = 0.7692
b. P(35 and 54) = 112/182 = 0.6154
c. P(male and 35 and 54) = 87/182 = 0.4780
d. P(female and over 54) = 3/182 = 0.0165
e. P(male or 35 and 54) = 140/182 + 112/182 − 87/182 = 0.9066
f. P(female or over 54) = 42/182 + 29/182 − 3/182 = 0.3736
g. P(male/under 35) = 27/41 = 0.6585
h. P(male/over 54) = 26/29 = 0.8966
i. P(over 54/male) = 26/140 = 0.1857
j. P(over 54/female) = 3/42 = 0.0714
k. P(m) = 140/182 = 0.769   P(m/35 to 54) = 87/112 = 0.777
    Probabilities are very close, they could be independent
l. P(f) = 42/182 = 0.2307   P(f/over 54) = 3/29 = 0.103
    The events are not independent
m. No, there are some members that are both female and over 54.
n. Yes, you must either be male or female

100. a. Using MINITAB
Rows: Pool   Column: Township

	1	2	3	4	5	All
0	9	8	7	11	3	38
1	6	12	18	18	13	67
All	15	20	25	29	16	105

1. P(1 or Pool) = 15/105 + 67/105 − 6/105 = 0.7238
2. P(Pool/3) = 18/25 = 0.72
3. P(3 and Pool) = 18/105 = 0.1714

b. Using MINITAB
Rows: Garage   Column: Township

	1	2	3	4	5	All
0	6	5	10	9	4	34
1	9	15	15	20	12	71
All	15	20	25	29	16	105

1. P(G) = 71/105 = 0.6762
2. P(NG/5) = 4/16 = 0.25
3. P(G and 3) = 15/105 = 0.1429
4. P(NG or 2) = 34/105 + 20/105 − 5/105 = 49/105 = 0.4667

101. a.

	< 1.5 million	1.5 up to 2.5	2.5 or more	Total
Losing	6	7	3	16
Winning	0	5	7	12
Total	6	12	10	28

1. P(Win) = 12/28 = 0.4826
2. P(Win or 2.5 or more) = 12/18 + 10/28 − 7/28 = 15/28 = 0.5357
3. P(Win|2.5 or more) = 0.70
4. P(Losing and < 1.5) = 6/28 = 0.2143

b.

	Grass	Turf	Total
Losing	10	6	16
Winning	10	2	12
Total	20	8	28

1. P(Turf) = 8/28 = 0.2857
2. P(W|Grass) = 10/20 = 0.50
3. P(W|Turf) = 2/8 = 0.25
4. P(Win or turf) = 12/28 + 8/28 − 2/28 = 18/28 = 0.6429

102.

	Circulation		
Male	<3000	3000 ≥	Total
≤ 50	14	11	25
50 >	20	3	23
	34	14	48

a. 23/48 = 0.4792
b. 3/48 = 0.0625
c. 23/38 + 14/48 − 3/48 = 34/48 = 0.7083
d. 3/14 = 0.2143

103. a. The first step is to group the 94 school districts by the percent of students on welfare.

Welfare Group	Frequency	Mean Percent Passing
Low	43	72.0
Moderate	32	64.0
High	19	54.0
Total	94	66.0

To explain these values, there were 19 districts in which the percent on welfare was more than ten percent. The mean passing rates in these 19 schools was 54.0.

1. From the above chart, among the 94 districts the mean percent passing is 66.0. So we estimate the probability that a randomly selected student passes the exam is 54.0.
2. From the above chart, among the low group, 72 percent passed the test. So we estimate the probability of passing the exam as 0.72.
3. The probability a student from a high welfare district passes is 0.54.
4. First to find the probability that a student is from a moderate district and failed the exam, we multiply the likelihood of being from the moderate group and failed. That is $32/94 = 0.34$ time the probability a student in the moderate group fails (1 – probability he or she passes = $1 – 0.66 = 0.34$). The result is $0.34 \times 0.34 = 0.12$. To find the probability a student failed or is from the moderate group: P(Moderate or Fail) = P(moderate) + P(fail) – P(moderate and fail) = $0.34 + 0.34 – 0.12 = 0.56$

b. First we create the following table, which shows the districts by welfare and size.

Welfare	Small	Medium	Large	Total
Low	22	17	4	43
Moderate	9	18	5	32
High	5	7	7	19
Total	36	42	16	94

1. P(Small) = 36/94(100) = 38%
2. P(Low|small) = 22/36(100) = 61%
3. P(Small and low) = 22/94(100) = 23%
4. P(Small or low) = 36/94 + 43/94 – 22/94 = 57/94 = 0.61
5. P(3 medium) = (42/94)(41/93)(40/92) = 0.0856

1.   Mean = 1.3   Variance = 0.81 found by:
      $\mu = \sum XP(X) = 0(.20) + 1(.40) + 2(.30) + 3(.10) = 1.3$
      $\sigma^2 = \sum(X - \mu)^2 P(X)$
      $\quad = (0 - 1.3)^2(.2) + (1 - 1.3)^2(.4) + (2 - 1.3)^2(.3) + (3 - 1.3)^2$
      $\quad = 0.81$

2.   Mean = 5.4   Variance = 12.04 found by:
      $\mu = \sum XP(X) = 2(.5) + 8(.3) + 10(.2) = 5.4$
      $\sigma^2 = \sum(X - \mu)^2 P(X)$
      $\quad = (2 - 5.4)^2(.5) + (8 - 5.4)^2(.3) + (10 - 5.4)^2(.2)$
      $\quad = 12.04$

3.   a.   The second or middle, one
      b.   0.20, 0.40, 0.90
      c. $\mu = 14.5$, $5(.1) + 10(.3) + 15(.2) + 20(.4) = 14.5$ Variance = 27.25
            $\sigma^2 = (5 - 14.5)^2(.1) + (10 - 14.5)^2(.3) + (15 - 14.5)^2(.2) + (20 - 14.5)^2(.4) = 27.25$
            $\sigma = 5.22$ found by $\sqrt{27.25}$

4.   a.   Discrete
      b.   Continuous
      c.   Discrete
      d.   Continuous
      e.   Discrete
      f.   Continuous

5. $\mu = 0(.3) + 1(.4) + 2(.2) + 3(.1) = 1.1$
      $\sigma^2 = (0 - 1.1)^2(.3) + (1 - 1.1)^2(.4) + (2 - 1.1)^2(.2) + (3 - 1.1)^2(.1) = 0.89$
      $\sigma = 0.943$

6. $\mu = 1000(.6) + 1200(.3) + 1500(.1) = 1110$
      $\sigma^2 = (1000 - 1110)^2(.6) + (1200 - 1110)^2(.3) + (1500 - 1110)^2(.1) = 24,900$
      $\sigma = 157.8$

7.   a.   0.20
      b.   0.55
      c.   0.95
      d. $\mu = 0(.45) + 10(.3) + 100(.2) + 500(0.05) = 48$
            $\sigma^2 = (0 - 48)^2(.45) + (10 - 48)^2(.3) + (100 - 48)^2(.2) + (500 - 48)^2(.05) = 12,226$
            $\sigma = 110.57$

8.   a.   0.5000

     b.   0.6667

     c.   0

     d.

$$\mu = 0(1/3) + 1(1/2) + 2(0) + 3(1/6) = 1$$
$$\sigma^2 = (0-1)^2(1/3) + (1-1)^2(1/2) + (2-1)^2(0) + (3-1)^2(1/6) = 1$$
$$\sigma = 1$$

9.   a.   0, 1, 2, 3

     b.

Number of Minority	Probability
0	0.1667
1	0.5000
2	0.3000
3	0.0333

     c.   0.5, 0.8333, 0.3333

     d.

$$\mu = 0(.1667) + 1(.5) + 2(.3) + 3(0.0333) = 1.1999$$
$$\sigma^2 = (0-1.1999)^2(.1667) + (1-1.1999)^2(.5) + (2-1.1999)^2(.3) + (3-1.1999)^2(.0333) = 0.5599$$
$$\sigma = 0.7483$$

10.   a.

Number of Tosses	Probability
1	0.5000
2	0.2500
3	0.1250
4	<u>0.1250</u>
	1.0000

     b.

$$\mu = 1(.5) + 2(.25) + 3(.125) + 4(.125) = 1.875$$
$$\sigma^2 = (1-1.875)^2(.5) + ... + (4-1.875)^2(.125) = 1.1094$$
$$\sigma = 1.0533$$

     c.   0.5000

11.   a.

$$P(2) = \frac{4!}{2!(4-2)!}(.25)^2(.75)^{4-2} = 0.2109$$

     b.

$$P(3) = \frac{4!}{3!(4-3)!}(.25)^3(.75)^{4-3} = 0.0469$$

12.   a.

$$P(2) = \frac{5!}{1!(5-1)!}(.4)^1(.6)^{5-1} = 0.2592$$

     b.

$$P(3) = \frac{5!}{2!(5-2)!}(.4)^2(.6)^{5-2} = 0.3456$$

13.   a.

x	$P(X)$
0	0.064
1	0.288
2	0.432
3	0.216

     b.

$$\mu = 0(0.064) + ... 3(0.216) = 1.8 \qquad \sigma^2 = (0-1.8)^2 0.064 + ... + (3-1.8)^2 0.216 = 0.72$$
$$\sigma = \sqrt{0.72} = 0.8485$$

14. a.

x	$P(r)$
0	0.168
1	0.360
2	0.309
3	0.132
4	0.028
5	0.002

b. $\mu = 0(0.168) + ... + 5(0.002) = 1.5 \quad \sigma^2 = (0-1.5)^2 0.168 + ... + (5-1.5)^2 0.002 = 1.05$

$\sigma = \sqrt{1.05} = 1.0247$

15. a. 0.2668, found by $P(2) = \dfrac{9!}{2!(9-2)!}(.3)^2(.7)^7$

b. 0.1715, found by $P(4) = \dfrac{9!}{4!(9-4)!}(.3)^4(.7)^5$

c. 0.0404, found by $P(0) = \dfrac{9!}{0!(9-0)!}(.3)^0(.7)^9$

16. a. 0.7351, found by $P(6) = \dfrac{6!}{6!(6-6)!}(.95)^6(.05)^0$

b. 0.2321, found by $P(5) = \dfrac{6!}{5!(6-5)!}(.95)^5(.05)^1$

c. $\mu = 5.7$, found by $6(.95)$

d. $\sigma^2 = 0.285$, found by $6(.95)(.05)$

17. a. 0.2824, found by $P(0) = \dfrac{12!}{0!(12-0)!}(.10)^0(.9)^{12}$

b. 0.3765, found by $P(1) = \dfrac{12!}{1!(12-1)!}(.10)^1(.9)^{11}$

c. 0.2301, found by $P(2) = \dfrac{12!}{2!(12-2)!}(.10)^2(.9)^{10}$

d. $\mu = 1.2$, found by $12(.10)$

18. a. 0.2311, found by $_{12}C_4(0.3)^4(0.7)^8$

b. 0.0138, found by $_{12}C_0(0.3)^0(0.7)^{12}$

c. 0.1678, found by $_{12}C_2(0.3)^2(0.7)^{10}$

d. 3.6, found by $12(0.3)$

e. 2.52, found by $12(0.3)(0.7)$ $\qquad \sigma = 1.587$, found by $\sqrt{2.52}$

19. a. Number of production employees absent

b. Discrete because the number absent can only assume certain values, such as 1, 2, 3, and so on. There cannot be a fractional number of employees absent on a particular day.

c. 0.349, found by referring to Appendix A, an n of 10, and x of 0, and a π of 0.10.

d.

x	P(x)
0	0.349
1	0.387
2	0.194
3	0.057
4	0.011
5	0.001

e. $\mu = 1.00$, found by $n\pi = 10(.10)$

$\sigma^2 = 0.90$, found by $n\pi(1-\pi) = (10)(.10)(.90)$

$\sigma = 0.949$, found by $\sqrt{0.90}$

20. a. 1/5 or 0.20
   b. Number of correct responses among the eight people.
   c. Discrete because there can only 0, 1, …, 8 people who identified the cereal correctly.
   d. 0.168 from Appendix A
   e.

Number Correct r	Probability of occurrence P(r)	Number correct r	Probability of occurrence P(r)
0	0.168	5	0.009
1	0.336	6	0.001
2	0.294	7	0.000
3	0.147	8	0.000
4	0.046	Total	1.000*

   * slight discrepancy due to rounding

   f. $\mu = 1.60$, found by 8(.20)   variance = 1.28   standard deviation = 1.13
   g.

   h. They were probably not guessing. The change that they would guess 7 out of 8 correct is practically zero.
   i. Outcome can only be right or wrong, probability distribution results from counts, probability of success remains the same from trial to trial. Trials are independent.

21. a. 0.296, found by using Appendix A with n of 8, π of 0.30 and x of 2.
   b. $P(x \le 2) = 0.058 + 0.198 + 0.296 = 0.552$
   c. 0.448, found by $P(x \ge 3) = 1 - P(x \le 2) = 1 - 0.552$

22. a. 0.101, found from Appendix A, $n = 12$, $x = 5$
   b. $P(x \le 5) = 0.002 + 0.012 + 0.042 + 0.101 = 0.157$
   c. $P(x \ge 6) = 1 - P(x \le 5) = 1 - 0.157 = 0.843$

23. a. 0.387, found from Appendix A with n of 9, π of 0.90, and an x of 9
     b. $P(x < 5) = 0.001$
     c. 0.992, found by $1 - 0.008$
     d. 0.947, found by $1 - 0.053$

24. a. 0.358, found from Appendix A with n of 20, π of 0.05, and an x of 0
     b. 0.642, found by $1 - 0.358$
     c. 0.076, found by $1 - [0.358 + 0.377 + 0.189]$

25. $$P(2) = \frac{[_6C_2][_4C_1]}{_{10}C_3} = \frac{15(4)}{120} = 0.50$$

26. $$P(3) = \frac{[_{10}C_3][_5C_1]}{_{15}C_4} = \frac{120(5)}{1365} = 0.4396$$

27. $$P(0) = \frac{[_7C_2][_3C_0]}{_{10}C_2} = \frac{21(1)}{45} = 0.4667$$

28. a. $$P(3) = \frac{[_6C_3][_2C_0]}{_8C_3} = \frac{20(1)}{56} = 0.3571$$
     b. $P(X \le 2) = 1 - P(X = 3) = 1 - 0.3571 = 0.6429$

29. $$P(2) = \frac{[_9C_3][_6C_2]}{_{15}C_5} = \frac{84(15)}{3003} = 0.4196$$

30. $$P(0) = \frac{[_{11}C_5][_4C_0]}{_{15}C_5} = \frac{462(1)}{3003} = 0.1538 \quad P(X \ge 1) = 1 - P(0) = 1 - 0.1538 = 0.8462$$

31. a. 0.6703
     b. 0.3297

32. a. 0.1465
     b. 0.2381
     c. 0.7619

33. a. 0.0613
     b. 0.0803

34. a. 0.1353
     b. 0.8647

35. $\mu = 6$, $P(X \ge 5) = 0.7149 = 1 - (.0025+.0149+.0446+.0892+.1339)$

36. 0.8088

37. a. $$P(2) = \frac{[_8C_2][_4C_2]}{_{12}C_4} = \frac{28(6)}{495} = 0.3394$$
     b. $$\frac{[_8C_0][_4C_4]}{_{12}C_4} = \frac{1}{495} = 0.0020$$

c. $P(1) = \dfrac{[_8C_3][_4C_1]}{_{12}C_4} = \dfrac{56(4)}{495} = 0.4525$ $P(0) = \dfrac{[_8C_4][_4C_0]}{_{12}C_4} = \dfrac{(70)1}{495} = 0.1414$

$P(X < 1) = P(0) + P(1) = 0.1414 + 0.4525 = 0.5939$

Using a binomial with $n = 12$, and $\pi = 4/12 = 0.33$

a. $P(2) = {}_4C_2(.33)^2(.67)^2 = 0.2933$

b. $P(4) = {}_4C_4(.33)^4(.67)^6 = 0.012$

c. $P(X \le 1) = {}_4C_0(.33)^0(.67)^4 + {}_4C_1(.33)^1(.67)^3$
$= 0.2015 + 0.3970 = 0.5985$

Binomial estimates are not very close.

38. The binomial distribution is a discrete probability distribution where the outcomes of the experiment can take only one of two forms. A second important part is that data collected is a result of counts. Additionally, one trial is independent from the next and the chance for success remains the same from one trial to the next.

39. When n is large and π is small the Poisson and the binomial distribution will yield approximately the same results.

40.

	Poisson	*Binomial*

a. 0.0384 found by $\dfrac{0.04^1(e)^{-0.04}}{1!}$ 0.0388 found by ${}_4C_1(.01)^1(.99)^3$

b. 0.0008 found by $\dfrac{0.04^2(e)^{-0.04}}{2!}$ 0.0006 found by ${}_4C_2(.01)^2(.99)^2$

c. 0.9608 found by $\dfrac{0.04^0(e)^{-0.04}}{0!}$ 0.9606 found by ${}_4C_0(.01)^0(.99)^4$

Binomial estimates are good

41. $\mu = 0(.1) + 1(.2) + 2(.3) + 3(.4) = 2.00$ $\sigma^2 = (0-2)^2(.1)+...+(3-2)^2(.40) = 1.0$ $\sigma = 1$

42. $\mu = 0.25(\$1000) + 0.60(\$2000) + 0.15(\$5000) = \$2200$

$\sigma^2 = (1000-2200)^2(.25)+...+(5000-2200)^2(.15) = 1,560,000$ $\sigma = 1249$

43. $\mu = 0(.4) + 1(.2) + 2(.2) + 3(.1) + 4(.1) = 1.3$ $\sigma^2 = (0-1.30)^2(.4)+...+(4-1.30)^2(.10) = 1.81$

$\sigma = 1.3454$

44. $\mu = 13.2$, found by $3.00 + 5.20 + 3.50 + 1.50$
$\sigma^2 = 0.86$, found by $0.36 + 0.016 + 0.16 + 0.324$
$\sigma = \sqrt{0.86} = 0.9274$

45. a. 0.001
     b. 0.001

46. The probability of exactly two Spanish-speaking Americans on the jury is 0.168 (Appendix A, $n = 12$, $\pi = 0.3$, and $x = 2$). One might argue that this is a sufficiently large chance and agree with the government lawyer.

47. $P(2) = \dfrac{[_6C_2][_4C_2]}{_{10}C_4} = \dfrac{15(6)}{210} = 0.4286$

48. a. $P(1) = \dfrac{[_{20}C_3][_5C_1]}{_{25}C_4} = \dfrac{1140(5)}{12,560} = 0.4506$

    b. 0.410, using Appendix A, $n = 4$, $x = 1$, $\pi = 0.20$

    c. 0.3595 found by $\mu = n\pi = 4(0.2) = 0.8$, $x = 1$

    d. The answers vary because of the different assumptions.

49. a. $P(1) = \dfrac{[_7C_2][_3C_1]}{_{10}C_3} = \dfrac{21(3)}{120} = 0.5250$

    b. $P(0) = \dfrac{[_7C_3][_3C_0]}{_{10}C_3} = \dfrac{35(1)}{120} = 0.2917$

    $P(X \geq 1) = 1 - P(0) = 1 - 0.2917 = 0.7083$

50. $P(X = 0) = \dfrac{[_5C_3][_4C_0]}{_9C_3} = \dfrac{10}{84} = 0.119$ $P(X = 1) = \dfrac{[_5C_2][_4C_1]}{_9C_3} = \dfrac{10(4)}{84} = 0.476$

    $P(X = 2) = \dfrac{[_5C_1][_4C_2]}{_9C_3} = \dfrac{5(6)}{84} = 0.357$ $P(X = 3) = \dfrac{[_5C_0][_4C_3]}{_9C_3} = \dfrac{4}{84} = 0.048$

    $P(X \geq 1) = 1 - P(X = 0) = 1 - 0.119 = 0.881$

51. $P(X = 0) = \dfrac{[_8C_4][_4C_0]}{_{12}C_4} = \dfrac{70}{495} = 0.141$

52. a. 0.60, found by $P(X = 1) = \dfrac{[_4C_2][_2C_1]}{_6C_3} = \dfrac{6(2)}{20}$

    b. 0.20, found by $P(X = 2) = \dfrac{[_4C_1][_2C_2]}{_6C_3} = \dfrac{4(1)}{20}$

53. a. 0.0498

    b. 0.7746, found by $(1 - 0.0498)^5$

54. a. $\mu = 3$, probability $= 0.0498$

    b. 0.5768, found by $1 - (0.0498 + 0.1494 + 0.2240)$

55. $\mu = 4.0$ from Appendix C

    a. 0.0183

    b. 0.1954

    c. 0.6289

    d. 0.5665

56.   a.   Referring to Appendix C and finding P(X < 5) = 0.1353 + 0.2707+0.2707+0.1804 + 0.0902 = 0.9473, which is very close to the goal of 0.95.

        b.

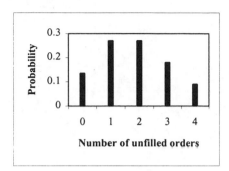

57.   For NASA, $\mu = n\pi = 25(1/60{,}000) = 0.0004$

$$P(0) = \frac{0.0004^0 e^{-0.0004}}{0!} = 0.9996 \qquad P(X \geq 1) = 1 - 0.9996 = 0.0004$$

For Air Force, $\mu = 25(1/35) = 0.7143$

$$P(0) = \frac{0.7143^0 e^{-0.7143}}{0!} = 0.4895 \qquad P(X \geq 1) = 1 - 0.4895 = 0.5105$$

Summarizing, Air Force estimate is 0.4895, and NASA estimate is 0.0004.

58.   Let $n = 34$, and $\pi = 29/34 = 0.8529$

$$P(5) = {}_{34}C_5 (0.8529)^{29}(0.1471)^5 = 0.1899$$

59.   Let $\mu = n\pi = 155(1/3709) = 0.042$

$$P(5) = \frac{0.042^5 e^{-0.042}}{5!} = 0.0000001 \qquad \text{Very Unlikely!}$$

60.   a.

Number	Count	P(X)	XP(X)	$(X - \mu)^2 P(X)$
2	24	0.2286	0.4571	0.7406
3	26	0.2476	0.7428	0.1585
4	26	0.2476	0.9905	0.0099
5	11	0.1048	0.5238	0.1509
6	14	0.1333	0.8000	0.6453
7	2	0.0191	0.1333	0.1951
8	2	0.0191	0.1524	0.3360
	105	1.000	3.8000	2.2362

$\mu = 3.80,$ $s = \sqrt{2.2362} = 1.4954$

        b.

Number	Count	P(X)	XP(X)	$(X - \mu)^2 P(X)$
1.5	16	0.1524	0.2286	0.0515
2.0	65	0.6191	1.2382	0.0041
2.5	15	0.1429	0.3573	0.0251
3.0	9	0.0857	02571	0.0723
	105	1.0001	2.0812	0.1530

$\mu = 2.0812,$ $\sigma = \sqrt{0.1530} = 0.3912$

61.   Eight of the 28 teams have turf home fields.

$$P(2) = \frac{_8C_2 \, _{20}C_3}{_{28}C_5} = \frac{(28)(1140)}{98,280} = 0.3248$$

THE NORMAL PROBABILITY DISTRIBUTION

1. The actual shape of a normal distribution depends on its mean and standard deviation. Thus, there is a normal distribution, and an accompanying normal curve, for a mean of 7 and a standard deviation of 2. There is a another normal curve for a mean of $25,000 and a standard deviation of $1742, and so on.

2. It is bell shaped and symmetrical about its mean. It is asymptotic. There is a family of normal curves. The mean, median, and the mode are equal.

3. a. 490 and 510, found by $500 \pm 1(10)$
   b. 480 and 520, found by $500 \pm 2(10)$
   c. 470 and 530, found by $500 \pm 3(10)$

4. a. about 68 percent
   b. about 95 percent
   c. over 99 percent

5. a. 1.25 found by $z = \dfrac{25-20}{4.0} = 1.25$
   b. 0.3944, found in Appendix D
   c. 0.3085, found by $z = \dfrac{18-20}{2.5} = -0.5$
      Find 0.1915 in Appendix D for $z = -0.5$ then $0.5000 - 0.1915 = 0.3085$

6. a. $z = 0.84$, found by $z = \dfrac{14.3-12.2}{2.5} = 0.84$
   b. 0.2995, found in Appendix D
   c. 0.1894, found by $z = \dfrac{10-12.5}{2.5} = -0.88$
      Find 0.3106 in Appendix D for $z = -0.88$, then $0.5000 - 0.3106 - 0.1894$

7. a. 0.3413, found by $z = \dfrac{\$20-\$16.50}{\$3.50} = 1.00$ Then find 0.3413 in Appendix D for a $z = 1$
   b. 0.1587, found by $0.5000 - 0.3413 = 0.1587$
   c. 0.3386, found by $z = \dfrac{\$15.00-\$16.50}{\$3.50} = -0.43$
      Find 0.1664 in Appendix D, for a $z = -0.43$, then $0.5000 - 0.1664 = 0.3336$

8. a. About 0.4332 from Appendix D, where $z = 1.50$
   b. About 0.1915, where $z = -0.50$
   c. About 0.3085, found by $0.5000 - 0.1915$

9.   a.   0.8276, first find $z = -1.5$, found by $((44 - 50)/4)$ and $z = 1.25 = (55 - 50)/4)$. The area between -1.5 and 0 is 0.4332 and the area between 0 and 1.25 is 0.3944, both from Appendix D. Then adding the two area we find that $0.4332 + 0.3944 = 0.8276$.

     b.   0.1056, found by $0.5000 - 0.3994$, where $z = 1.25$

     c.   0.2029, recall that the area for $z = 1.25$ is 0.3944, and the area for $z = 0.5$, found by $((52 - 50)/4)$ is 0.1915. Then subtract $0.3944 - 0.1915$ and find 0.2029.

     d.   X = 56.60, found by adding 0.5000(the area left of the mean) and then finding a z value that forces 45% of the data to fall inside the curve. Solving for X: $1.65 = (X - 50)/4 = 56.60$.

10.   a.   0.4017, first find $z = -0.36$, found by $((75 - 80)/14)$ and $z = 0.71(((90 - 80)/14)$. The area between -0.36 and 0 is 0.1406 and the area between 0 and 0.71 is 0.2611, both from Appendix D. then adding the two area we find $0.1406 + 0.2611 = 0.4017$.

     b.   0.3594, found by $0.5000 - 0.1406$, where $z = -0.36$

     c.   0.2022 found by $z = (55 - 80)/14 = -1.79$, for which the area is 0.4633. The z-value for 70 is -0.71 and the corresponding area is 0.2661. So $0.4633 - 0.2611 = 0.2022$

     d.
$$-0.84 = \frac{X - 80}{14}$$
$$X = 80.00 - 11.76 = 68.24$$

11.   a.   0.1525, found by subtracting $0.4938 - 0.3413$, which are the areas associated with z values of 2.5 and 1, respectively.

     b.   0.0062, found by $0.5000 - 0.4938$

     c.   0.9710, found by recalling that the area of the z value of 2.5 is 0.4938. Then find $z = -2.00$ found by $((6.8 - 7.0)/0.1)$. Thus, $0.4938 + 0.4772 = 0.9710$.

     d.   7.233, find a z value where 0.4900 of area is between 0 and z. That value is $z = 2.33$, then solve for X: $(X - 7)/0.1$ so $X = 7.233$

12.   a.   0.3085, found by $z = (\$80,000 - \$70,000)/\$20,000 = 0.50$. The area is 0.1915. Then $0.5000 - 0.1915 = 0.3085$

     b.   0.2902, found by $z = ((80,000 - 70,000)/20,000) = 0.50$, the area is 0.1915
$z = ((65,000 - 70,000)/20,000) = -0.25$, the area is 0.0987
Adding these values together: $0.1915 + 0.0987 = 0.2902$

     c.   0.5987, found by the area under the curve with a $z = -0.25$, $0.0987 + 0.5000 = 0.5987$

     d.   \$86,800, first find a z value that forces 30% of the area to fall below the z value ($z = 0.84$). Then solve for X in the equation $0.84 = (X - \$70,000)/\$20,000 = \$86,800$.

13.   a.   0.0764, found by $z = (20 - 15)/3.5 = 1.43$, then $0.5000 - 0.4236 = 0.0764$

     b.   0.9236, found by $0.5000 + 0.4236$, where $z = 1.43$

     c.   0.1185, found by $z = (12 - 15)/3.5 = -0.86$. The area under the curve is 0.3051, then $z = ((10 - 15/3.5) = -1.43$. The area is 0.4236, finally, $0.4236 - 0.3051 = 0.1185$

     d.   About 16.82 minutes, found by solving for X where $z = 0.52$. This point forces 0.20 of the area to fall under the curve between 0 and z. First multiplying 0.52×3.5 and then adding 15, we find $X = 16.82$.

14.   a.   2.28%, found by $(200 - 160)/20 = 2$. The area is 0.4772. Then $0.500 = 0.4772 = 0.228$.

     b.   69.15%, found by $(150 - 160)/20 = -0.5$. The area is 0.1915. Then $0.1915 + 0.5000 = 0.6915$

     c.   143.2, found by solving for X for a $z = -0.84$, which forces 0.30 of the area to fall under the curve. First multiplying $-0.84(20)$ and then adding 160, so $X = 143.2$

15. a. $\mu = n\pi = 50(0.25) = 12.5$

$\sigma^2 = n\pi(1 - \pi) = 12.5(1 - 0.25) = 9.375 \qquad \sigma = \sqrt{9.375} = 3.0619$

   b. 0.2578, found by $(14.5 - 12.5)/3.0619 = 0.65$, the area is 0.2422, then $0.5000 - 0.2422 = 0.2578$

   c. 0.2578, found by $(10.5 - 12.5)/3.0619 = -0.65$. The area is 0.2422. Then $0.5000 - 0.2422 = 0.2578$.

16. a. $\mu = (40)(0.55) = 22 \qquad \sigma^2 = 9.9 \qquad \sigma = 3.15$

   b. 0.2148, found by $(24.5 - 22)/3.15 = 0.79$. The area is 0.2852. Then $0.5000 - 0.2852 = 0.2148$

   c. 0.0197, found by $(15.5 - 22)/3.15 = -2.06$. The area is 0.4803. Then $0.5000 - 0.4803 = 0.0197$

   d. $z = (14.5 - 22.0)/3.15 = -2.38$ and $(25.5 - 22.0)/3.15 = 1.1$, so 0.8578, found by $0.4913 + 0.3665 = 0.8578$

17. a. 0.0655, found by $(9.5 - 6)/2.32 = 1.51$. The area is 0.4345. Then $0.5000 - 0.4345 = 0.0655$

   b. 0.1401, found by $(8.5 - 6)/2.32 = 1.08$. The area is 0.3599. Then $0.5000 - 0.3599 = 0.1401$

   c. 0.0746, found by $0.4345 - 0.3599 = 0.0746$. This is the probability of getting exactly 9 errors.

18. a. 10, which is the same as μ

   b. 0.1894, found by $((7.5 - 10)/2.828) = -0.88$. The area is 0.3106. Then $0.5000 - 0.3106 = 0.1894$

   c. 0.2981, found by $((8.5 - 10)/2.828) = -0.53$. The area is 0.2019. Then $0.5000 - 0.2019 = 0.2981$

   d. 0.1087, found by $0.3106 - 0.2019$

19. a. Yes. (1) There are two mutually exclusive outcomes-overweight and not overweight. (2) It is the result of counting the number of successes (overweight members). (3) Each trial is independent. (4) The probability of 0.30 remains the same for each trial.

   b. 0.0084, found by $\mu = 500(0.30) = 150 \qquad \sigma^2 = 0.0500(0.30)(0.70) = 0.0105$

$\sigma = \sqrt{105} = 10.24695 \qquad z = \dfrac{X - \mu}{\sigma} = \dfrac{174.5 - 150}{10.24695} = 2.39$

The area under the curve for 2.39 is 0.4916. Then $0.5000 - 0.4916 = 0.0084$

   c. 0.8461, found by $z = \dfrac{139.5 - 150}{10.24695} = -1.02$

The area between 139.5 and 150 is 0.3461. Adding $0.3461 + 0.5000 = 0.8461$

20. a. About 0.9599, found by $\mu = 100(0.38) = 38 \qquad \sigma^2 = 100(0.38)(1 - 0.38) = 23.56$

$\sigma = \sqrt{23.56} = 4.85 \qquad$ Then $(29.5 - 38)/4.85) = -1.75$. Area under the curve for -1.75 is 0.4599. Adding $0.4599 + 0.5000 = 0.9599$

   b. 0.6985, found by $(40.5 - 38)/4.85) = 0.52$, for which the area is 0.1985. Then $0.5000 + 0.1985 = 0.6985$

   c. 0.6584, found by $0.4599 + 0.1985$

21. a. 46.41%, found by (20.27 – 20.00)/0.15 = 1.8
    b. 3.59%, found by 0.5000 – 0.4641
    c. 81.85%, found by 0.3413 + 0.4772
    d. 27.43%, found by 0.5000 – 0.2257

22. a. About 34.13%, found by (34 – 32)/2 = 1.00, the area for 1.00 is 0.3413
    b. About 4.95%, found by (28.7 – 32)2 = – 1.65. The area for – 1.65 is 0.4505, then 0.5000 – 0.4505 = 0.0495
    c. About 77.45%, found by (29 – 32)/2 = – 1.5. The area for – 1.5 is 0.4332. Then 0.4332 + 0.3413(from part a) = 0.7745
    d. About 35.3 hours, found by 1.65 = (X – 32)/2

23. a. – 0.4 for net sales, found by (170 – 180)/25 and 2.92 for employees, found by (1850 – 1500)/120
    b. Net sales are 0.4 standard deviations below the mean. Employees is 2.92 standard deviations above the mean.
    c. 65.54% of the aluminum fabricators have greater net sales compared with Clarion, found by 0.1554 + 0.5000. Only 0.18% have more employees than Clarion, found by 0.5000 – 0.4982

24. Only 1.92% had a mechanical aptitude score greater than Shawn. (1310 – 1000)/150 = 2.07. The area for 2.07 is 0.4808. Then 0.500 – 0.4808 = 0.0192. About 11.51% had an IQ greater than Shawn, found by (122 – 110)/10 = 1.2. The area for 1.2 is 0.3849. Then 0.5000 – 0.3849 = 0.1151

25. a. 15.87%, found by (15 – 20)/5 = – 1.0. The area for –1.0 is 0.3413. Then 0.5000 – 0.3413 = 0.1587
    b. 0.5403, first, the area between 18 and 20 is 0.1554. The area between 20 and 26 is 0.3849. 0.1554 + 0.3849 = 0.5403
    c. About 1 person, found by z = (7 – 20)/5 = – 2.6, for which the area is 0.4953. Then 0.5000 – 0.4953 = 0.0047. Finally, 200(0.0047) = 0.94, which is about 1 person.

26. 60.06%, found by (42,000 – 40,000)/5000 = 0.40. The area under the curve for 0.40 is 0.1554. similarly, the area between 32,000 and 40,000 is 0.4452. 0.1554 + 0.4452 = 0.6006

27. a. (860 – 1000)/50 = – 2.8. The area below 860 is 0.0026, found by 0.5000 – 0.4974, or 0.26 percent
    b. (1055 – 1000)/50 = 1.1. The area between 1000 and 1055 is 0.3643. The area between 1000 and 1100 is 0.4772. Subtracting: 0.4772 – 0.3643 = 0.1129 or 11.29%.

28. a. 39.44%, found by (1970 – 1820)/120 = 1.25. The area for a z is 0.3944
    b. 10.56%, found by 0.5000 – 0.3944
    c. 3.36%, found by 0.5000 – 0.4664 = 0.0336

29. About 4099 units found by solving for X. 1.65 = (X – 4000)/60

30. a. About 0.47% (65,200 – 60,000)/2000 = 2.6. Then 0.5000 – 0.4953 = 0.0047
    b. About 22 trucks, (55,000 – 60,000)/2000 = – 2.5. Then 0.5000 – 0.4938 = 0.0062. Multiplying, 0.0062 x 3500 = 21.7
    c. About 2945, (62,000 – 60,000)/2000 = 1.00. then 0.5000 + 0.3413 = 0.8413. Multiplying 0.8413 x 3500 = 2944.55

31. a.   Only 2.28% earn more than John: $(30,400 - 28,000)/1200 = 2.00$. Then $0.5000 - 0.4772 = 0.0228$

     b.   Of the other supervisors, 97.72% have more service. $(10 - 20)/5 = -2.00$. Then $0.4772 + 0.5000 = 0.9772$

32. a.   26.43%, found by $(30 - 35)/8 = -0.63$, Then $0.500 - 0.2357 = 0.2643$

     b.   26.43%, found by $(40 - 35)/8 = 0.63$. Then $0.5000 - 0.2357 = 0.2643$

     c.   The normal distribution is continuous. Thus, the probability of an exact value is very small.

     d.   About 4.26%. You could find the probability of 39.5 and 40.5
          $z = (39.5 - 35)/8 = 0.56$. Area is 0.2123
          $z = (40.5 - 35)/8 = 0.69$. Area is 0.2549   Subtracting: $0.2549 - 0.2123 = 0.0426$

     e.   45.24 minutes or longer, found by solving for X. $1.28 = (X - 35)/8$

33. a.   15.39%, found by $(8 - 10.3)/2.25 = -1.02$, then $0.5000 - 0.3461 = 0.1539$

     b.   17.31%, found by:
          $z = (12 - 10.3)/2.25 = 0.76$. Area is 0.2764
          $z = (14 - 10.3)/2.25 = 1.64$. Area is 0.4495
          The area between 12 and 14 is 0.1731, found by $0.4495 - 0.2764$.

     c.   Yes, but it is rather remote. Reasoning: On 99.73% of the days, returns are between 3.55 and 17..03, found by $10.3 \pm 3(2.25)$. Thus, the chance of less than 3.55 returns is rather remote.

34. a.   0.0262, found by: $\mu = 50(0.20) = 10$
          $\sigma^2 = 50(0.20)(0.80) = 8$ $\sigma = \sqrt{8} = 2.83$ Then $(4.5 - 10)2.83 = -1.94$, for which the area is 0.4738. Then $0.5000 - 0.4738 = 0.0262$

     b.   0.9441, found by $(5.5 - 10)/2.83 = -1.59$, for which the area is 0.4441. Then $0.5000 + 0.4441 = 0.9441$

     c.   0.0297, found by $(4.5 - 10)/2.828 = -1.94$ and $(5.5 - 10)/2.828 = -1.59$. Then $0.4738 - 0.4441 = 0.0297$

     d.   0.8882, found by adding the area between $z = -1.59$ and $z = 1.59$. Then $2(0.4441) = 0.8882$

35. a.   0.9678, found by: $\mu = 60(0.64) = 38.4$
          $\sigma^2 = 60(0.64)(0.36) = 13.824$ $\sigma = \sqrt{13.824} = 3.72$ Then $(31.5 - 38.4)/3.72 = -1.85$, for which the area is 0.4678. Then $0.5000 + 0.4678 = 0.9678$

     b.   0.0853, found by $(43.5 - 38.4)/3.72 = 1.37$, for which the area is 0.4147. Then $0.5000 - 0.4147 = 0.0853$

     c.   0.8084, found by $0.441 + 0.3643$

     d.   0.0348 found by $0.4495 - 0.4147$

36. $\mu = np = 100(0.05) = 5$ $\sigma^2 = np(1 - p) = 100(0.05)(0.95) = 4.75$
     $\sigma = \sqrt{4.75} = 2.18$

     a.   0.1215, found by $(7.5 - 5)/2.18 = 1.15$. The area is 0.3749. Then $0.5000 - 0.3749 = 0.1215$

     b.   0.1192, found by $(10.5 - 5)/2.18 = 2.52$. The area is 0.4941. Subtracting $0.4941 - 0.3749 = 0.1192$

     c.   0.0714 calculating the probability of 8.5 and 7.5, then find the difference, probability of $8.5 = 0.4463$, 7.5 is 0.3749 so $0.4463 - 0.3749 = 0.0714$

     d.   0.0197, found by $0.5000 - 0.4803$

37. a. 0.8106, where μ =10, variance = 8, standard deviation = 2.8284, $z = (7.5 - 10)/2.8284 =$
       -0.88. The area is 0.3106, then $0.5000 + 0.3106 = 0.8106$
     b. 0.1087, found by $z = (8.5 - 10)/2.8284 = -0.53$, then $0.3106 - 0.2019 = 0.1087$
     c. 0.2981, found by $0.5000 - 0.2019$

38. a. μ =60(0.10) = 6 $\qquad$ $\sigma = \sqrt{60(0.1)(0.9)} = 2.32$
       $z = (1.5 - 6)/2.32 = -1.94$ $\qquad$ $z = (2.5 - 6)/2.32 = -1.51$
       Probability is $0.4738 - 0.4345 = 0.0393$
     b. 0.9738, found by $0.5000 + 0.4738$

39. 0.0968, found by: μ =50(0.40) = 20
     $\sigma^2 = 50(0.40)(0.60) = 12$ $\qquad$ $\sigma = \sqrt{12} = 3.4641$
     $z = (24.5 - 20)/3.4641 = 1.30$. The area is 0.4032. Then for 25 or more, $0.5000 - 0.4032 =$
     0.0968

40. μ =800(0.80) = 640 $\qquad$ $\sigma = \sqrt{800(0.80)(0.20)} = 11.3137$

     $z = \dfrac{664.5 - 640}{11.3137} = 2.17$ $\qquad$ Probability is $0.5000 - 0.4850 = 0.0150$

41. a. $1.65 = (45 - \mu)/5$ $\qquad$ μ =36.75
     b. $1.65 = (45 - \mu)/10$ $\qquad$ μ =28.5
     c. $z = (30 - 28.5)/10 = 0.15$, then $0.5000 + 0.0596 = 0.5596$

42. μ =25(1/35) = 0.714 $\qquad$ $\sigma = \sqrt{25\left(\dfrac{1}{35}\right)\left(\dfrac{34}{35}\right)} = 0.833$

     $z = \dfrac{0.5000 - 0.714}{0.8333} = -0.26$ $\qquad$ Then $0.5000 + 0.1026 = 0.6026$

43. a. 0.6687, found by $z = (2.00 - 2.80)/0.40 = -2.00$ and $(3.00 - 2.80)/0.40 = 0.50$. Then
       $0.4772 + 0.1915 = 0.6687$
     b. 0.0228, found by $(2.00 - 2.80)/0.40 = -2.00$, The probability is $= 0.5000 - 0.4772 =$
       0.0228
     c. 122, found by $z = (3.70 - 2.80)/0.40 = 2.25$, so $0.5000 - 0.4878 = 0.0122$. Then 10,000 x
       $0.0122 = 122$
     d. 3.312, found by $1.28 = (X - 2.8)/0.40$

44. Karrie is the 88 percentile, George is the 48 percentile. Scores are normally distributed.
     $2.05 = \dfrac{30 - 18.3}{\sigma}$ thus σ = 5.71   For Karrie: $25 - 18.3/5.71 = 1.17$, then $0.5000 + 0.3790 =$
     0.8790 or 88th percentile. For George: $(18 - 18.3)/5.71 = -0.05$, then $0.5000 - 0.0199 = 0.4801$
     or 48th percentile.

45. a. 21.19 percent found by $z = (9.00 - 9.20)/0.25 = -0.80$; so $0.5000 - 0.2881 = 0.2119$
   b. Increase the mean. $z = (9.00 - 9.20)/0.25 = 1.00$; probability is $0.5000 - 0.3413 = 0.1587$
   Reduce the standard deviation. $\sigma = (9.00 - 9.20)/0.15 = 1.33$; the probability $= 0.500 - 0.4082 = 0.0918$
   Reducing the standard deviation is better because a smaller percent of the hams will be below the limit.

46. $0.5000 - 0.3333 = 0.1667$ so $z = 0.43$ $\qquad -0.43 = \dfrac{40 - 43.9}{\sigma} \qquad \sigma = 9.07$

   $0.5000 - 0.2000 = 0.3000$, so $z = 0.84$ $\qquad 0.84 = \dfrac{49 - 43.9}{\sigma} \qquad \sigma = 6.07$

   There is about a 50 percent difference between the two standard deviations. The distribution is not normal.

47. a. $z = (52 - 60)/5 = 1.60$, so $0.5000 - 0.4452 = 0.0548$
   b. Let $z = 0.67$, so $0.67 = (X - 52)/5$ and $X = 55.35$, set mileage at 55,350
   c. $z = (45 - 52)/5 = -1.40$, so $0.5000 - 0.4192 = 0.0808$

48. a. $z = (45.00 - 42.000)/2.25 = 1.33$, $p(z > 1.33) = 0.5000 - 0.4082 = 0.0918$. It is over \$45 about 22 days, found by $240(0.0918)$.
   b. $z = (38.00 - 42.00)/2.25 = -1.78$ and $z = (40.00 - 42.00)/2.25 = -0.89$. So $0.4625 - 0.3133 = 0.1492$ or 14.92 percent of the days.
   c. $15/240 = 0.5000 - 0.0625 = 0.4375$. The z value corresponding to 0.4375 is about 1.54. $1.54 = (X - 42.00)/2.25$ and $X = 42.00 + 3.465 = 45.465$.

49. $\dfrac{470 - \mu}{\sigma} = 0.25 \qquad \dfrac{500 - \mu}{\sigma} = 1.28 \qquad \sigma = 29.126$ and $\mu = 462.719$

50. 32.56 found by $-1.28 = (X - 36.84)/3.34$

51. $\mu = 150(0.15) = 22.5 \qquad \sigma\sqrt{150(0.15)(0.85)} = 4.3732$
   $z = (30.5 - 22.5)/4.3732 = 1.83 \qquad P(z > 1.83) = 0.5000 - 0.4664 = 0.0336$

52. a. $z = (280.0 - 221.10)/47.11 = 1.25 \qquad P(z > 1.25) = 0.5000 - 0.3944 = 0.1056$
   There are 14 homes or 13.3%, that actually sell for more than \$280,000, so the approximation is close.
   b. $z = (18 - 14.629)/4.874 = 0.69 \qquad z = (22 - 14.629)/4.874 = 1.51$
   Probability is $0.4345 - 0.2549 = 0.1796$
   There are actually 24 homes or 23 percent. The normal approximation under estimates the actual percent by about 5 percentage points.

53. a. $z = (3.5 - 2.257)0.792 = 1.57 \qquad P(z > 1.57) = 0.5000 - 0.4418 = 0.0582$
   Two of the 28 teams, or 7 percent had attendance of over 2.0 million. The approximation is quite accurate.
   b. $z = (50.0 - 38.58)/13.74 = 0.83 \qquad P(z > 0.83) = 0.5000 - 0.2967 = 0.2033$
   Five teams had salaries of over \$50.0 million. The actual percent is 18, versus an estimate of 20 percent.

54.   a. $z = (5000 - 3048)/3756 = 0.52$ $P(z > 0.52) = 0.5000 - 0.1985 = 0.3015$
Seven out of the 48 magazines or about 15 percent is the actual. Estimate is not very accurate.

      b. $z = (75 - 42.75)/13.74 = 2.35$ $P(z > 2.35) = 0.5000 - 0.4906 = 0.0094$
There is only one observation greater than 75, so the approximation is quite good.

55.   a. $z = (3000 - 2725)/1095 = 0.25$ $P(z > 0.25) = 0.5000 - 0.0987 = 0.4013$
Only eight schools or 8.5 percent, spent more than 3000 per student. Estimate is not very accurate.

      b. $z = (2000 - 2134)/3895 = -0.03$ $P(z > -0.03) = 0.0120 + 0.5000 = 0.5120$
There are actually 30 school districts, or about 32 percent so the estimate is not accurate.

CHAPTER 8

SAMPLING METHODS AND SAMPLING DISTRIBUTIONS

1. a. 303 Louisiana, 5155 S. Main, 3501 Monroe, 2652 W. Central
    b. Answers will vary
    c. 630 Dixie Hwy, 835 S. McCord Rd., 4624 Woodville Rd.
    d. Answers will vary

2. a. Childrens Hospital Medical Center, St. Francis-St. George Hospital, Bethesda North, Good Samaritan Hospital, Mercy Hospital-Hamilton
    b. Answers will vary
    c. Jewish Hospital-Kenwood, Mercy Hospital-Anderson, Good Samaritan Hospital, St. Elizabeth Medical Center-North unit, Emerson Behavioral Service, Shriners Burns Institute
    d. Answers will vary

3. a. Bob Schmidt Chevrolet, Great Lakes Ford Nisson, Grogan Towne Chrysler, Southside Lincoln Mercury, Rowen Chrysler Plymouth Jeep Eagle
    b. Answers will vary
    c. Yark Automotive, Thayer Chevrolet Geo Toyota, Franklin Park Lincoln Mercury, Matthews Ford Oregon, Inc., Valiton Chrysler Plymouth

4. a. Denker, Brett; Wood, Tom; Keisser, Keith; Priest, Harvey
    b. Answers will vary
    c. Denker, Brett; Glemser, Cathy; Joehlin, Bob; O'Donnell, Jim; Smithers, Bob

5. a.

Sample	Values	Sum	Mean
1	12, 12	24	12
2	12, 14	26	13
3	12, 16	28	14
4	12, 14	26	13
5	12, 16	28	14
6	14, 16	30	15

   b. $\mu_{\bar{X}} = (12 + 13 + 14 + 13 + 14 + 15) / 6 = 13.5$ $\mu = (12 + 12 + 14 + 16)/4 = 13.5$

   c. More dispersion with population compared to the sample means. The sample means vary from 12 to 15 whereas the population varies from 12 to 16.

6. a.

Sample	Values	Sum	Mean
1	2,2	4	2
2	2,4	6	3
3	2,4	6	3
4	2,8	10	5
5	2,4	6	3
6	2,4	6	3
7	2,8	10	5
8	4,4	8	4
9	4,8	12	6
10	4,8	12	6

b. $\mu = (2+2+4+4+8)/5 = 4$ $\mu_{\bar{x}} = (2+3+3+5+3+3+5+4+6+6)/10 = 4$

c.   They are equal. The dispersion for the population is greater than that for the sample means. The population varies from 2 to 8, whereas the sample means only vary from 2 to 6.

7.   a.

Sample	Values	Sum	Mean
1	12,12,14	38	12.66
2	12,12,15	39	13.0
3	12,12,20	44	14.66
4	14,15,20	49	16.33
5	12,14,15	41	13.66
6	12,14,15	41	13.66
7	12,15,20	47	15.66
8	12,15,20	47	15.66
9	12,14,20	46	15.33
10	12,14,20	46	15.33

b. $\mu_{\bar{x}} = (12.66+13.0+...+15.33+15.33)/10 = 14.6$

       $\mu = (12+12+14+15+20)/5 = 14.6$

c.   The dispersion of the population is greater than that of the sample means. the sample means vary from 12.6 to 16.3 where as the population varies from 12 to 20.

8.   a.

Sample	Values	Sum	Mean
1	0,0,1	1	0.33
2	0,0,3	3	1.00
3	0,0,6	6	2.00
4	0,1,3	4	1.33
5	0,3,6	9	3.00
6	0,1,3	4	1.33
7	0,3,6	9	3.00
8	1,3,6	10	3.33
9	0,1,6	7	2.33
10	0,1,6	7	2.33

b. $\mu_{\bar{x}} = (0.33+1.00+...+2.33+2.33)/10 = 2$ $\mu = (0+0+1+3+6)/5 = 2$

c.   The dispersion of the population is greater than the sample means. The sample means vary from 0.33 to 3.33, the population varies from 0 to 6.

9.   a.   20 found by $_6C_3$

     b.

Sample	Cases	Sum	Mean
Ruud,Austin,Sass	3,6,3	12	4.0
Ruud,Sass,Palmer	3,3,3	9	3.0
Ruud,Palmer,Wilhelms	3,3,0	6	2.0
Ruud,Wilhelms,Schueller	3,0,1	4	1.33
Austin,Sass,Palmer	6,3,3	12	4.0
Austin,Palmer,Wilhelms	6,3,0	9	3.0
Austin,Wilhelms,Schueller	6,0,1	7	2.33
Sass,Palmer,Wilhelms	3,3,0	6	2.0
Sass,Wilhelms,Schueller	3,0,1	4	1.33
Palmer,Wilhelms,Schueller	3,0,1	4	1.33
Palmer,Schueller,Ruud	3,1,3	7	2.33

Ruud,Austin,Palmer	3,6,3	12	4.0
Ruud,Austin,Wilhelms	3,6,0	9	3.0
Ruud,Austin,Schueller	3,6,1	10	3.33
Ruud,Sass,Wilhelms	3,3,0	6	2.0
Ruud,Sass,Schueller	3,3,1	7	2.33
Ruud,Palmer,Schueller	3,3,1	7	2.33
Austin,Sass,Schueller	6,3,1	10	3.33
Austin,Palmer,Schueller	6,3,1	10	3.33
Sass,Palmer,Schueller	3,3,1	7	2.33

c. $\mu_{\bar{X}} = \dfrac{52.63}{20} = 2.63$ $\mu = (3 + 6 + 3 + 3 + 1)/6 = 2.66$ They are equal

d.

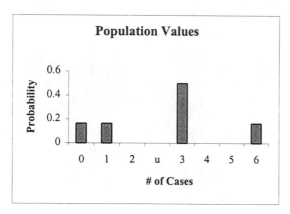

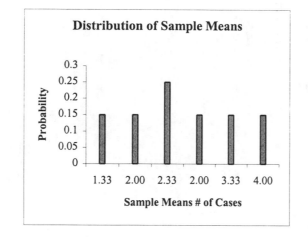

Sample Mean	Number of Means	Probability
1.33	3	0.1500
2.00	3	0.1500
2.33	5	0.2500
3.00	3	0.1500
3.33	3	0.1500
4.00	3	0.1500
	20	1.0000

More of a dispersion in population compared to sample means. The sample means vary
from 1.33 to 4.0. The population varies from 0 to 6.

10. a.   10, found by (5!)/3!2!

b.
Cars sold	Sample mean	Cars sold	Sample mean
8,6	7	6,10	8
8,4	6	6,6	6
8,10	9	4,10	7
8,6	7	4,6	5
6,4	5	10,6	8

c.   6.8 for population, 6.8 for sample means. They are identical.

d.

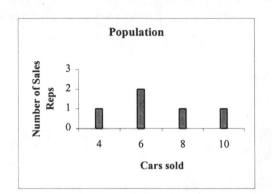

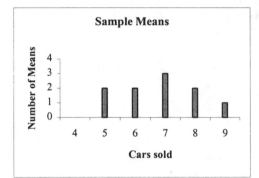

11. a. $\mu = \dfrac{0+1+...+9}{10} = 4.5$

b.

Sample	Sum	$\overline{X}$
1	11	2.2
2	31	6.2
3	21	4.2
4	24	4.8
5	21	4.2
6	20	4.0
7	23	4.6
8	29	5.8
9	35	7.0
10	27	5.4

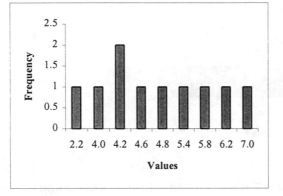

The mean of the 10 sample means is 4.84, which is close to the population mean of 4.5. The sample means range form 2.2 to 7.0, where as the population values range from 0 to 9. From the above graph, the sample means tend to cluster between 4 and 5.

12. a.

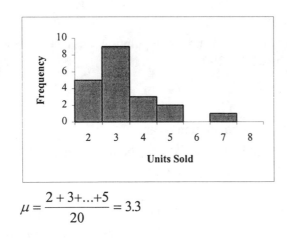

b. $\mu = \dfrac{2 + 3 + ... + 5}{20} = 3.3$

c.   Answers will vary, below is one sample

Sample	Sample Values	Sum	$\overline{X}$
1	2,3,2,3,3	12	2.6
2	3,3,4,2,4	16	3.2
3	3,3,4,4,2	16	3.2
4	3,2,5,5,3	18	3.6
5	3,4,4,2,7	20	4.0

$$\mu_{\overline{X}} = \frac{2.6 + 3.2 + 3.2 + 3.6 + 4.0}{5} = 3.32$$

d.   Sample mean is very close to the population mean. It is not to be expected that they are exact.

e.

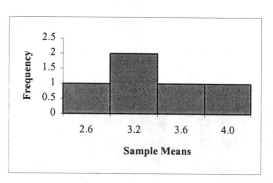

There is less dispersion in the sample means than the population.

13.   51.314 and 58.686, found by $55 \pm 2.58(10 / \sqrt{49})$

14.   38.911 and 41.089, found by $40 \pm 1.96(5 / \sqrt{81})$

15.   a.   1.581, found by $\sigma_{\overline{X}} = 5 / \sqrt{10}$
       b.   The population is normally distributed and the population variance is known.
       c.   16.901 and 23.099, found by 20 ± 3.099

16.   1.65, found in Appendix D.

17.   a. $20. It is our best estimate of the population mean.
       b. $18.60 and $21.40, found by $20 \pm 1.96(\$5 / \sqrt{49})$ about 95 percent of the intervals similarly constructed will include the population mean.

18.   a. $18.775 and $21.225, found by $20 \pm 1.96(\$5 / \sqrt{64})$
       b.   The confidence interval is based on the standard error computed by $s / \sqrt{n}$. As n, the sample size, increases (in this case from 49 to 64) the standard error decreases and the confidence interval becomes smaller.

19.   a.   8.60 gallons

        b.   7.83 and 9.37, found by $8.60 \pm 2.58(2.30 / \sqrt{60})$

        c.   If 100 such intervals were determined, the population mean would be included in about 99 intervals.

20.   5.29 and 6.81 errors found by $6.05 \pm 1.96(2.44 / \sqrt{40})$

21.   a.   0.80, found by 80/100

        b.   0.7216 and 0.8784, found by $0.80 \pm 1.96 \sqrt{\dfrac{(.80)(.20)}{100}}$

22.   a.   0.75, found by 300/400

        b.   0.694 and 0.806, found by $0.75 \pm 2.58 \sqrt{\dfrac{(.75)(.25)}{400}}$

        c.   She is almost assured of receiving more than 50 percent of the votes.

23.   a.   0.625, found by 250/400

        b.   0.578 and 0.672, found by $0.625 \pm 1.96 \sqrt{\dfrac{(.625)(.375)}{400}}$

24.   a.   0.15, found by 30/200

        b.   0.101 and 0.199, found by $0.15 \pm 1.96 \sqrt{\dfrac{(.15)(.85)}{200}}$

25.   33.465 and 36.535, found by $35 \pm 1.96 \left(\dfrac{5}{\sqrt{36}} \right) \sqrt{\dfrac{300 - 36}{300 - 1}}$

26.   36.846 and 43.154, found by $40 \pm 2.58 \left(\dfrac{9}{\sqrt{49}} \right) \sqrt{\dfrac{500 - 49}{500 - 1}}$

27.   1.689 up to 2.031, found by $1.86 \pm 2.58 \left(\dfrac{0.50}{\sqrt{50}} \right) \sqrt{\dfrac{400 - 50}{400 - 1}}$

28.   0.43 and 0.77, found by $0.60 \pm 1.96 \sqrt{\dfrac{(.60)(.40)}{30}} \sqrt{\dfrac{300 - 30}{300 - 1}}$

29.   97, found by $n = \left(\dfrac{1.96 \times 10}{2} \right)^2 = 96.04$

30.   60, found by $n = \left(\dfrac{2.58 \times 15}{5} \right)^2 = 59.91$

31.   196, found by $n = 0.15(0.85)\left(\dfrac{1.96}{0.05}\right)^2 = 195.9216$

32.   165, found by $n = 0.45(0.55)\left(\dfrac{2.58}{0.10}\right)^2 = 164.75$

33.   554, found by $n = \left(\dfrac{1.96 \times 3}{0.25}\right)^2 = 553.19$

34.   25, found by $n = \left(\dfrac{1.96 \times 0.5}{0.2}\right)^2 = 24.01$

35.   a.   577, found by $n = 0.60(0.40)\left(\dfrac{1.96}{0.04}\right)^2 = 576.24$

       b.   601, found by $n = 0.50(0.50)\left(\dfrac{1.96}{0.04}\right)^2 = 600.25$

36.   a.   5718, found by $n = 0.30(0.70)\left(\dfrac{1.65}{0.01}\right)^2 = 5717.25$

       b.   Increase the allowable error from 0.01 to 0.05. Thus the sample size would be reduced to

            229, found by $n = 0.30(0.70)\left(\dfrac{1.65}{0.05}\right)^2 = 228.69$

37.   a.   Formal Man, Summit Stationers, Bootleggers, Leather Ltd., Petries
       b.   Answers will vary
       c.   Elder-Beerman, Frederick's of Hollywood, Summit Stationers, Lion Store, Leather Ltd., Things Remembered, County Seat, Coach House Gifts, Regis Hairstylists

38.   a.   Jeanne Fiorito, Douglas Smucker, Jeanine S. Huttner, Harry Mayhew, Mark Steinmetz, and Paul Langenkamp.
       b.   One randomly selected group of numbers is 05, 06, 74, 64, 66, 55, 27, and 22. The members of the sample are Janet Arrowsmith, David DeFrance, Mark Zilkoski, and Larry Johnson.
       c.   Francis Aona, Paul Langenkamp, Ricardo Pena, and so on.
       d.   Answers will vary.

39.   The difference between a sample statistic and the population parameter. Yes, the difference could be zero. The sample mean and the population parameter are equal.

40.   1.   Destructive nature of some tests
       2.   Physically impossible to check all items
       3.   Costly to check all items
       4.   Time consuming to check all items

41. Use of either a proportional or nonproportional stratified random sample would be appropriate. For example, suppose the number of banks in Region 111 were as follows:

Assets	Number	Percent of Total
$500 million and more	20	2.0
$100-499 million	324	32.4
less than $100 million	656	65.6
	1000	100

For a proportional stratified sample, if the sample size is 100, then two banks worth assets of $500 million would be selected, 32 medium-sized banks and 66 small banks. For a nonproportional sample, 10 or even all-20 large banks could be selected and fewer medium and small size banks and the sample results weighted by the appropriate percents of the total.

42. A simple random sample would be appropriate, but this means each 10-foot length would have to be numbered 1, 2, 3, ..., 720. A faster method would be to (1) select a pipe from the first say, 20 pipes produced, and (2) select every 20th pipe produced thereafter and measure its inside diameter. Thus, the sample would include about 36 PVC pipes.

43. a. We selected 60, 104, 75, 72, and 48. Answers will vary.
    b. We selected the third observation. So the sample consists of 75, 72, 68, 82, 48. Answers will vary.
    c. Number the first 20 motels from 00 to 19. Randomly select three numbers. Then number the last five numbers 20 to 24. Randomly select two numbers from that group.

44. Answers will vary

45. a. 15 found by $_6C_2$
    b.

Sample	Value	Sum	Mean
1	79,64	143	71.5
2	79,84	163	81.5
3	79,82	161	80.5
4	79,92	171	85.5
5	79,77	156	78.0
6	64,84	148	74.0
7	64,82	146	73.0
8	64,92	156	78.0
9	64,77	141	70.5
10	84,82	166	83.0
11	84,92	176	88.0
12	84,77	161	80.5
13	82,92	174	87.0
14	82,77	159	79.5
15	92,77	169	84.5
			1195.0

   c. $\mu_{\bar{x}} = \dfrac{1195}{15} = 79.67$ $\mu = 478/6 = 79.67$ They are equal

   d. No, the student is not graded on all available information. He/she is as likely to get a lower grade based on the sample as a higher grade.

46. a. 10, found by $_5C_2$

b.
Sample	Value	Sum	Mean
1	2,3	5	2.5
2	2,5	7	3.5
3	2,3	5	2.5
4	2,5	7	3.5
5	3,5	8	4.0
6	3,3	6	3.0
7	3,5	8	4.0
8	5,3	8	4.0
9	5,5	10	5.0
10	3,5	8	4.0
			36.0

c. $\mu_{\bar{X}} = 36/10 = 3.6$ $\mu = 18/5 = 3.6$ They are equal

47. a. 10, found by $_5C_2$

b.
Number correct	Mean	Number correct	Mean
4,3	3.5	3,3	3.0
4,5	4.5	3,2	2.5
4,3	3.5	5,3	4.0
4,2	3.0	5,2	3.5
3,5	4.0	3,2	2.5

c.
Sample Mean	Frequency	Probability
2.5	2	0.20
3.0	2	0.20
3.5	3	0.30
4.0	2	0.20
4.5	1	0.10

d. $\mu_{\bar{X}} = (3.5 + 4.5 + ... + 2.5)/10 = 3.4$ $\mu = (4 + 3 + 5 + 3 + 2)/5 = 3.4$
The two means are equal.

e. The population values are uniform in shape. The distribution of the sample means tends toward normality.

48. a. 15, found by $_6C_2$

b.
Ages	Mean	Ages	Mean
54,50	52	50,52	51
54,52	53	52,48	50
54,48	51	52,50	51
54,50	52	52,52	52
54,52	53	48,50	49
50,52	51	48,52	50
50,48	49	50,52	51
50,50	50		

c.
Sample Means	Frequency	Probability
49	2	0.13
50	3	0.20
51	5	0.33
52	3	0.20
53	2	0.13

d. $\mu = 51$ $\mu_{\bar{X}} = 51$

e.   Tending toward normal

f.   Sample means. Somewhat normal

49.   6.14 years to 6.86 years, found by $6.5 \pm 1.96(1.7 / \sqrt{85})$

50.   a.   3.01 pounds

         b.   3.0002 and 3.0198 pounds, found by $3.01 \pm 1.96(0.03 / \sqrt{36})$
                   About 95 percent of similarly constructed intervals would include the population mean.

51. $1.168 and $1.190, found by $1.179 \pm 2.58(0.03 / \sqrt{50})$

52.   24.28 weeks up to 27.72 weeks, found by $26.0 \pm 1.96(6.2 / \sqrt{50})$

53.   a.   The driveway, because it has the smallest standard deviation.

         b.   driveway: 10.776 and 13.224, found by $12 \pm 2.58(3 / \sqrt{40})$

                   patio: 9.553 and 14.448, found by $12 \pm 2.58(6 / \sqrt{40})$

                   deck: 8.737 and 15.263, found by $12 \pm 2.58(8 / \sqrt{40})$

54.   2.55 up to 2.97 meals, found by $2.76 \pm 2.17(0.75 / \sqrt{60})$

55.   a.   65.61 up to 71.59 hours, found by $68.6 \pm 2.58(8.2 / \sqrt{50})$

         b.   The value suggested by the NCAA is included in the confidence interval, therefore it is reasonable.

         c.   Changing the confidence interval to 95 would reduce the width of the interval. The value of 2.58 would change to 1.96.

56.   a.   From $1627 to $2013, found by $1820 \pm 1.96(660 / \sqrt{45})$

         b.   The population mean could be $1700 because it is in the interval constructed above.

57.   0.42 and 0.50, found by $0.46 \pm 2.58 \sqrt{\dfrac{0.46(1 - 0.46)}{900}}$

58.   0.647 and 0.753, found by $0.70 \pm 2.58 \sqrt{\dfrac{0.70(1 - 0.70)}{500}}$

Note that the finite-population correction factor was not applied because n/N is less than 0.05.

59.   0.633 and 0.687, found by $0.66 \pm 1.96 \sqrt{\dfrac{0.66(0.34)}{1200}}$

60.   a.   25.36 up to 29.04, found by $27.2 \pm 1.96 \dfrac{10.3}{\sqrt{120}}$

         b.   0.096 up to 0.204, found by $0.15 \pm 1.65 \sqrt{\dfrac{0.15(0.85)}{120}}$

61. a. $p = 560/1000 = 0.560$, from 0.53 up to 0.59, found by $0.56 \pm 1.96 \sqrt{\dfrac{0.56(0.44)}{1000}}$

 b. The lower point of the interval is greater than 0.50. So we can conclude the majority feel the President is doing a good job.

62. $52.56 and $55.44, found by $54.00 \pm 1.96 \dfrac{\$4.50}{\sqrt{35}} \sqrt{\dfrac{(500-35)}{500-1}}$

63. 0.345 and 0.695, found by $0.52 \pm 2.58 \sqrt{\dfrac{(0.52)(0.48)}{50}} \sqrt{\dfrac{(650-50)}{650-1}}$

64. 369, found by $n = 0.60(1-0.60)[1.96/0.05]^2$

65. 134, found by $[(1.65 \times 14)/2\}^2 = 133.4$

66. 97, found by $\left(\dfrac{1.96 \times 500}{100}\right)^2$

67. 865, found by $0.10(0.90)\left(\dfrac{1.96}{0.02}\right)^2$

68. a. 708.13, rounded up to 709, found by: $0.21(1-0.21)[1.96/0.03]^2$

 b. 1068, found by $0.50(0.50)[1.96/0.03]^2$

69. a. 25%, found by 25/100

 b. 0.172 to 0.328, found by $0.25 \pm 1.96 \sqrt{\dfrac{(0.25)(0.75)}{100}} \sqrt{\dfrac{605-100}{604}}$ No, 0.40 not in interval

 c. 1.65, found by 165/100

 d. 1.387 to 1.913, found by $1.65 \pm 1.96 \dfrac{1.4659}{\sqrt{100}} \sqrt{\dfrac{505}{604}}$ Note: $s = 1.4659$

 e. No, because 0 is not in the interval between 1.387 and 1.91.

70. Answers will vary. The results of problem 64 in chapter 3 were used as the selling price. The five stocks random by selected sold for $122.00, $63.387, $105.00, $75.813, and $65.250. The sample mean is $86.387. The population mean is $67.26, so the sample error is $19.127.

71. a. For selling price: 212.09 up to 230.11 found by $221.1 \pm (1.96)\dfrac{47.11}{\sqrt{105}} = 221.1 \pm 9.01$

 b. For distance: 13.697 up to 15.561 found by $14.629 \pm (1.96)\dfrac{4.874}{\sqrt{105}} = 14.629 \pm 0.932$

 c. For garage: 0.5867 up to 0.7657 found by

 $0.6762 \pm (1.96)\sqrt{\dfrac{0.6762(1-0.6762)}{105}} = 0.6762 \pm 0.0895$

72. a. The population standard deviation is not known and the sample size is less than 30, so strictly speaking the estimate should not be made. However, the 30 value is arbitrary and the sample size is 28, so the estimate would be reasonable.

b. 107.61 up to 128.67, found by $118.14 \pm 1.65 \dfrac{33.77}{\sqrt{28}}$

73. a. The interval is from 2.394 up to 3.414 found by $2.904 \pm (1.96) \dfrac{1.804}{\sqrt{48}} = 2.904 \pm 0.510$

b. The interval is from \$21,287 up to \$31,957 found by

$26{,}622 \pm (1.96) \dfrac{18{,}858}{\sqrt{48}} = 26{,}622 \pm 5335$

c. The interval is from 38.86 up to 46.64 found by $42.75 \pm (1.96) \dfrac{13.74}{\sqrt{48}} = 42.75 \pm 3.89$

74. Deleting four school districts in question, the mean percent on welfare is 6.197, with a standard deviation of 3.956, for a sample of 90. The 99 percent confidence level is:

$6.197 \pm (2.58) \dfrac{3.956}{\sqrt{90}} = 6.197 \pm 1.076$ So the endpoints of the confidence interval are 5.121 and

7.273. All four of the school districts are outside the interval. We conclude that these districts are different from the others.

1. a.   Two-tailed
    b   Reject H_o and accept H_1 when z does not fall in the region from -1.96 and 1.96
    c. -1.2, found by $z = \dfrac{49 - 50}{(5/\sqrt{36})}$
    d.   Fail to reject H_o
    e. $p = 0.2302$, found by $2(0.5000 - 0.3849)$. A 23.02% chance of finding a z value this large when H_o is true.

2. a.   One-tail
    b.   Reject H_o when $z > 2.05$
    c.   4, found by $z = \dfrac{12 - 10}{(3/\sqrt{36})}$
    d.   Reject H_o and conclude that $\mu > 10$
    e. p-value is very close to 0, given a z value of 4.00. Very little chance H_o is true.

3. a.   One-tailed
    b.   Reject H_o and accept H_1 when $z > 1.65$
    c.   1.2, found by $z = \dfrac{21 - 20}{(5/\sqrt{36})}$
    d.   Fail to reject the H_o at the 0.05 significance level.
    e. $p = 0.1151$, found by $0.5000 - 0.3849$. An 11.51% chance of finding a z-value this large or larger.

4. a.   One-tailed
    b.   Reject H_o and accept H_1 where $z < -1.88$
    c. -2.67, found by $z = \dfrac{215 - 220}{(15/\sqrt{64})}$
    d.   Reject H_o and conclude that the population mean is less than 220 at the 0.03 significance level.
    e. $p = 0.0038$, found by $0.5000 - 0.4962$. Less than 0.5% chance H_o is true.

5. a. H_o: $\mu = 60,000$ H_1: $\mu \neq 60,000$
    b.   Reject H_o if $z < -1.96$ or $z > 1.96$
    c. -0.69, found by $z = \dfrac{59,500 - 60,000}{(5000/\sqrt{48})}$
    d.   Do not reject H_o
    e. $p = 0.4902$, found by $2(0.5000 - 0.2549)$. Crosset's experience is not different from that claimed by the manufacturer. If the H_o is true, the probability of finding a value more extreme than this is 0.4902.

6.   a. $H_0: \mu \geq 3$ $H_1: \mu < 3$
     b.   Reject H_0 if $z < -1.65$
     c. -1.77, found by $z = \dfrac{2.75 - 3.0}{(1/\sqrt{50})}$
     d.   Reject H_0
     e. $p = 0.0384$, found by $(0.5000 - 0.4616)$. We conclude that the mean waiting time is less than three minutes. When H_0 is true, the probability of obtaining a value smaller than 2.75 is 0.0384.

7.   a. $H_0: \mu \geq 6.8$ $H_1: \mu < 6.8$
     b.   Reject H_0 if $z < -1.65$
     c. -7.2, found by $z = \dfrac{6.2 - 6.8}{(0.5/\sqrt{36})}$
     d. H_0 is rejected
     e. $p = 0$. The mean number of videos watched is less than 6.8 per month. If H_0 is true, there is virtually no chance of getting a statistic this small.

8.   a. $H_0: \mu \leq 20$ $H_1: \mu > 20$
     b.   Reject H_0 if $z > 2.33$
     c. 8.86, found by $z = \dfrac{\$24.85 - \$20.00}{(\$3.24/\sqrt{35})}$
     d.   Reject H_0
     e. $p = 0.0000$. The mean amount of tips per day is larger than $20.00. If H_0 is true, the probability of obtaining a sample mean this far above 20 is virtually zero.

9.   a.   Two-tailed test
     b.   Reject H_0 if $z < -2.05$ or $z > 2.05$
     c. 2.59, found by $z = \dfrac{102 - 99}{\sqrt{\dfrac{5^2}{40} + \dfrac{6^2}{50}}}$
     d.   Reject H_0 and accept H_1
     e. $p = 0.0096$, found by $2(0.5000 - 0.4952)$

10.   a.   One-tailed test
     b.   Reject H_0 and accept H_1 if $z > 1.41$
     c. 0.607 found by $z = \dfrac{2.67 - 2.59}{\sqrt{\dfrac{(0.75)^2}{65} + \dfrac{(0.66)^2}{50}}}$
     d.   Fail to reject H_0
     e. $p = 0.2709$, found by $0.5000 - 0.2291$

11. Step 1: H_o: $\mu_1 \geq \mu_2$ $\qquad$ H_1: $\mu_1 < \mu_2$
Step 2: The 0.05 significance level was chosen
Step 3: Reject H_o and accept H_1 if $z < -1.65$
Step 4: -0.94, found by $z = \dfrac{7.6 - 8.1}{\sqrt{\dfrac{(2.3)^2}{40} + \dfrac{(2.9)^2}{55}}}$
Step 5: Fail to reject H_o. No difference in lengths of time that owners occupied their homes. $p = 0.1736$ found by $0.5000 - 0.3264$

12. Step 1: H_o: $\mu_c = \mu_p$ $\qquad$ H_1: $\mu_c \neq \mu_p$
Step 2: The 0.05 significance level was chosen
Step 3: Reject H_o and accept H_1 if z less than -1.96 or greater than 1.96
Step 4: -1.53, found by $z = \dfrac{\$370 - \$380}{\sqrt{\dfrac{(\$30)^2}{35} + \dfrac{(\$26)^2}{40}}}$
Step 5: Fail to reject H_o. There is no difference in the mean cost of the apartments. The p-value is 0.126 found by $2(0.5000 - 0.4370)$

13. a. Two-tailed test. Because we are trying to show a difference exists between two means.
b. Reject H_o if $z < -2.58$ or $z > 2.58$
c. -2.66, found by $z = \dfrac{31.4 - 34.9}{\sqrt{\dfrac{(5.1)^2}{32} + \dfrac{(6.7)^2}{49}}}$ $\qquad$ Reject H_o at the 0.01 level. There is a difference in the mean turnover rate.

14. a. H_o is rejected if $z > 1.65$
b. 1.09, found by $z = \dfrac{0.75 - 0.70}{\sqrt{\dfrac{0.70(0.30)}{100}}}$
c. H_o is not rejected

15. a. H_o is rejected if $z < -1.96$ or $z > 1.96$
b. -2.24, found by $z = \dfrac{0.30 - 0.40}{\sqrt{\dfrac{0.40(0.60)}{120}}}$
c. H_o is rejected

16. a. H_o: $\pi \leq 0.52$ $\qquad$ H_1: $\pi > 0.52$
b. H_o is rejected if $z > 2.33$
c. 1.62, found by $z = \dfrac{0.5667 - 0.52}{\sqrt{\dfrac{0.52(0.48)}{300}}}$
d. H_o is not rejected. We cannot conclude that the proportion of men driving on the Ohio Turnpike is not larger than 0.52.

17. H_o: $\pi \le 0.33$ H_1: $\pi > 0.33$
H_o is rejected if $z > 2.05$

2.00, found by $z = \dfrac{0.40 - 0.3333}{\sqrt{\dfrac{0.3333(0.6667)}{200}}}$

H_o is not rejected. The proportion of students with jobs is not larger at your school.

18.   a. H_o: $\pi \ge 0.90$ H_1: $\pi < 0.90$
  b. H_o is rejected if $z < -1.28$

  c. -2.67, found by $z = \dfrac{0.82 - 0.90}{\sqrt{\dfrac{0.90(0.10)}{100}}}$

  d. H_o is rejected. Less than 90% of the customers receive their orders in less than 10 minutes.

19. H_o: $\pi \ge 0.50$ H_1: $\pi < 0.50$
H_o is rejected if $z < -1.65$

-0.40, found by $z = \dfrac{0.48 - 0.50}{\sqrt{\dfrac{0.50(0.50)}{100}}}$

H_o is not rejected. The proportion of student changing their major has not changed.

20.   a. H_o is rejected if $z > 1.65$

  b.   0.64, found by $p_c = \dfrac{70 + 90}{100 + 150}$

  c.   1.61, found by $z = \dfrac{0.70 - 0.60}{\sqrt{\dfrac{(0.64)(0.36)}{100} + \dfrac{(0.64)(0.36)}{150}}}$

  d. H_o is not rejected

21.   a. H_o is rejected if $z < -1.96$ or $z > 1.96$

  b.   0.80, found by $p_c = \dfrac{170 + 110}{200 + 150}$

  c.   2.70, found by $z = \dfrac{0.85 - 0.7333}{\sqrt{\dfrac{(0.80)(0.20)}{200} + \dfrac{(0.80)(0.20)}{150}}}$

  d. H_o is rejected

22.   a. H_o: $\pi_1 = \pi_2$ H_1: $\pi_1 \ne \pi_2$
  b. H_o is rejected if $z < -1.96$ or $z > 1.96$

  c. $\bar{p}_c = \dfrac{24 + 40}{400 + 400} = 0.08$

  d. -2.09, found by $z = \dfrac{0.06 - 0.10}{\sqrt{\dfrac{(0.08)(0.92)}{400} + \dfrac{(0.08)(0.92)}{400}}}$

  e. H_o is rejected. The proportion infested is not the same in the two fields.

23.   a. H_0: $\pi_1 \geq \pi_2$ H_1: $\pi_1 < \pi_2$

     b. H_0 is rejected if $z < -1.65$ $\bar{p}_c = \dfrac{1530 + 2010}{3000 + 3000} = 0.59$

     c. -12.60, found by $z = \dfrac{0.51 - 0.67}{\sqrt{\dfrac{(0.59)(0.41)}{3000} + \dfrac{(0.59)(0.41)}{3000}}}$

     d. H_0 is rejected. The proportion of women who think men are thoughtful has declined.

24. H_0: $\pi_d \leq \pi_r$ H_1: $\pi_d > \pi_r$

     H_0 is rejected if $z > 2.05$ $\bar{p}_c = \dfrac{168 + 200}{800 + 1000} = 0.2044$

$$z = \dfrac{0.21 - 0.20}{\sqrt{\dfrac{(0.2044)(0.7956)}{800} + \dfrac{(0.2044)(0.7956)}{1000}}} = 0.52$$

     H_0 is not rejected. There is no difference in the proportion of Democrats and Republicans who favor lowering the standards.

25. H_0: $\pi_s = \pi_m$ H_1: $\pi_s \neq \pi_m$

     H_0 is rejected if $z < -1.96$ or $z > 1.96$ $\bar{p}_c = \dfrac{120 + 150}{400 + 600} = 0.27$

$$z = \dfrac{0.30 - 0.25}{\sqrt{\dfrac{(0.27)(0.73)}{400} + \dfrac{(0.27)(0.73)}{600}}} = 1.74$$

     H_0 is not rejected. There is no difference in the proportion of married and single drivers who have accidents.

26. 1.05, found by $z = (9922 - 9880) / 400 / \sqrt{100}$. Then $0.5000 - 0.3531 = 0.1469$, which is the probability of a Type II error.

27. -0.45, found by $z = (9922 - 9940) / 400 / \sqrt{100}$. Then the area of $0.1736 + 0.5000 = 0.6736$, which is the probability of a Type II error.

28. H_0: $\mu \geq 10$ H_1: $\mu < 10$

     Reject H_0 if $z < -1.65$ $z = \dfrac{9.0 - 10.0}{2.8 / \sqrt{50}} = -2.53$

     Reject H_0. The mean weight loss is less than 10 pounds. p-value $= 0.5000 - 0.4943 = 0.0057$.

29. H_0: $\mu \leq 16$ H_1: $\mu > 16$

     Reject H_0 if $z > 1.65$ $z = \dfrac{16.05 - 16.0}{0.03 / \sqrt{50}} = 11.79$

     Reject H_0. The cans are being overfilled. p-value is very close to 0.

30. H_o: $\mu \le \$15,000$ H_1: $\mu > \$15,000$

Reject H_o if $z > 1.65$ $z = \dfrac{\$17,000 - \$15,000}{\$3000 / \sqrt{75}} = 5.77$

Reject H_o. At the 0.05 level we can conclude that the mean household income is greater than $15,000.

31. H_o: $\mu \le 90$ H_1: $\mu > 90$ Reject H_o if $z > 1.28$

$z = \dfrac{94 - 90}{22 / \sqrt{100}} = 1.82$

Reject H_o. At the 0.10 level we can conclude that the farm selling time has increased.

32. H_o: $\mu = \$30,000$ H_1: $\mu \ne \$30,000$

Reject H_o if $z < 1.65$ or $z > 1.65$ $z = \dfrac{\$30,500 - \$30,000}{\$3000 / \sqrt{120}} = 1.83$

Reject H_o. We can conclude that the mean salary is not $30,000. p-value is 0.0672, found by 2(0.5000 – 0.4664)

33. H_o: $\mu \ge 40$ H_1: $\mu < 40$ Reject H_o if $z < -1.65$

$z = \dfrac{37.8 - 40}{12.2 / \sqrt{60}} = -1.40$

H_o is not rejected. The p-value = 0.5000 – 0.4192 = 0.0808. We cannot conclude that the mean leisure time is less than 40 hours per week.

34. H_o: $\mu \le 1.25$ H_1: $\mu > 1.25$ Reject H_o if $z > 1.65$

$z = \dfrac{1.27 - 1.25}{0.05 / \sqrt{35}} = 2.37$

Reject H_o. The mean price of gasoline is greater than $1.25. The p-value = 0.5000 – 0.4911 = 0.0089

35.   a. H_o: $\mu \ge 50$ H_1: $\mu < 50$ Reject H_o if $z \le -2.33$ $\overline{X} = 48.18$

         $z = \dfrac{48.18 - 50}{3.00 / \sqrt{10}} = -1.92$

         H_o is not rejected. The mean weight is not less than 50 pounds.

   b.   Mr. Rutter can use the z distribution as the test statistic because the population standard deviation ($\sigma = 3$) is known. And the population is normal.

   c. p-value = 0.5000 – 0.4726 = 0.0274

36. H_o: $\mu = \$3.65$ H_1: $\mu \ne \$3.65$

Reject H_o where z does not fall in the range between –1.96 and 1.96

$z = \dfrac{\$3.69 - \$3.65}{\$0.24 / \sqrt{45}} = 1.12$

Fail to reject H_o. There is no difference in the mean allowance for 9-year-olds in the Tampa area and the rest of the United States.

37. H_o: $\mu_1 = \mu_2$ $\qquad\qquad$ H_1: $\mu_1 \neq \mu_2$ $\qquad\qquad$ Reject H_o if $z < -2.05$ or $z > 2.05$

$$z = \frac{114.6 - 117.9}{\sqrt{\frac{(9.1)^2}{40} + \frac{(10.4)^2}{50}}} = -1.60$$

Fail to reject H_o. There is no difference in the test scores. The p-value is 0.1096, found by $2(0.5000 - 0.4452)$

38. H_o: $\mu_1 = \mu_2$ $\qquad\qquad$ H_1: $\mu_1 \neq \mu_2$ $\qquad\qquad$ Reject H_o if $z < -1.96$ or $z > 1.96$

$$z = \frac{20 - 21}{\sqrt{\frac{(4)^2}{45} + \frac{(3)^2}{50}}} = -1.37$$

Do not reject H_o. There is no difference in delivery times. The p-value is 0.1706, found by $2(0.5000 - 0.4147)$

39. H_o: $\mu_1 = \mu_2$ $\qquad\qquad$ H_1: $\mu_1 \neq \mu_2$ $\qquad\qquad$ Reject H_o if $z < -2.58$ or $z > 2.58$

$$z = \frac{36.2 - 37.0}{\sqrt{\frac{(1.14)^2}{35} + \frac{(1.30)^2}{40}}} = -2.84$$

Reject H_o. There is a difference in the useful life of the two brands of paint. The p-value is 0.0046, found by $2(0.5000 - 0.4977)$

40. H_o: $\mu_1 \geq \mu_2$ $\qquad\qquad$ H_1: $\mu_1 < \mu_2$ $\qquad\qquad$ Reject H_o if $z < -1.65$

$$z = \frac{345 - 351}{\sqrt{\frac{(21)^2}{54} + \frac{(28)^2}{60}}} = -1.30$$

Fail to reject H_o. There is not enough evidence to conclude that more units are produced on the afternoon shift.

41. H_o: $\mu_1 = \mu_2$ $\qquad\qquad$ H_1: $\mu_1 \neq \mu_2$ $\qquad\qquad$ Reject H_o if $z < -1.96$ or $z > 1.96$

$$z = \frac{4.77 - 5.02}{\sqrt{\frac{(1.05)^2}{40} + \frac{(1.23)^2}{50}}} = -1.04$$

H_o is not rejected. There is no difference in the mean number of calls. p-value $= 2(0.5000 - 0.3508) = 0.2984$

42. H_o: $\mu_1 \geq \mu_2$ $\qquad\qquad$ H_1: $\mu_1 < \mu_2$ $\qquad\qquad$ Reject H_o if $z < -2.33$

$$z = \frac{4.35 - 5.84}{\sqrt{\frac{(1.20)^2}{50} + \frac{(1.36)^2}{40}}} = 5.44$$

H_o is rejected. The mean number of cups for regular coffee drinkers is less. p-value $= 2(0.5000 - 0.5000) = 0.0000$

43. $H_o: \mu_1 \le \mu_2$ $\qquad$ $H_1: \mu_1 > \mu_2$ $\qquad$ Reject H_o if $z > 2.05$

$$z = \frac{11.00 - 7.67}{\sqrt{\dfrac{(3.88)^2}{30} + \dfrac{(4.42)^2}{40}}} = 3.35$$

H_o is rejected. Those with smaller boats use their boats more often. The p-value is less than 0.0001

44. $H_o: \mu_1 \le \mu_2$ $\qquad$ $H_1: \mu_1 > \mu_2$ $\qquad$ Reject H_o if $z > 2.33$

$$z = \frac{11.00 - 8.90}{\sqrt{\dfrac{2.65^2}{36} + \dfrac{1.64^2}{40}}} = 4.10$$

Reject H_o and conclude that the fog index is higher in scientific journals.

45. $H_o: \pi \le 0.60$ $\qquad$ $H_1: \pi > 0.60$ $\qquad$ H_o is rejected if $z > 2.33$

$$z = \frac{0.70 - 0.60}{\sqrt{\dfrac{0.60(0.40)}{200}}} = 2.89$$

H_o is rejected. Ms. Dennis is correct. More than 60% of the accounts are more than 3 months old.

46. $H_o: \pi \le 0.55$ $\qquad$ $H_1: \pi > 0.55$ $\qquad$ H_o is rejected if $z > 1.65$

$$z = \frac{0.60 - 0.55}{\sqrt{\dfrac{0.55(0.45)}{70}}} = \frac{0.05}{0.0595} = 0.841$$

H_o is not rejected. We cannot conclude that more than 55% of the commuters would use the route.

47. $H_o: \pi \le 0.44$ $\qquad$ $H_1: \pi > 0.44$ $\qquad$ H_o is rejected if $z > 1.65$

$$z = \frac{0.480 - 0.44}{\sqrt{\dfrac{0.44(0.56)}{1000}}} = 2.55$$

H_o is rejected. We conclude that there has been an increase in the proportion of people wanting to go to Europe.

48. $H_o: \pi \le 0.10$ $\qquad$ $H_1: \pi > 0.10$ $\qquad$ H_o is rejected if $z > 1.65$

$$z = \frac{\dfrac{9}{50} - 0.10}{\sqrt{\dfrac{0.10(0.90)}{50}}} = 1.89$$

H_o is rejected. More than 10 percent of the sets need repair. p-value $= 0.5000 - 0.4706 = 0.0294$

49. H_0: $\pi \le 0.20$ $\qquad$ H_1: $\pi > 0.20$ $\qquad$ H_0 is rejected if $z > 2.33$

$$z = \frac{\frac{56}{200} - 0.20}{\sqrt{\frac{0.20(0.80)}{200}}} = 2.83$$

H_0 is rejected. More than 20 percent of the owners move during a particular year. p-value = $0.5000 - 0.4977 = 0.0023$

50. H_0: $\pi_1 \le \pi_2$ $\qquad$ H_1: $\pi_1 > \pi_2$ $\qquad$ Reject H_0 if $z > 1.65$

$$\bar{p}_c = \frac{180 + 261}{200 + 300} = 0.882 \qquad z = \frac{0.90 - 0.87}{\sqrt{\frac{0.882(0.118)}{200} + \frac{0.882(0.118)}{300}}} = 1.019$$

H_0 is not rejected. There is no difference in the proportions that found relief in the new and the old drugs.

51. H_0: $\pi_a = \pi_f$ $\qquad$ H_1: $\pi_a \ne \pi_f$ $\qquad$ Reject H_0 if $z < -1.96$ or $z > 1.96$

$$\bar{p}_c = \frac{198 + 117}{1000 + 500} = 0.21 \qquad z = \frac{0.198 - 0.234}{\sqrt{\frac{0.21(0.79)}{1000} + \frac{0.21(0.79)}{500}}} = -1.61$$

H_0 is not rejected. There is no difference in the proportion of American-born citizens and foreign-born citizens who favor resumption of diplomatic relations with Cuba.

52. H_0: $\pi_m = \pi_w$ $\qquad$ H_1: $\pi_m \ne \pi_w$ $\qquad$ Reject H_0 if $z < -1.96$ or $z > 1.96$

$$\bar{p}_c = \frac{70 + 72}{500 + 400} = 0.1578 \qquad z = \frac{0.14 - 0.18}{\sqrt{\frac{0.1578(0.8422)}{500} + \frac{0.1578(0.8422)}{400}}} = -1.636$$

H_0 is not rejected. There is no difference in the proportion of smokers.

53. a. Reject H_0 where $z > 1.65$

$$z = \frac{24{,}421 - 24{,}000}{(1944 / \sqrt{35})} = 1.28 \qquad \text{Fail to reject } H_0$$

    b. 24,542, found by: $1.65 = \dfrac{\bar{X}_c - 24{,}000}{(1944 / \sqrt{35})}$

$$\bar{X}_c = 24{,}542$$

    c. $z = \dfrac{24{,}542 - 25{,}000}{(1944 / \sqrt{35})} = -1.39 \qquad 0.5000 - 0.4177 = 0.0823$

54. a. $9.00 \pm 1.65(1 / \sqrt{36}) = 9.00 \pm 0.275$ $\qquad$ So the limits are 8.725 and 9.275

    b. $z = (8.725 - 8.900) / (1 / \sqrt{36}) = -1.05$ $\qquad$ $P(z > -1.05) = 0.5000 + 0.3531 = 0.8531$

    c. $z = (9.275 - 9.300) / (1 / \sqrt{36}) = -0.15$ $\qquad$ $P(z > -0.15) = 0.5000 - 0.0596 = 0.4404$

55. a. $H_0: \mu \le 0.75$ $H_1: \mu > 0.75$ Reject H_0 if $z > 1.65$

$$z = \frac{0.80 - 0.75}{0.1 / \sqrt{45}} = 3.35$$

Reject H_0. The mean time spent in the mall is more than 0.75 hours.

b. $1.65 = (\overline{X}_c - 0.75) / (0.1 / \sqrt{45})$

$\overline{X}_c = 0.0246 + 0.75 = 0.7746$

then $z = (0.7746 - 0.77) / (0.1 / \sqrt{45}) = 0.31$ $P(z < 0.31) = 0.1217 + 0.5000 = 0.6217$

c. Increase the significance level to 0.10

56. $50 + 2.33 \left(\dfrac{10}{\sqrt{n}} \right) = 55 \quad (0.525) \left(\dfrac{10}{\sqrt{n}} \right)$ Let $n = 33$

$$n = (5.71)^2 = 32.6$$

57. a. $H_0: \mu \ge 100$ $H_1: \mu < 100$ Reject H_0 if $z < -1.65$

From MINITAB system $\overline{X} = 93.27$ and $s = 40.85$

$$z = \frac{93.27 - 100}{40.85 / \sqrt{52}} = -1.19$$

H_0 is not rejected. We cannot conclude that the mean number of bids per facility is less than 100. The p-value is 0.1170, found by $0.5000 - 0.3830$.

b. $H_0: \mu \le 150$ $H_1: \mu > 150$ Reject H_0 if $z > 1.65$

From MINITAB system $\overline{X} = 183.9$ and $s = 87.0$

$$z = \frac{183.9 - 150}{87.0 / \sqrt{52}} = 2.81$$

Reject H_0. The mean number of annual medical in-patient days is more than 150 (hundreds) per facility. The p-value is 0.0025, found by $0.5000 - 0.4975$. H_0 is rejected at either significance level.

58. The answers will vary. Because the Cleveland Indians are the favorite team of one of the authors. Here is the test based on players on the active roster and the disabled list.

$\overline{X} = 1885.9$ $s = 1921.2$ $n = 31$

$$z = \frac{1885.9 - 1500}{1921.2 / \sqrt{31}} = 1.12$$

Do not reject H_0. We cannot conclude that the mean salary is more than \$1,500,000. The p-value is 0.1314, found by $0.5000 - 0.3686$.

59. a. $H_0: \mu \le 220.0$ $H_1: \mu > 220.0$ Reject H_0 if $z > 2.33$

$$z = \frac{221.0 - 220.0}{47.11 / \sqrt{105}} = 0.24$$

Do not reject H_0. We cannot conclude that the mean selling price is more than \$220,000. The p-value is 0.4052, found by $0.5000 - 0.0948$

b. $H_0: \mu \le 2100$ $H_1: \mu > 2100$ Reject H_0 if $z > 2.33$

$$z = \frac{2231.4 - 210.0}{249.3 / \sqrt{105}} = 5.40$$

Reject H_0. The mean size of the home is greater than 2100 square feet. The p-value is 0.

c. H_0: $\pi \le 0.60$ H_1: $\pi > 0.60$ H_0 is rejected if $z > 1.65$ Seventy-one homes have an attached garage, so $p = 71/105 = 0.6762$

$$z = \frac{0.6762 - 0.60}{\sqrt{\dfrac{0.60(0.40)}{105}}} = 1.59$$

Do not reject H_0. We cannot conclude that more than 60 percent of the homes have an attached garage. The p-value is 0.0559, found by $0.5000 - 0.4441$.

d. H_0: $\pi \le 0.60$ H_1: $\pi > 0.60$ H_0 is rejected if $z > 1.65$
$p = 67/105 = 0.6381$

$$z = \frac{0.6381 - 0.60}{\sqrt{\dfrac{0.60(0.40)}{105}}} = 0.80$$

Do not reject H_0. We cannot conclude that more than 60 percent of the homes have a pool. The p-value is 0.2119, found by $0.5000 - 0.2881$.

60. To use the standard normal distribution as the test statistic, several assumptions are required. First the population must follow the normal distribution. The team salaries are somewhat positively skewed, but overall the normality assumption is not seriously violated. Second, the population standard deviation must be known or estimated from a large (greater than 30) sample. In this case the population standard deviation is not known and the sample size is less than 30. So using the standard normal distribution is not warranted.

61. a. H_0: $\mu \le 2.5$ H_1: $\mu > 2.5$ H_0 is rejected if $z > 1.65$

$$z = \frac{2.75 - 2.50}{1.859 / \sqrt{48}} = 0.93$$

H_0 is not rejected. The mean number of magazines read is not greater than 2.5 for men.

b. H_0: $\mu \ge 40$ H_1: $\mu < 40$ H_0 is rejected if $z > 2.33$

$$z = \frac{35.167 - 40.00}{5.200 / \sqrt{48}} = -6.44$$

Reject H_0. The mean age of readers is less than 40 years.

62. a. H_0: $\mu \ge 35,000$ H_1: $\mu < 35,000$ H_0 is rejected if $z < -2.33$

$$z = \frac{33,181 - 35,000}{3549 / \sqrt{94}} = -4.97$$ Reject H_0. The p-value is 0.

b. H_0: $\mu \ge 0.10$ H_1: $\mu < 0.10$ H_0 is rejected if $z < -2.33$

$$z = \frac{7.233 - 10.0}{6.522 / \sqrt{94}} = -4.11$$

Reject H_0. The mean percent on welfare is less than ten percent. The p-value is 0.

c. H_0: $\mu \le 60$ H_1: $\mu > 60$ H_0 is rejected if $z > 2.33$

$$z = \frac{65.86 - 60.0}{13.61 / \sqrt{94}} = 4.18$$

Reject H_0. The mean passing rate among the districts is greater than 60 percent.

d. H_o: $\mu_1 = \mu_2$ H_1: $\mu_1 \neq \mu_2$ Reject H_o if $z < -2.58$ or $z > 2.58$
Population 1 is the smaller schools

$$z = \frac{68.98 - 59.20}{\sqrt{\dfrac{11.81^2}{64} + \dfrac{14.94^2}{30}}} = 3.15$$

Reject H_o. There is a difference in the mean percent of students passing the examination in the larger and the smaller school districts.

CHAPTER 10

TESTS OF HYPOTHESIS: SMALL SAMPLES

1.   a.   Reject H_o where $t > 1.833$

         b. $t = \dfrac{12 - 10}{(3 / \sqrt{10})} = 2.108$

         c.   Reject H_o, the mean is greater than 10.

2.   a.   Reject H_o if $t < -3.106$ or $t > 3.106$

         b. $t = \dfrac{407 - 400}{(6 / \sqrt{12})} = 4.042$

         c.   Reject H_o, the mean does not equal 400.

3. H_o: $\mu \le 40$ H_1: $\mu > 40$ Reject H_o if $t > 1.703$

    $t = \dfrac{42 - 40}{(2.1 / \sqrt{28})} = 5.040$

    Reject H_o and conclude that the mean number of calls is greater than 40 per week.

4. H_o: $\mu \ge 42.3$ H_1: $\mu < 42.3$ Reject H_o if $t < -1.319$

    $t = \dfrac{40.6 - 42.3}{(2.7 / \sqrt{24})} = -3.084$

    Reject H_o. The mean assembly time is less than 42.3 minutes.

5. H_o: $\mu \le 22{,}100$ H_1: $\mu > 22{,}100$ Reject H_o if $t > 1.740$

    $t = \dfrac{23{,}400 - 22{,}100}{(1500 / \sqrt{18})} = 3.680$

    Reject H_o and conclude that the mean life of the spark plugs is greater than 22,100 miles.

6. H_o: $\mu \le 15$ H_1: $\mu > 15$ Reject H_o if $t > 1.725$

    $t = \dfrac{18 - 15}{(1 / \sqrt{21})} = 13.75$

    Reject H_o and conclude that the mean service time is greater than 15 minutes.

7.   a.   Reject H_o if $t < -3.747$

         b. $\overline{X} = 17$ and $s = \sqrt{\dfrac{1495 - \dfrac{(85)^2}{5}}{5 - 1}} = 3.536$ $t = \dfrac{17 - 20}{3.536 / \sqrt{5}} = -1.90$

         c.   Do not reject H_o. We cannot conclude the population mean is less than 20.

         d.   Between 0.05 and 0.10, about 0.065

8.   a.   Reject H_0 if $t < -2.571$ or $t > 2.571$

      b. $t = \dfrac{111.667 - 100}{6.055 / \sqrt{6}} = 4.72$

      c.   Reject H_0. The population mean is not equal to 100

      d.   less than 0.01 (between 0.001 and 0.01)

9. H_0: $\mu \le 4.35$ H_1: $\mu > 4.35$ Reject H_0 if $t > 2.821$

$$t = \frac{4.368 - 4.35}{(0.0339 / \sqrt{10})} = 1.68$$

Do not reject H_0. The additive did not increase the mean weight of the chickens. The p-value is between 0.10 and 0.05.

10. H_0: $\mu \le 2160$ H_1: $\mu > 2160$ Reject H_0 if $t > 2.306$

$$t = \frac{2172.44 - 2160}{(9.3823 / \sqrt{9})} = 3.98$$

Reject H_0. The mean chlorine shelf life has increased. The p-value is less than 0.005.

11. H_0: $\mu \le 4.0$ H_1: $\mu > 4.0$ Reject H_0 if $t > 1.796$

$$t = \frac{4.50 - 4.0}{(2.68 / \sqrt{12})} = 0.65$$

Do not reject H_0. Mean number of fish caught has not been shown to be greater than 4.0. The p-value is greater than 0.10.

12. H_0: $\mu \le 53$ H_1: $\mu > 53$ Reject H_0 if $t > 1.761$

$$t = \frac{56.4 - 53.0}{(3.7378 / \sqrt{15})} = 3.52$$

Reject H_0. The mean number of surveys conducted is greater than 53. The p-value is less than 0.005.

13.   a.   Reject H_0 if $t > 2.120$ or $t < -2.120$ $df = 10 + 8 - 2 = 16$

      b. $s_p^2 = \dfrac{(10-1)(4)^2 + (8-1)(5)^2}{10 + 8 - 2} = 19.9375$

      c. $t = \dfrac{23 - 26}{\sqrt{19.9375\left(\dfrac{1}{10} + \dfrac{1}{8}\right)}} = -1.416$

      d.   Do not reject H_0.

      e. p-value is greater than 0.10 and less than 0.20

14.   a.   Reject H_0 if $t > 1.697$ or $t < -1.697$ $df = 17 + 15 - 2 = 30$

      b. $s_p^2 = \dfrac{(15-1)(12)^2 + (17-1)(15)^2}{15 + 17 - 2} = 187.20$

c. $$t = \frac{350 - 342}{\sqrt{187.2\left(\frac{1}{15} + \frac{1}{17}\right)}} = 1.651$$

d. Do not reject H_o.

e. p-value is greater than 0.10 and less than 0.20

15. H_o: $\mu_f \leq \mu_m$ H_1: $\mu_f > \mu_m$ $df = 9 + 7 - 2 = 14$ Reject H_o if $t > 2.624$

$$s_p^2 = \frac{(7-1)(6.88)^2 + (9-1)(9.49)^2}{9+7-2} = 71.749 \qquad t = \frac{79 - 78}{\sqrt{71.749\left(\frac{1}{7} + \frac{1}{9}\right)}} = 0.234$$

Do not reject H_o. There is no difference in the mean grades.

16. H_o: $\mu_s \leq \mu_d$ H_1: $\mu_s > \mu_d$ $df = 15 + 12 - 2 = 25$ Reject H_o if $t > 2.485$

$$s_p^2 = \frac{(15-1)(15.5)^2 + (12-1)(18.1)^2}{15+12-2} = 278.69 \qquad t = \frac{61 - 48.4}{\sqrt{278.69\left(\frac{1}{15} + \frac{1}{12}\right)}} = 1.949$$

Do not reject H_o. There is no difference in the mean amount of time spent watching television.

17. H_o: $\mu_s \leq \mu_a$ H_1: $\mu_s > \mu_a$ $df = 6 + 7 - 2 = 11$ Reject H_o if $t > 1.363$

$$s_p^2 = \frac{(6-1)(12.2)^2 + (7-1)(15.8)^2}{6+7-2} = 203.82 \qquad t = \frac{142.5 - 130.3}{\sqrt{203.82\left(\frac{1}{6} + \frac{1}{7}\right)}} = 1.536$$

Reject H_o. The mean daily expenses are greater for the sales staff. The p-value is between 0.05 and 0.10.

18. H_o: $\mu_n \leq \mu_t$ H_1: $\mu_n > \mu_t$ $df = 12 + 8 - 2 = 18$ Reject H_o if $t > 2.552$

$$s_p^2 = \frac{(12-1)(22.8)^2 + (8-1)(34.4)^2}{12+8-2} = 777.88 \qquad t = \frac{535.8 - 526.8}{\sqrt{777.88\left(\frac{1}{8} + \frac{1}{12}\right)}} = 0.707$$

Do not reject H_o. There is no difference in the mean salary of nurses and grade school teachers. The p-value is greater than 0.10.

19. a. Reject H_o if $t > 2.353$

b. $\bar{d} = \frac{12}{4} = 3.00$ $s_d = \sqrt{\frac{38 - \frac{(12)^2}{4}}{3}} = 0.816$

c. $t = \frac{3.00}{0.816 / \sqrt{4}} = 7.35$

d. Reject the H_o. There are more defective parts produced on the say shift.

e. p-value is less than 0.005, but greater than 0.0005

20. a.   Reject H_o if $t < -2.776$ or $t > 2.776$

b. $d = \dfrac{23}{5} = 4.6$ $s_d = \sqrt{\dfrac{115 - \dfrac{(23)^2}{5}}{4}} = 1.52$

c. $t = \dfrac{4.6}{1.52 / \sqrt{5}} = 6.767$

d.   Reject the H_o. There is a difference in the mean number of citations given by the two officers.

e. p-value is less than 0.01, but greater than 0.001

21. $H_o: \mu_d \le 0$ $H_1: \mu > 0$ Reject H_o if $t > 2.764$

     $\bar{d} = 7.3636$ $s_d = 8.3699$

     $t = \dfrac{7.3636}{8.3699 / \sqrt{11}} = 2.92$ Reject H_o. The weights have increased

22. $H_o: \mu_d \le 0$ $H_1: \mu > 0$ Reject H_o if $t > 1.796$

     $\bar{d} = 25.917$ $s_d = 40.791$

     $t = \dfrac{25.917}{40.791 / \sqrt{12}} = 2.20$

Reject H_o. The incentive plan resulted in an increase in daily income. The p-value is about 0.025.

23. $H_o: \mu_d \le 0$ $H_1: \mu > 0$ Reject H_o if $t > 2.821$

     $\bar{d} = 0.10$ $s_d = 4.28$

     $t = \dfrac{0.10}{4.28 / \sqrt{10}} = 0.07$ Fail to reject H_o. There has been no reduction.

24. $H_o: \mu_d \ge 0$ $H_1: \mu_d < 0$ Reject H_o if $t < -2.998$

     $\bar{d} = -3.625$ $s_d = 4.8385$

     $t = \dfrac{-3.625}{4.8385 / \sqrt{8}} = -2.12$ Do not reject H_o. The p-value is about 0.035

25. $H_o: \mu \ge 87$ $H_1: \mu < 87$ Reject H_o if $t < -1.895$

     $\bar{X} = \dfrac{664}{8} = 83.0$ $s = \sqrt{\dfrac{55{,}244 - (664)^2 / 8}{8 - 1}} = 4.3425$

     $t = \dfrac{83 - 87}{4.3425 / \sqrt{8}} = -2.61$ Reject H_o. The mileage is less than advertised.

26. $H_o: \mu \le 42$ $H_1: \mu > 42$ Reject H_o if $t > 1.796$

     $t = \dfrac{51 - 42}{8 / \sqrt{12}} = 3.90$

Reject H_o. The mean time for delivery is more than 42 days. The p-value is less than 0.005

27. H_o: $\mu \leq 9$ H_1: $\mu > 9$ Reject H_o if $t > 2.998$
$\bar{X} = 9.488$ $s = 0.467$

$$t = \frac{9.488 - 9.00}{0.467 / \sqrt{8}} = 2.95$$

Do not reject H_o. The mean prime rate for small banks is 9.0 percent. The p-value is less than 0.025.

28. H_o: $\mu = 2.25$ H_1: $\mu \neq 2.25$ Reject H_o if $t < -2.201$ or $t > 2.201$
$\bar{X} = 2.087$ $s_d = 0.4048$

$$t = \frac{2.087 - 2.25}{0.4048 / \sqrt{12}} = -1.395$$

Do not reject H_o. There is not a difference in the mean amount of coffee consumed at Northwestern State.

29. H_o: $\mu \leq 25$ H_1: $\mu > 25$ Reject H_o if $t > 2.624$
$\bar{X} = 26.07$ $s = 1.5337$

$$t = \frac{26.07 - 25.00}{1.5337 / \sqrt{15}} = 2.702$$

Reject H_o. The mean number of patients per day is more than 25. The p-value is less than 0.01.

30. H_o: $\mu \geq 6.5$ H_1: $\mu < 6.5$ Reject H_o if $t < -2.718$
$\bar{X} = 5.1667$ $s = 3.1575$

$$t = \frac{5.1667 - 6.5}{3.1575 / \sqrt{12}} = -1.463$$

Do not reject H_o. The p-value is greater than 0.05.

31. H_o: $\mu \geq 3.5$ H_1: $\mu < 3.5$ Reject H_o if $t < -1.746$

$$t = \frac{2.9553 - 3.5}{0.5596 / \sqrt{17}} = -4.013$$

Reject H_o. The mean time to complete a game is less than 3.5 hours.

32. H_o: $\mu = 0$ H_1: $\mu \neq 0$ Reject H_o if $t < -2.110$ or $t > 2.110$
$\bar{X} = -0.2322$ $s = 0.3120$

$$t = \frac{-0.2322 - 0}{0.3120 / \sqrt{18}} = -3.158$$

Reject H_o. The mean gain or loss does not equal 0. The p-value is less than 0.01, but greater than 0.001.

33. H_o: $\mu \leq 4.5\%$ H_1: $\mu > 4.5\%$ Reject H_o if $t > 1.796$
$\bar{X} = 4.5717$ $s = 0.2405$

$$t = \frac{4.5717 - 4.50}{0.2405 / \sqrt{12}} = 1.033$$

Do not reject H_o. The mean number rate of return is not more than 4.5%.

34. H_o: $\mu_1 = \mu_2$ $\qquad$ H_1: $\mu_1 \neq \mu_2$ $\qquad$ Reject H_o if $t < -2.060$ or $t > 2.060$

$$s_p^2 = \frac{(15-1)(2.6)^2 + (12-1)(3.3)^2}{15+12-2} = 8.5772 \qquad t = \frac{17.6-16.2}{\sqrt{8.5772\left(\frac{1}{15}+\frac{1}{12}\right)}} = 1.23$$

Do not reject H_o. There is no difference in the mean percent of salaries spent by employees on the two health packages.

35. H_o: $\mu_e \leq \mu_b$ $\qquad$ H_1: $\mu_e > \mu_b$ $\qquad$ Reject H_o if $t > 1.701$

$$s_p^2 = \frac{(20-1)(5.84)^2 + (10-1)(5.67)^2}{20+10-2} = 33.4767 \qquad t = \frac{24.80-20.25}{\sqrt{33.4767\left(\frac{1}{10}+\frac{1}{20}\right)}} = 2.031$$

H_o is rejected. The mean weight of the packages at the end of the month is larger.

36. H_o: $\mu_n = \mu_s$ $\qquad$ H_1: $\mu_n \neq \mu_s$ $\qquad$ Reject H_o if $t < -2.086$ or $t > 2.086$

$$s_p^2 = \frac{(10-1)(10.5)^2 + (12-1)(14.25)^2}{10+12-2} = 161.2969 \qquad t = \frac{83.55-78.8}{\sqrt{161.2969\left(\frac{1}{10}+\frac{1}{12}\right)}} = 0.874$$

Do not reject H_o. There is no difference in the mean number of hamburgers sold at the two locations.

37. H_o: $\mu_1 \leq \mu_2$ $\qquad$ H_1: $\mu_1 > \mu_2$ $\qquad$ Reject H_o if $t > 2.567$

$$s_p^2 = \frac{(8-1)(2.2638)^2 + (11-1)(2.4606)^2}{8+11-2} = 5.672 \qquad t = \frac{10.375-5.636}{\sqrt{5.672\left(\frac{1}{8}+\frac{1}{11}\right)}} = 4.28$$

Reject H_o. The mean number of transaction by the young adults is more than for the senior citizens.

38. H_o: $\mu_1 = \mu_2$ $\qquad$ H_1: $\mu_1 \neq \mu_2$ $\qquad$ Reject H_o if $t > 2.086$ or $t < -2.086$

$\overline{X}_1 = 12.17$ $\qquad$ $s_1 = 1.0563$ $\qquad$ $\overline{X}_2 = 14.875$ $\qquad$ $s_2 = 2.2079$

$$s_p^2 = \frac{(10-1)(1.0563)^2 + (12-1)(2.2079)^2}{10+12-2} = 3.1832 \qquad t = \frac{12.17-14.875}{\sqrt{3.1832\left(\frac{1}{10}+\frac{1}{12}\right)}} = -3.541$$

Reject H_o. There is a difference in the mean race times.

39. H_o: $\mu_1 \leq \mu_2$ $\qquad$ H_1: $\mu_1 > \mu_2$ $\qquad$ Reject H_o if $t > 2.650$

$\overline{X}_1 = 125.125$ $\qquad$ $s_1 = 15.094$ $\qquad$ $\overline{X}_2 = 117.714$ $\qquad$ $s_2 = 19.914$

$$s_p^2 = \frac{(8-1)(15.094)^2 + (7-1)(19.914)^2}{8+7-2} = 305.708 \qquad t = \frac{125.125-117.714}{\sqrt{305.708\left(\frac{1}{8}+\frac{1}{7}\right)}} = 0.819$$

H_o is not rejected. There is no difference in the mean number sold at the regular price and the mean number sold at reduced price.

40. H_o: $\mu_1 = \mu_2$ H_1: $\mu_1 \neq \mu_2$ Reject H_o if $t > 1.717$ or $t < -1.717$

$$s_p^2 = \frac{(10-1)(13.68)^2 + (14-1)(6.71)^2}{10+14-2} = 103.16 \qquad t = \frac{83.8 - 79.29}{\sqrt{103.16\left(\frac{1}{10} + \frac{1}{14}\right)}} = 1.07$$

Do not reject H_o. There is no difference in the mean number of hours for the two treatments.

41. H_o: $\mu_1 = \mu_2$ H_1: $\mu_1 \neq \mu_2$ Reject H_o if $t > 2.819$ or $t < -2.819$

$$s_p^2 = \frac{(10-1)(2.33)^2 + (14-1)(2.55)^2}{10+14-2} = 6.06 \qquad t = \frac{15.87 - 18.29}{\sqrt{6.06\left(\frac{1}{10} + \frac{1}{14}\right)}} = -2.374$$

Do not reject H_o. There is no difference in the mean amount purchased.

42. H_o: $\mu_d \geq 0$ H_1: $\mu_d < 0$ Reject H_o if $t < -2.998$

$\overline{d} = -2.5$ $s_d = 2.928$

$$t = \frac{-2.5}{2.928 / \sqrt{8}} = -2.415$$

Do not reject H_o. There mean number of accidents has not been reduced.

43. H_o: $\mu_d \leq 0$ H_1: $\mu_d > 0$ Reject H_o if $t > 1.895$

$\overline{d} = 1.75$ $s_d = 2.9155$

$$t = \frac{1.75}{2.9155 / \sqrt{8}} = 1.698$$

Do not reject H_o. There is no difference in the mean number of absences. The p-value is greater than 0.05.

44. H_o: $\mu_d \leq 0$ H_1: $\mu_d > 0$ Reject H_o if $t > 1.796$

$\overline{d} = 0.1908$ $s_d = 0.3260$

$$t = \frac{0.1908}{0.3260 / \sqrt{12}} = 2.027$$

Reject H_o. The chip reduced the mean processing time. The p-value is greater than 0.025.

45. H_o: $\mu_d \leq 0$ H_1: $\mu_d > 0$ Reject H_o if $t > 1.833$

$\overline{d} = 0.027$ $s_d = 0.2661$

$$t = \frac{0.027}{0.2661 / \sqrt{10}} = 0.321$$

Do not reject H_o. We have not shown a decline in grades.

46. H_o: $\mu_d = 0$ H_1: $\mu_d \neq 0$ Reject H_o if $z < -1.761$ or $z > 1.761$

$\overline{d} = -247.67$ $s_d = 548.04$

$$t = \frac{-247.67}{548.04 / \sqrt{15}} = -1.75$$

Do not reject H_o. There is no difference in the mean insurance price.

47. $H_0: \mu_d \le 0$ $\qquad H_1: \mu_d > 0$ $\qquad$ Reject H_0 if $t > 2.764$

$\bar{d} = 4.02$ $\qquad s_d = 6.41$

$$t = \frac{4.02}{6.41 / \sqrt{11}} = 2.080$$

Do not reject H_0. Stock prices have not significantly increased.

48. Answers will vary. Answer developed February 10, 1998

$H_0: \mu_d \le 0$ $\qquad H_1: \mu_d > 0$ $\qquad$ Reject H_0 if $t > 1.860$

$\bar{d} = 2.99$ $\qquad s_d = 3.38$

$$t = \frac{2.99}{3.38 / \sqrt{9}} = 2.654$$

Reject H_0. The mean price of the stock increased.

49. a. μ_1 = without pool $\qquad \mu_2$ = with pool

$H_0: \mu_1 = \mu_2$ $\qquad H_1: \mu_1 \ne \mu_2$ $\qquad$ Reject H_0 if $t > 2.000$ or $t < -2.000$

$\bar{X}_1 = 202.79$ $\qquad s_1 = 33.71$ $\qquad n = 38$

$\bar{X}_2 = 231.48$ $\qquad s_2 = 50.48$ $\qquad n = 67$

$$s_p^2 = \frac{(38-1)(33.71)^2 + (67-1)(50.48)^2}{38 + 67 - 2} = 2041.05$$

$$t = \frac{202.79 - 231.48}{\sqrt{2041.05\left(\dfrac{1}{38} + \dfrac{1}{67}\right)}} = -3.12$$

Reject H_0. There is a difference in mean selling price for homes with and without a pool.

b. μ_1 = without garage $\qquad \mu_2$ = with garage

$H_0: \mu_1 = \mu_2$ $\qquad H_1: \mu_1 \ne \mu_2$ $\qquad$ Reject H_0 if $t > 2.000$ or $t < -2.000$

$\alpha = 0.05$ $\qquad$ df $= 34 + 71 - 2 = 103$

$\bar{X}_1 = 185.44$ $\qquad s_1 = 28.01$ $\qquad \bar{X}_2 = 238.18$ $\qquad s_2 = 44.88$

$$s_p^2 = \frac{(34-1)(28.01)^2 + (71-1)(44.88)^2}{103} = 1620.25$$

$$t = \frac{185.44 - 238.18}{\sqrt{1620.25\left(\dfrac{1}{34} + \dfrac{1}{71}\right)}} = -6.28$$

Reject H_0. There is a difference in mean selling price for homes with and without a garage.

c. H_o: $\mu_1 = \mu_2$ H_1: $\mu_1 \neq \mu_2$ Reject H_o if $t > 2.036$ or $t < -2.036$

$\overline{X}_1 = 196.92$ $s_1 = 35.79$ $n = 15$

$\overline{X}_2 = 227.45$ $s_2 = 44.2$ $n = 20$

$$s_p^2 = \frac{(15-1)(35.79)^2 + (20-1)(44.2)^2}{15+20-2} = 1668.24$$

$$t = \frac{196.92 - 227.45}{\sqrt{1668.24\left(\frac{1}{15} + \frac{1}{20}\right)}} = -2.188$$

Reject H_o. There is a difference in mean selling price for homes in Township 1 and Township 2.

50.   a. H_o: $\mu_n = \mu_a$ H_1: $\mu_n \neq \mu_a$ Reject H_o if $t > 2.056$ or $t < -2.056$

$\overline{X}_1 = 129.79$ $s_1 = 32.85$ $n = 14$

$\overline{X}_2 = 106.50$ $s_2 = 31.59$ $n = 14$

$$s_p^2 = \frac{(14-1)(32.85)^2 + (14-1)(31.59)^2}{14+14-2} = 1038.52$$

$$t = \frac{129.75 - 106.50}{\sqrt{1038.52\left(\frac{1}{14} + \frac{1}{14}\right)}} = 1.909$$

Do not reject H_o. There is no difference in mean number of stolen bases per team by league.

b. H_o: $\mu_n = \mu_a$ H_1: $\mu_n \neq \mu_a$ Reject H_o if $t > 2.056$ or $t < -2.056$

$\overline{X}_1 = 0.263$ $s_1 = 0.009$ $\overline{X}_2 = 0.271$ $s_2 = 0.013$

$$s_p^2 = \frac{(14-1)(0.009)^2 + (14-1)(0.013)^2}{14+14-2} = 0.000125$$

$$t = \frac{0.263 - 0.271}{\sqrt{0.000125\left(\frac{1}{14} + \frac{1}{14}\right)}} = -1.893$$

Do not reject H_o. There is no difference in mean team batting average.

c. H_o: $\mu_n = \mu_a$ H_1: $\mu_n \neq \mu_a$ Reject H_o if $t > 2.056$ or $t < -2.056$

$\overline{X}_1 = 2.279$ $s_1 = 0.774$ $\overline{X}_2 = 2.235$ $s_2 = 0.837$

$$s_p^2 = \frac{(14-1)(0.774)^2 + (14-1)(0.837)^2}{14+14-2} = 0.650$$

$$t = \frac{2.279 - 2.235}{\sqrt{0.650\left(\frac{1}{14} + \frac{1}{14}\right)}} = 0.144$$

Do not reject H_o. There is no difference in mean attendance between the two leagues.

d. H_o: $\mu_T = \mu_G$ H_1: $\mu_T \neq \mu_G$ Reject H_o if $t > 2.056$ or $t < -2.056$

$\overline{X}_T = 132.8$ $s_T = 42.6$ $n = 8$

$\overline{X}_G = 112.3$ $s_G = 28.73$ $n = 20$

$$s_p^2 = \frac{(8-1)(42.6)^2 + (20-1)(28.73)^2}{8 + 20 - 2} = 1091.78$$

$$t = \frac{132.8 - 112.3}{\sqrt{1091.78\left(\dfrac{1}{8} + \dfrac{1}{20}\right)}} = 1.483$$

Do not reject H_o. There is no difference in mean number of stolen bases per team among teams with turf stadiums versus grass stadiums.

51.   a.   Let population 1 refer to less than 50%.

H_o: $\mu_1 = \mu_2$ H_1: $\mu_1 \neq \mu_2$ Reject H_o if $t > 2.021$ or $t < -2.021$

Less than 50% male: $\overline{X}_1 = 37.620$ $s_1 = 24.527$ $n = 25$

50% or more: $\overline{X}_2 = 35.551$ $s_2 = 21.653$ $n = 23$

$$s_p^2 = \frac{(25-1)(24.527)^2 + (23-1)(21.653)^2}{25 + 23 - 2} = 538.098$$

$$t = \frac{37.620 - 35.551}{\sqrt{538.098\left(\dfrac{1}{25} + \dfrac{1}{23}\right)}} = 0.309$$

Do not reject H_o. There is no difference in the mean cost of the two groups.

b. H_o: $\mu_1 = \mu_2$ H_1: $\mu_1 \neq \mu_2$ Reject H_o if $t > 2.021$ or $t < -2.021$

Less than 50% male: $\overline{X}_1 = 4142$ $s_1 = 4679$ $n = 25$

50% or more: $\overline{X}_2 = 1858$ $s_2 = 1850$ $n = 23$

$$s_p^2 = \frac{(25-1)(4679)^2 + (23-1)(1850)^2}{25 + 23 - 2} = 13{,}059{,}304$$

$$t = \frac{4142 - 1858}{\sqrt{13{,}059{,}304\left(\dfrac{1}{25} + \dfrac{1}{23}\right)}} = -2.187$$

Reject H_o. There mean circulation is not the same for the two groups of magazines.

c. H_o: $\mu_1 = \mu_2$ H_1: $\mu_1 \neq \mu_2$ Reject H_o if $t > 2.021$ or $t < -2.021$

Less than 50% male: $\overline{X}_1 = 35.20$ $s_1 = 5.23$ $n = 25$

50% or more: $\overline{X}_2 = 35.13$ $s_2 = 5.29$ $n = 23$

$$s_p^2 = \frac{(25-1)(5.23)^2 + (23-1)(5.29)^2}{25 + 23 - 2} = 27.6548$$

$$t = \frac{35.20 - 35.13}{\sqrt{27.6548\left(\dfrac{1}{25} + \dfrac{1}{23}\right)}} = 0.046$$

Do not reject H_o. There is no difference in the mean age of the two groups.

52. a. H_o: $\mu_1 = 3000$ H_1: $\mu_1 \neq 3000$ Reject H_o if $t > 2.101$ or $t < -2.101$

$\overline{X}_1 = \$2928.47$ $s_1 = \$2031.81$ $n = 19$

$$t = \frac{2928.47 - 3000}{2031.81 / \sqrt{9}} = -0.153$$

H_o is not rejected. Cannot reject H_o that the mean about spent on instruction is $3000.

b. H_o: $\mu_s = \mu_l$ H_1: $\mu_s \neq \mu_l$ Reject H_o if $t > 2.01$ or $t < -2.01$

Small: $\overline{X}_s = 30,820$ $s = 2961$ $n = 36$

Large: $\overline{X}_l = 36,677$ $s_2 = 2530$ $n = 16$

$$s_p^2 = \frac{(36-1)(2961)^2 + (16-1)(2530)^2}{36+16-2} = 8,057,534.7$$

$$t = \frac{30,820 - 36,677}{\sqrt{8,057,534.7\left(\frac{1}{36} + \frac{1}{16}\right)}} = -6.867$$

Reject H_o. There is a difference in the mean salary per school in the large and small schools.

c. H_o: $\mu_s = \mu_l$ H_1: $\mu_s \neq \mu_l$ Reject H_o if $t > 2.01$ or $t < -2.01$

Small: $\overline{X}_s = 2888$ $s = 1723$ $n = 36$

Large: $\overline{X}_l = 2812.2$ $s_2 = 367.4$ $n = 16$

$$s_p^2 = \frac{(36-1)(1723)^2 + (16-1)(367.4)^2}{36+16-2} = 2,118,605.128$$

$$t = \frac{288 - 2812.2}{\sqrt{2,118,605.128\left(\frac{1}{36} + \frac{1}{16}\right)}} = 0.173$$

H_o is not rejected. There is no difference in the mean amount spent in the large and small schools.

d. H_o: $\mu_s = \mu_l$ H_1: $\mu_s \neq \mu_l$ Reject H_o if $t > 2.01$ or $t < -2.01$

Small: $\overline{X}_s = 95.772$ $s = 1.010$ $n = 36$

Large: $\overline{X}_l = 94.213$ $s_2 = 1.326$ $n = 16$

$$s_p^2 = \frac{(36-1)(1.010)^2 + (16-1)(1.326)^2}{36+16-2} = 1.2415$$

$$t = \frac{95.772 - 94.213}{\sqrt{1.2415\left(\frac{1}{36} + \frac{1}{16}\right)}} = 4.657$$

Reject H_o. There is a difference in the mean attendance rate between large and small schools.

1. 9.01 from Appendix G

2. 9.78

3. Reject H_o if $F > 10.5$, where df in numerator are 7 and 5 in the denominator.

    $F = 2.04$, found by: $F = \dfrac{s_1^2}{s_2^2} = \dfrac{(10)^2}{(7)^2} = 2.04$

    Do not reject H_o. There is no difference in the variations of the two populations.

4. Reject H_o if $F > 9.15$, where df in numerator are 4 and 6 in the denominator.

    $F = 2.94$, found by: $F = \dfrac{s_1^2}{s_2^2} = \dfrac{(12)^2}{(7)^2} = 2.94$

    Do not reject H_o. There is no difference in the variations of the two populations.

5. H_o: $\sigma_1^2 = \sigma_2^2$ $\qquad$ H_1: $\sigma_1^2 \neq \sigma_2^2$
    Reject H_o where $F > 3.10$ (3.10 is about halfway between 3.14 and 3.07)

    $F = 1.44$, found by $F = \dfrac{(12)^2}{(10)^2} = 1.44$

    Do not reject H_o. There is no difference in the variations of the two populations.

6. H_o: $\sigma_1^2 \leq \sigma_2^2$ $\qquad$ H_1: $\sigma_1^2 > \sigma_2^2$

    Reject H_o when $F > 3.68$ $\qquad$ $F = 1.24$, found by $F = \dfrac{(3.9)^2}{(3.5)^2} = 1.24$

    Do not reject H_o. The variations in the stocks is the same.

7. a. H_o: $\mu_1 = \mu_2 = \mu_3$ $\qquad$ H_1: Treatment means are not all the same
    b. Reject H_o if $F > 4.26$
    c & d

Source	SS	df	MS	F
Treatment	62.17	2	31.08	21.94
Error	12.75	9	1.42	
Total	74.92	11		

    e. Reject H_o. The treatment means are not all the same.

8. a. H_o: $\mu_1 = \mu_2 = \mu_3$ $\qquad$ H_1: Treatment means are not all the same
    b. Reject H_o if $F > 3.89$
    c & d

Source	SS	df	MS	F
Treatment	70.40	2	35.20	5.12
Error	82.53	12	6.88	
Total	152.93	14		

    e. Reject H_o. The treatment means are not all the same.

9. H_0: $\mu_1 = \mu_2 = \mu_3$ H_1: Treatment means are not all the same
Reject H_0 if $F > 4.26$

Source	SS	df	MS	F
Treatment	276.50	2	138.25	14.18
Error	87.75	9	9.75	

Reject H_0. The treatment means are not all the same.

10. H_0: $\mu_1 = \mu_2 = \mu_3$ H_1: Treatment means are not all the same
Reject H_0 if $F > 3.89$

Source	SS	df	MS	F
Treatment	22.93	2	11.4560	5.7325
Error	24.00	12	2.0	

Reject H_0 5.7325 > 3.89. The mean number of hours spent on a terminal are not equal.

11. a. H_0: $\mu_1 = \mu_2 = \mu_3$ H_1: Treatment means are not all the same
    b.   Reject H_0 if $F > 4.26$
    c.   SST = 107.20   SSE = 9.47   SS total = 116.67
    d.

Source	SS	df	MS	F
Treatment	107.20	2	53.600	50.96
Error	9.47	9	1.052	
Total	116.67	11		

    e.   Since 50.96 > 4.26, H_0 is rejected. At least one of the means differ.
    f.
$$(\bar{X}_1 - \bar{X}_2) \pm \sqrt{MSE(1/n_1 + 1/n_2)}$$
$$(9.667 - 2.20) \pm 2.262\sqrt{1.052(1/3 + 1/5)}$$
$$7.467 \pm 1.69$$
[5.777, 9.157] Yes, we can conclude that the treatments 1 and 2 have different means.

12. a. H_0: $\mu_1 = \mu_2 = \mu_3$ H_1: Treatment means are not all the same
    b.   Reject H_0 if $F > 3.47$
    c.   SST = 46.96   SSE = 53.00   SS total = 99.96
    d.

Source	SS	df	MS	F
Treatment	46.96	2	23.48	9.30
Error	53.00	21	2.52	
Total	99.96	23		

    e.   Since 9.30 > 3.47, H_0 is rejected. At least one of the means differ.
    f.
$$(\bar{X}_1 - \bar{X}_2) \pm \sqrt{MSE(1/n_1 + 1/n_2)}$$
$$(6.0 - 4.25) \pm 2.080\sqrt{2.52(1/10 + 1/8)}$$
$$1.75 \pm 1.57$$
[0.18, 3.32] Yes, we can conclude that the treatments 2 and 3 are different.

13   H_0: $\mu_1 = \mu_2 = \mu_3 = \mu_4$ H_1: Treatment means are not all equal
Reject H_0 if $F > 3.71$

Source	SS	df	MS	F
Treatment	32.33	3	10.77	2.36
Error	45.67	10	4.567	
Total	78.00	13		

Since 2.36 is less than 3.71, H_0 is not rejected. There is no difference in the mean number of weeks.

14. a. H_0: $\mu_1 = \mu_2 = \mu_3$ H_1: At least one mean differs   Reject H_0 if $F > 3.81$

Source	SS	df	MS	F
Treatment	86.49	2	43.245	13.09
Error	42.95	13	3.3038	
Total	129.44	15		

Since $13.09 > 3.81$, H_0 is rejected. At least one mean rate of return differs.

b. $(17.40 - 11.62) \pm 2.160\sqrt{3.3038(1/5 + 1/5)}$

5.78 ± 2.48

[3.30, 8.26] These treatment means differ.

15. a. H_0: $\mu_1 = \mu_2$ H_1: Not all treatment means are equal
    b. Reject H_0 where $F > 18.5$
    c. H_0: $\mu_1 = \mu_2 = \mu_3$ H_1: Not all block means are equal   Reject H_0 if $F > 19.0$

    d. $SST = \dfrac{(127)^2}{3} + \dfrac{(92)^2}{3} - \dfrac{(219)^2}{3} = 204.167$

    $SSB = \dfrac{(77)^2}{2} + \dfrac{(63)^2}{2} + \dfrac{(79)^2}{2} - \dfrac{(219)^2}{6} = 76$

    SS total $= 8283 - (219)^2/6 = 289.5$

    $SSE = 289.5 - 204.167 - 76 = 9.333$

    e.

Source	SS	df	MS	F
Treatment	204.167	1	204.167	43.75
Blocks	76.000	2	38.000	8.14
Error	9.333	2	4.667	
Total	289.5000	5		

    f. $43.75 > 18.5$, so reject H_0. There is a difference in the treatments. $8.14 < 19.0$, so fail to reject H_0 for blocks. There is no difference between blocks.

16. a. H_0: $\mu_1 = \mu_2 = \mu_3$ H_1: Not all treatment means are equal
    b. Reject H_0 where $F > 6.94$
    c. H_0: $\mu_1 = \mu_2 = \mu_3$ H_1: Not all block means are equal   Reject H_0 if $F > 6.94$

    d. $SST = \dfrac{(28)^2}{3} + \dfrac{(33)^2}{3} + \dfrac{(25)^2}{3} - \dfrac{(86)^2}{9} = 10.889$

    $SSB = \dfrac{(34)^2}{3} + \dfrac{(29)^2}{3} + \dfrac{(23)^2}{3} - \dfrac{(86)^2}{9} = 20.222$

    SS total $= 864 - (86)^2/9 = 42.222$

    $SSE = 42.222 - 20.222 - 10.889 = 11.111$

    e.

Source	SS	df	MS	F
Treatment	10.889	2	5.444	1.96
Blocks	20.222	2	10.111	3.64
Error	11.111	4	2.778	
Total	42.222	8		

    f. $1.96 < 6.94$, so fail to reject H_0. There is no difference in the treatments. $3.64 < 6.94$, so fail to reject H_0 for blocks. There is no difference between blocks.

17. For treatment   For blocks
    H_0: $\mu_1 = \mu_2 = \mu_3$ H_0: $\mu_1 = \mu_2 = \mu_3 = \mu_4 = \mu_5$
    H_1: Not all means equal H_1: Not all means are equal
    Reject if $F > 4.46$ Reject if $F > 3.84$

Chapter 11

Source	SS	df	MS	F
Treatment	62.53	2	31.265	5.75
Blocks	33.73	4	8.4325	1.55
Error	43.47	8	5.4338	
Total	139.73			

There is a difference in shifts, but not by employee.

18. For treatment

H_0: $\mu_1 = \mu_2 = \mu_3$

H_1: Not all means equal

Reject if $F > 4.46$

For blocks

H_0: $\mu_1 = \mu_2 = \mu_3 = \mu_4 = \mu_5$

H_1: Not all means are equal

Reject if $F > 3.84$

Source	SS	df	MS	F
Treatment	58.13	2	29.0650	1.97
Blocks	75.73	4	18.9325	1.29
Error	117.87	8	14.73	
Total	251.73	14		

Since $1.97 < 4.46$ the H_0 for treatments is not rejected. Likewise, since $1.29 < 3.84$ H_0 for blocks is not rejected. There is no difference in the mean number of surgeries by hospital or by day of the week.

19. H_0: $\sigma_1^2 \le \sigma_2^2$ H_1: $\sigma_1^2 > \sigma_2^2$

$df_1 = 21 - 1 = 20$ $df_2 = 18 - 1 = 17$ H_0 is rejected if $F > 3.16$

$F = \dfrac{(45,600)^2}{(21,330)^2} = 4.57$ Reject H_0. There is more variation in selling price of ocean front homes.

20. H_0: $\sigma_n^2 \le \sigma_o^2$ H_1: $\sigma_n^2 > \sigma_o^2$

$df_1 = 16 - 1 = 15$ $df_2 = 16 - 1 = 15$ H_0 is rejected if $F > 2.40$

$F = \dfrac{(22)^2}{(12)^2} = 3.36$ Reject H_0. There is more variation in processing time of the new machine.

21. Sharkey: $n = 7$ $s_d = 14.79$

White: $n = 8$ $s_d = 22.95$

H_0: $\sigma_w^2 \le \sigma_s^2$ H_1: $\sigma_w^2 > \sigma_s^2$

$df_s = 7 - 1 = 6$ $df_w = 8 - 1 = 7$ H_0 is rejected if $F > 8.26$

$F = \dfrac{(22.95)^2}{(14.79)^2} = 2.41$ Cannot reject H_0. There is no difference in the variation of the weekly sales.

22.   a. H_0: $\mu_1 = \mu_2 = \mu_3$ H_1: Treatment means are not all equal

   b. $\alpha = 0.05$ Reject if $F > 3.89$

   c.
Source	SS	df	MS	F
Treatment	40	2	20	4
Error	60	12	5	
Total	100	14		

   d.   Reject H_0. The treatment means are not all equal.

23.   a. H_0: $\mu_1 = \mu_2 = \mu_3 = \mu_4$ H_1: Treatment means are not all equal

      b. $\alpha = 0.05$ Reject if $F > 3.10$

      c.

Source	SS	df	MS	F
Treatment	50	3	50/3	1.67
Error	200	20	10	
Total	250	23		

      d.   Do not reject H_0.

24.

Source	SS	df	MS	F
Treatment	320	2	160	8.00
Error	180	9	20	
Total	500	11		

      a.   3

      b.   12

      c.   4.26

      d. H_0: $\mu_1 = \mu_2 = \mu_3$ H_1: Not all means are equal

      e. H_0 is rejected. The treatment means differ.

25. H_0: $\mu_1 = \mu_2 = \mu_3$ H_1: Not all means are equal

   H_0 is rejected if $F > 3.89$

Source	SS	df	MS	F
Treatment	63.33	2	31.667	13.38
Error	28.40	12	2.367	
Total	91.73	14		

H_0 is rejected. There is a difference in the treatment means.

26. H_0: $\mu_1 = \mu_2 = \mu_3$ H_1: Not all means are equal

   H_0 is rejected if $F > 3.89$

Source	SS	df	MS	F
Treatment	26.13	2	13.067	13.52
Error	11.60	12	0.967	
Total	37.73	14		

H_0 is rejected since $13.52 > 3.89$. There is a difference in the mean weight loss among the three diets.

27. H_0: $\mu_1 = \mu_2 = \mu_3 = \mu_4$ H_1: Not all means are equal

   H_0 is rejected if $F > 3.10$

Source	SS	df	MS	F
Factor	87.79	3	29.26	9.12
Error	64.17	20	3.21	
Total	151.96	23		

Since computed F of $9.12 > 3.10$, the null hypothesis of no difference is rejected at the 0.05 level.

28.   a. H_0: $\mu_1 = \mu_2 = \mu_3$ H_1: Not all means are equal

      H_0 is rejected if $F > 3.68$

Source	SS	df	MS	F
Treatment	116.3	2	58.2	5.09
Error	171.5	15	11.4	
Total	287.8	17		

      Reject H_0. There is a difference in the mean scores

b.   Yes, because both endpoints are positive.

$$(33.29 - 28.4) \pm 2.131\sqrt{11.4(1/7 + 1/5)} = 0.68 \text{ and } 9.10$$

The mean perfectionism scores for those from a rural background differs from those with an urban background.

29.   a. $H_o: \mu_1 = \mu_2$ $H_1: \mu_1 \neq \mu_2$ Critical value of $F = 4.75$

Source	SS	df	MS	F
Treatment	219.43	1	219.43	23.10
Error	114.00	12	9.5	
Total	333.43	13		

     b. $t = \dfrac{19 - 27}{\sqrt{9.51\left(\dfrac{1}{6} + \dfrac{1}{8}\right)}} = -4.80$

Since $t^2 = F$. That is $(-4.80)^2 \approx 23.10$ (actually 23.14, difference due to rounding).

     c. H_o is rejected. There is a difference in the mean scores.

30. $H_o: \mu_1 = \mu_2 = \mu_3$ H_1: The means are not all equal   Critical value of $F = 3.44$

ANALYSIS OF VARIANCE

Source	df	SS	MS	F
Treatment	2	3872	1936	10.18
Error	22	4182	190	
Total	24	8054		

Since the computed value of 10.18 exceeds the critical value of 3.44, the null hypothesis is rejected. The mean salary for those with high school or less is $49,000, it is $74,670 for those with an undergraduate degree, and $78,330 for those with a Master's degree or more. The salary for those with only high school differs from both the other groups. The salaries for those with college work do no differ. The confidence interval for the difference between high school and undergraduate is computed as follows:

$$(49.00 - 74.67) \pm 2.074\sqrt{190\left(\frac{1}{7} + \frac{1}{9}\right)} = -25.67 \pm 14.41$$

for $\overline{X}_1$ and $\overline{X}_3$: $(\overline{X}_1 - \overline{X}_3) \pm 2.074\sqrt{190\left(\frac{1}{7} + \frac{1}{9}\right)} = -29.333 \pm 14.41$

31.   For color the critical value of F is 4.76, for size it is 5.14

Source	SS	df	MS	F
Treatment	25.0	3	8.3333	5.88
Blocks	21.5	2	10.75	7.59
Error	8.5	6	1.4167	
Total	55.0	11		

H_o for both treatments and blocks (color and size) is rejected. At least one mean differs for color and at least one mean differs for size.

32.   a. $H_o: \mu_1 = \mu_2 = \mu_3 = \mu_4$ Reject if $F > 3.29$,
Do not reject H_o because computed F (2.865) is less than 3.29.

b. H_o: $\mu_1 = \mu_2 = \mu_3 = \mu_4 = \mu_5 = \mu_6$ Reject if $F > 2.90$

Source	SS	df	MS	F
Treat	31533.00	3	10511	2.865
Blocks	35402.83	5	7080.57	1.930
Error	55033.50	15	3668.90	
Total	121969.50	23		

For a and b, do not reject H_o. There is no difference in the mean by location or by week.

33. a.   Critical value of F is 3.49. Computed F is 0.668, do not reject H_o.
     b.   Critical value of F is 3.26. Computed F is 100.204, Reject H_o for block means.

34. *For Cars*   *For Gasoline*
H_o: $\mu_1 = \mu_2 = \mu_3$ H_o: $\mu_1 = \mu_2 = \mu_3 = \mu_4$
H_1: Means not equal H_1: Means not equal
H_o is rejected if $F > 5.14$ H_o is rejected if $F > 4.76$

Source	SS	df	MS	F
Treatment	3.92	2	1.96	1.39
Blocks	10.21	3	3.40	2.41
Error	8.46	6	1.41	
Total	22.59	11		

a.   There is no difference between the two types of gasoline because 2.41 is less than 4.76.
b.   There is no difference in the cars because 1.39 is less than 5.14.

35. *For Gasoline*   *For Automobile*
H_o: $\mu_1 = \mu_2 = \mu_3$ H_o: $\mu_1 = \mu_2 = \dots \mu_7$
H_1: Mean mileage is not the same H_1: Mean mileage is not the same
H_o is rejected if $F > 3.89$ H_o is rejected if $F > 3.00$

Source	SS	df	MS	F
Gasoline	44.095	2	22.048	26.71
Autos	77.238	6	12.873	15.60
Error	9.905	12	0.825	

There is a difference in both autos and gasoline.

36. H_o: $\mu_1 = \mu_2 = \mu_3$ H_1: There is a difference in the store means   Reject H_o if $F > 3.63$
     H_o: $\mu_1 = \mu_2 = \dots \mu_9$ H_1: There is a difference in the items   Reject H_o if $F > 2.59$

Source	SS	df	MS	F
Stores	0.1370	2	0.0685	3.10
Items	71.6136	8	8.9517	405.62
Error	0.3531	16	0.0221	
Total	72.103			

There is a difference in the items but not in the stores

37. H_o: $\mu_1 = \mu_2 = \mu_3 = \mu_4 = \mu_5 = \mu_6$ H_1: The treatment means are not equal
     Reject H_o if $F > 2.37$

Source	SS	df	MS	F
Treat	0.03478	5	0.00696	3.86
Error	0.10439	58	0.0180	
Total	0.13917	63		

H_o is rejected. There is a difference in the mean weight of the colors.

38. a. Recall that $\bar{X} = \sum X / n$ so $\bar{X}(n) = \sum X$ For the first treatment
$\bar{X}(n) = 51.32(10)$, so $\sum X = 513.2$ $SST = 300.65$ found by

$$SST = \frac{(513.2)^2}{10} + \frac{(446.4)^2}{10} + \frac{(472.0)^2}{10} + \frac{(508.5)^2}{10} - \frac{(1940.1)^2}{40} = 300.65$$

  b. $650.75 - 300.645 = 350.105$
  c.

Source	SS	df	MS	F
Treat	300.645	3	100.215	10.304
Error	350.105	36	9.725	
Total	650.750			

  d. $10.304 > 2.89$, so reject H_0. There is a difference in the treatment means.
  e. $(51.32 - 50.85) \pm 2.03\sqrt{9.725(1/10 + 1/10)} = 0.470 \pm 2.831$

[−2.361, 3.301] We cannot conclude that the number of minutes of music differ between $\bar{X}_1$ and $\bar{X}_4$

39. For calories: H_0: $\mu_B = \mu_M = \mu_P$ H_1: not all means are the same
Reject H_0 if $F > 3.18$

Source	SS	df	MS	F
Type	17,692	2	8846	16.07
Error	28,067	51	550	
Total	45,759	53		

Reject H_0. There is a difference in the mean number of calories. Poultry differs from both beef and meat.
For Sodium: H_0: $\mu_B = \mu_M = \mu_P$ H_1: not all means are the same
Reject H_0 if $F > 3.18$

Source	SS	df	MS	F
Type	31,739	2	15,869	1.78
Error	455,249	51	8926	

Do not reject H_0. Failed to show a difference in sodium for the three types.

40. H_0: $\mu_1 = \mu_2 = \mu_3$ H_1: Treatment means are not all the same
Reject H_0 if $F > 3.98$, there are 14 cottages that meet the criteria. [Note: answers may vary due to changes in rental rates]

Source	SS	df	MS	F
Type	182,351	2	91,176	0.58
Error	1,734,292	11	157,663	
Total	1,916,643	13		

Do not reject H_0. There is no difference in the mean rental price based on the number of bedrooms.

41. a. H_0: $\sigma_p^2 = \sigma_{np}^2$ H_1: $\sigma_p^2 \neq \sigma_{np}^2$
Reject H_0 if $F > 2.20$ (estimated) $df_1 = 67 - 1 = 66$ $df_2 = 38 - 1 = 37$

$$F = \frac{(50.58)^2}{(33.71)^2} = 2.25$$

Reject H_0. There is a difference in the variance of the two selling prices.

b. H_0: $\sigma_g^2 = \sigma_{ng}^2$ H_1: $\sigma_g^2 \neq \sigma_{ng}^2$ Reject H_0 if $F > 2.20$ (estimated)

$$F = \frac{(44.88)^2}{(28.01)^2} = 2.56$$

Reject H_0. There is a difference in the variance of the two selling prices.

c. H_0: $\mu_1 = \mu_2 = \mu_3 = \mu_4 = \mu_5$ H_1: Not all treatment means are equal
Reject H_0 if $F > 2.50$

Source	SS	df	MS	F
Township	13,258	4	3314	1.52
Error	217,555	100	2176	
Total	230,812	104		

Do not reject H_0. There is no difference in the mean selling price of the five townships.

42.   a. H_0: $\sigma_a^2 = \sigma_g^2$ H_1: $\sigma_a^2 \neq \sigma_g^2$ Reject H_0 if $F > 2.54$

$$F = \frac{(42.64)^2}{(28.73)^2} = 2.20$$ Do not reject H_0. There is no difference in the two variances.

b. H_0: $\mu_1 = \mu_2 = \mu_3$ H_1: Not all treatment means are equal
Reject H_0 if $F > 3.39$

Source	SS	df	MS	F
Treatment	824.9	2	412.5	6.19
Error	1666.9	25	66.7	
Total	2491.9	27		

Reject H_0. There is a difference in the mean number of games won, based on the three attendance levels.

c. H_0: $\mu_1 = \mu_2 = \mu_3$ H_1: Not all treatment means are equal
Reject H_0 if $F > 3.39$

Source	SS	df	MS	F
Treatment	857	2	428	0.36
Error	29941	25	1198	
Total	2491.9	27		

Do not reject H_0. There is no difference in the mean number of bases stolen.

d. H_0: $\mu_1 = \mu_2 = \mu_3$ H_1: Not all treatment means are equal
Reject H_0 if $F > 3.39$

Source	SS	df	MS	F
Treatment	2328	2	1164	10.52
Error	2768	25	111	
Total	5096	27		

Reject H_0. There is a difference in the mean team salary, based on attendance.

43.   a. H_0: $\mu_1 = \mu_2 = \mu_3$ H_1: Not all treatment means are equal
Reject H_0 if $F > 3.23$

Source	SS	df	MS	F
Treatment	105877149	2	52938574	4.27
Error	557332745	45	12385172	
Total	663209894	47		

Reject H_0. There is a difference in the treatment means. There is a difference between the 33 up to 67 percent male and the more than 67 percent male groups.

b. H_o: $\mu_1 = \mu_2 = \mu_3$ H_1: Not all treatment means are equal
Reject H_o if $F > 3.23$

Source	SS	df	MS	F
Treatment	3.194E+09	2	1.597E+09	3.33
Error	2.161E+10	45	480212090	
Total	2.480E+10	47		

The null hypothesis of equal treatment means is rejected. However, the p-value of 0.045 is very close to the significance level and we cannot identify any treatment means that differ.

c. H_o: $\sigma_1^2 = \sigma_2^2$ H_1: $\sigma_1^2 \neq \sigma_2^2$ Population 1 is the more than 67 percent group.
Reject H_o if $F > 3.31$

$$F = \frac{(4429)^2}{(2345)^2} = 3.57$$ H_o is rejected. The variation is not the same in the two groups.

44.   a. H_o: $\mu_1 = \mu_2 = \mu_3$ H_1: Not all treatment means are equal
Reject H_o if $F > 3.10$

Source	SS	df	MS	F	P
Treatment	2348101	2	1174051	0.98	0.380
Error	109205611	91	120062		
Total	111553712	93			

Do not reject H_o. There is no difference in the treatment means.

b. H_o: $\mu_1 = \mu_2 = \mu_3$ H_1: Not all treatment means are equal
Reject H_o if $F > 3.10$

Source	SS	df	MS	F	P
Treatment	416321491	2	208160746	25.10	0.000
Error	754723654	91	8293667		
Total	1.171E+09	93			

Do not reject H_o. There is no difference in the mean salaries of the three groups.

1. $\sum X = 28$ $\qquad \sum Y = 29$ $\qquad \sum X^2 = 186$ $\qquad \sum XY = 173$ $\qquad \sum Y^2 = 175$

$$r = \frac{5(173) - (28)(29)}{\sqrt{[5(186) - (28)^2][5(175) - (29)^2]}} = 0.75$$

The 0.75 coefficient indicates a rather strong positive correlation between X and Y. The coefficient of determination is 0.5625, found by $(0.75)^2$. X accounts for more than 56 percent of the variation in Y.

2. $\sum X = 39$ $\qquad \sum Y = 85$ $\qquad \sum X^2 = 211$ $\qquad \sum XY = 378$ $\qquad \sum Y^2 = 983$

$$r = \frac{8(378) - (39)(85)}{\sqrt{[8(211) - (39)^2][8(983) - (85)^2]}} = -0.89$$

The −0.89 indicates a very strong negative relationship between X and Y. The coefficient of determination if 0.7921, found by $(-0.89)^2$. Nearly X accounts for 80 percent of the variation in Y.

3. a. Sales
   b.

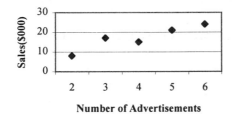

Number of Advertisements

   c. $n = 5$ $\quad \sum X = 20$ $\qquad \sum Y = 85$ $\qquad \sum X^2 = 90$ $\qquad \sum XY = 376$ $\qquad \sum Y^2 = 1595$

$$r = \frac{5(376) - (20)(85)}{\sqrt{[5(90) - (20)^2][5(1595) - (85)^2]}} = 0.93$$

   d. The coefficient of determination is 0.8649, found by $(0.93)^2$
   e. There is a strong positive association between the variables. The number of airings explains about 86 percent of the variation in sales.

4. a.

   (figure: Production vs. Assemblers scatter plot)

   Assemblers

b. Yes, as the number of assemblers increases, so does the production.

c. $n = 5$ $\sum X = 15$ $\sum Y = 120$ $\sum X^2 = 55$ $\sum XY = 430$ $\sum Y^2 = 3450$

$$r = \frac{5(430) - (15)(120)}{\sqrt{[5(55) - (15)^2][5(3450) - (120)^2]}} = 0.927$$

d. The r^2 is 0.8593, so about 86 percent of the variation in production is explained by the variation in the number of assemblers.

5. a. Police is the independent variable and crime is the dependent variable

b.

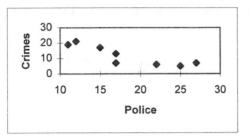

c. $n = 8$ $\sum X = 146$ $\sum Y = 95$ $\sum X^2 = 2906$ $\sum XY = 1502$ $\sum Y^2 = 1419$

$$r = \frac{8(1502) - (146)(95)}{\sqrt{[8(2906) - (146)^2][8(1419) - (95)^2]}} = -0.874$$

d. 0.76, found by $(-0.874)^2$

e. Strong inverse relationship. As the number of police increase, the crime decreases.

6. a. Age is the independent variable and price is the dependent variable.

b.

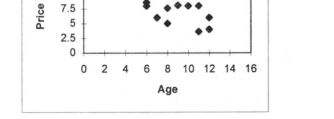

c. $n = 12$ $\sum X = 107$ $\sum Y = 82.9$ $\sum X^2 = 1009$ $\sum XY = 712.9$ $\sum Y^2 = 615.29$

$$r = \frac{12(712.9) - (107)(82.9)}{\sqrt{[12(1009) - (107)^2][12(615.29) - (82.9)^2]}} = -0.544$$

d. 0.296, found by $(-0.544)^2$

e. Moderate correlation between age of car and selling price. So, 29 percent of the variation in the selling price is explained by the variation in the age of the car.

7. Reject H_o if $t > 1.812$

$$t = \frac{0.32\sqrt{12-2}}{\sqrt{1-(0.32)^2}} = 1.07 \qquad \text{Do not reject } H_o.$$

8. Reject H_o if $t < -1.771$

$$t = \frac{-0.46\sqrt{15-2}}{\sqrt{1-(-0.46)^2}} = -1.868 \qquad \text{Reject } H_o.$$

9. $H_o:\ \rho \le 0 \qquad H_1:\ \rho > 0 \qquad \text{Reject } H_o \text{ if } t > 2.552 \qquad df = 18$

$$t = \frac{0.78\sqrt{20-2}}{\sqrt{1-(0.78)^2}} - 5.288$$

Reject H_o. There is a positive correlation between gallons sold and the pump price.

10. $H_o:\ \rho \le 0 \qquad H_1:\ \rho > 0 \qquad \text{Reject } H_o \text{ if } t > 1.734 \qquad df = 18$

$$t = \frac{0.86\sqrt{20-2}}{\sqrt{1-(0.86)^2}} = 7.150$$

Reject H_o. There is a positive correlation between assets and pretax profit.

11. a. $Y' = 3.7671 + 0.3630X$

$$b = \frac{5(173)-(28)(29)}{5(186)-(28)^2} = 0.3630 \qquad a = \frac{29}{5} - (0.363)\frac{28}{5} = 3.7671$$

   b. 6.3081, found by $Y' = 3.7671 + 0.3630(7)$

12. a. $Y' = 19.1198 - 1.7425X$

$$b = \frac{8(378)-(39)(85)}{8(211)-(39)^2} = -1.7425 \qquad a = \frac{85}{8} - (-1.74)\frac{39}{8} = 19.1198$$

   b. 6.9223, found by $19.1198 - 1.7425(7)$

13. a. $$b = \frac{10(718)-(91)(74)}{10(895)-(91)^2} = \frac{446}{669} = 0.667 \qquad a = \frac{74}{10} - (0.667)\frac{91}{10} = 1.333$$

   b. $Y' = 1.333 + 0.667(6) = 5.335$

14. a. $$b = \frac{10(26,584)-(334)(611)}{10(13,970)-(334)^2} = 2.1946 \qquad a = \frac{611}{10} - (2.1946)\frac{334}{10} = -12.201$$

   b. $Y' = -12.201 + 2.1946(40) = 75.583$

15. a.

b. $r = \dfrac{12(3306.35) - (501.10)(64.1)}{\sqrt{[12(28{,}459) - (501.10)^2][12(458.41) - (64.1)^2]}} = 0.673$

c. $r^2 = (0.673)^2 = 0.4529$

d. A strong positive association between the variables. About 45 percent of the variation in earnings are accounted for by sales.

e. $b = \dfrac{12(3306.35) - (501.1)(64.1)}{5(28{,}459) - (501.1)^2} = 0.0836$ $a = \dfrac{64.1}{12} - (0.0836)\dfrac{501.10}{12} = 1.8507$

f. $Y' = 1.8507 + 0.0836(50.0) = 6.0307$ ($ million)

16. a.

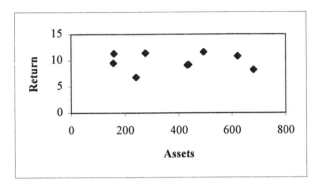

b. $r = \dfrac{9(34{,}111) - (3504.5)(87.9)}{\sqrt{[9(1{,}659{,}866) - (3504.5)^2][9(880.03) - (87.9)^2]}} = -0.046$

c. $r^2 = (-0.046)^2 = 0.002$

d. There is very little association between the variables.

e. $b = \dfrac{9(34{,}111) - (3504.5)(87.9)}{9(1{,}659{,}866) - (3504.5)^2} = -0.000393$

     $a = \dfrac{87.9}{9} - (-0.000393)\dfrac{3504.5}{9} = 9.9197$

f. $Y' = 9.9197 - 0.000393(400.0) = 9.7625$ The equation should be used with caution. Assets do not account for much of the variation in the rate of return.

17. a. $b = \dfrac{8(1502) - (146)(95)}{8(2906) - (146)^2} = -0.9596$ $a = \dfrac{95}{8} - (-0.9596)\dfrac{146}{8} = 29.3877$

b. 10.1957 found by $29.3877 - 0.9596(20)$

c. For each policeman added, crime goes down by one.

18. a. $b = \dfrac{12(712.9) - (107)(82.9)}{12(1009) - (107)^2} = -0.479$ $a = \dfrac{82.9}{12} - (-0.479)\dfrac{107}{12} = 11.179$

b. 6.389 found by $11.179 - 0.479(10)$

c. For each additional year the car decreases $479 in value.

19. a. 0.993, found by $\sqrt{\dfrac{175 - 3.767(29) - 0.363(173)}{5 - 2}}$

b. $Y' \pm 0.993$

20. a. 1.6578, found by $s_{y \cdot x} = \sqrt{\dfrac{983 - 19.1197(85) - (-1.7425)(378)}{8-2}}$

 b. $Y' \pm 3.3156$

21. a. 0.898, found by $\sqrt{\dfrac{584 - 1.333(74) - 0.667(718)}{10-2}}$

 b. $Y' \pm 1.796$

22. a. 9.3178, found by $\sqrt{\dfrac{51{,}581 - (-12.201)(611) - 2.1946(26{,}584)}{10-2}}$

 b. $Y' \pm 18.6356$

23. 3.355, found by $\sqrt{\dfrac{1419 - 29.3977(95) - (-0.9596)(1502)}{8-2}}$

24. 1.733, found by $\sqrt{\dfrac{615.29 - 11.179(82.9) - (-0.479)(712.9)}{12-2}}$

25. a. $6.308 \pm (3.182)(0.993)\sqrt{0.2 + \dfrac{(7-5.6)^2}{186 - (784/5)}} = 6.308 \pm 1.633$

   $= [4.675, 7.941]$

 b. $6.308 \pm (3.182)(0.933)\sqrt{1 + 1/5 + 0.0671} = [2.751, 9.865]$

26. a. $6.9222 \pm (2.447)(1.6578)\sqrt{\dfrac{1}{8} + \dfrac{(7.0 - 4.875)^2}{211 - (39)^2/8)}} = 6.9222 \pm 2.37007$

   $= [4.5522, 9.2923]$

 b. $6.9222 \pm (2.447)(1.6578)\sqrt{1 + \dfrac{1}{8} + \dfrac{(7.0 - 4.875)^2}{211 - (39)^2/8}} = 6.9222 \pm 4.6982$

   $[2.2238, 11.6208]$

27. a. $[4.2939, 6.3721]$
 b. $[2.9854, 7.6806]$

28. a. $[68.2887, 82.8805]$
 b. $[52.9089, 98.2603]$

29. Coefficient of correlation $r = 0.8944$, found by $\dfrac{(5)(340) - (50)(30)}{\sqrt{[(5)(600) - (50)^2][(5)(200) - (30)^2]}}$

 Then $(0.8944)^2 = 0.80$, the coefficient of determination.

30.   a.

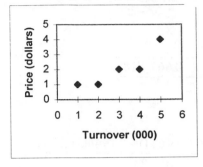

b.   0.8167, found by $(6 – 1.1)/6$ $\sum(Y – Y')^2 = 1.1$ and $\sum(Y – \bar{Y})^2 = 6$

c. $r = \dfrac{(5)(37) – (15)(10)}{\sqrt{[(5)(55) – (15)^2][(5)(26) – (10)^2]}} = 0.9037$ and $r^2 = 0.8167$

d.   Turnover accounts for 81.67 percent of the variation in price.

31.   a. $r^2 = 1000/1500 = 0.667$

b.   0.82, found by $\sqrt{0.667}$

c.   6.20, found by $s_{y \cdot x} = \sqrt{\dfrac{500}{15 – 2}}$

32.

Source	DF	SS	MS
Regression	1	7200	7200
Error	18	1800	100
Total	19	9000	

33. H_o: $\rho \le 0$ H_1: $\rho > 0$ Reject H_o if $t > 1.714$

$t = \dfrac{0.94\sqrt{25 – 2}}{\sqrt{1 – (0.94)^2}} = 13.213$

Reject H_o there is a positive correlation between passengers and weight of luggage.

34. H_o: $\rho \le 0$ H_1: $\rho > 0$ Reject H_o if $t > 2.552$

$t = \dfrac{0.40\sqrt{20 – 2}}{\sqrt{1 – (0.40)^2}} = 1.852$

Do not reject H_o. We cannot conclude that there is a positive correlation between GPA and family income.

35. H_o: $\rho \le 0$ H_1: $\rho > 0$ Reject H_o if $t > 2.764$

$t = \dfrac{0.47\sqrt{12 – 2}}{\sqrt{1 – (0.47)^2}} = 1.684$

Do not reject H_o. There is not a positive correlation between engine size and performance. p-value is greater than 0.05, but less than 0.10.

36. H_o: $\rho \le 0$ H_1: $\rho > 0$ Reject H_o if $t > 1.734$

$$t = \frac{0.21\sqrt{20-2}}{\sqrt{1-(0.21)^2}} = 0.911$$

Do not reject H_o. There is not a positive correlation between shots attempted and shots scored. The p-value is greater than 0.10.

37. H_o: $\rho \ge 0$ H_1: $\rho < 0$ Reject H_o if $t < -1.701$ $df = 28$

$$t = \frac{-0.45\sqrt{30-2}}{\sqrt{1-0.2025}} = -2.67$$

Reject H_o. There is a negative correlation between the selling price and the number of miles driven.

38. H_o: $\rho \ge 0$ H_1: $\rho < 0$ Reject H_o if $t < -1.697$

$$t = \frac{-0.363\sqrt{32-2}}{\sqrt{1-0.1318}} = -2.13$$

Reject H_o. There is a negative correlation between square feet and rental rate.

39. a. $r = 0.589$
     b. $r^2 = (0.589)^2 = 0.3469$
     c. H_o: $\rho \le 0$ H_1: $\rho > 0$ Reject H_o if $t > 1.860$

$$t = \frac{0.589\sqrt{10-2}}{\sqrt{1-(0.589)^2}} = 2.062$$

   H_o is rejected. There is a positive association between family size and the amount spent on food.

40. a. $r = 0.307$
     b. $r^2 = (0.307)^2 = 0.0942$
     c. H_o: $\rho \le 0$ H_1: $\rho > 0$ Reject H_o if $t > 1.812$

$$t = \frac{0.307\sqrt{12-2}}{\sqrt{1-(0.307)^2}} = 1.020$$

   H_o is not rejected. We have not shown this to be a relationship between the variables.

41. a. There is an inverse relationship between the variables. As the months owned increases the number of hours exercised decreases.

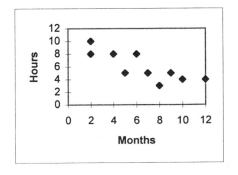

Chapter 12

b. $r = \dfrac{10(313) - (65)(58)}{\sqrt{[10(523) - (65)^2][10(396) - (58)^2]}} = -0.827$

c. $H_0: \rho \geq 0 \qquad H_1: \rho < 0 \qquad$ Reject H_0 if $t < -2.896$

$t = \dfrac{-0.827\sqrt{10-2}}{\sqrt{1-(-0.827)^2}} = -4.16$

Reject H_0. We can conclude that there is a negative association between months owned and hours exercised.

42.

Source	SS	df	MS	F
Regression	300	1	300	54.0
Error	100	18	5.556	
Total	400	19		

a. $s_{y \cdot x} = \sqrt{\dfrac{100}{18}} = 2.3570$

b. $r^2 = 300/400 = 0.75$

c. $r = \sqrt{0.75} = -0.866 \qquad$ The sign of r is negative because the sign of b is negative.

43. a.

Source	SS	df	MS	F
Regression	50	1	50	2.5556
Error	450	23	19.5652	
Total	500	24		

b. $n = 25$

c. $s_{y \cdot x} = \sqrt{19.5652} = 4.4233$

d. $r^2 = 50/500 = 0.10$

44. a. $Y' = 17.08 + 0.16(50) = 25.08$

b. $25.08 \pm (3.182)(4.05)\sqrt{1 + \dfrac{1}{5} + \dfrac{(50-42)^2}{9850 - \dfrac{(210)^2}{5}}} = 25.08 \pm 14.48$

[10.60, 39.56]

45. a. $n = 15 \qquad \sum X = 107 \qquad \sum X^2 = 837 \qquad \sum Y = 118.6$

$\sum Y^2 = 969.92 \qquad \sum XY = 811.60 \qquad s_{y \cdot x} = 1.114$

$b = \dfrac{15(811.60) - (107)(118.6)}{15(837.0) - (107)^2} = \dfrac{-516.2}{1106.0} = -0.4667$

$a = \dfrac{118.6}{15} - (-0.4667)\dfrac{107}{15} = 11.2358$

b. $Y' = 11.2358 - 0.4667(7.0) = 7.9689$

c. $7.9689 \pm (2.160)(1.114)\sqrt{1 + \dfrac{1}{15} + \dfrac{(7-7.1333)^2}{837 - \dfrac{(107)^2}{15}}} = 7.9689 \pm 2.4854$

[5.4835, 10.4543]

d. $r^2 = 0.499$. The number of bidders explains nearly 50 percent of the variation in the amount of the bid.

46. a. $$b = \frac{15(13,114.64) - (1193.8)(163.60)}{15(126,252.04) - (1193)^2} = 0.0030$$

$$a = \frac{163.6}{15} - (0.0030)\frac{1193.8}{15} = 10.6678$$

b. $r^2 = (0.466)^2 = 0.2172$

47. a. There appears to be a relationship between the two variables. As the distance increases, so does the shipping time.

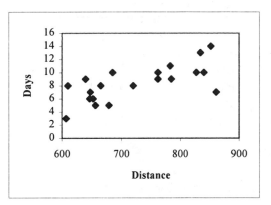

b. $r = 0.692$ $\qquad$ H_o: $\rho \leq 0$ $\qquad$ H_1: $\rho > 0$ $\qquad$ Reject H_o if $t > 1.734$

$$t = \frac{0.692\sqrt{20-2}}{\sqrt{1-(0.692)^2}} = 4.067$$

H_o is rejected. There is a positive association between shipping distance and shipping time.

c. $r^2 = 0.479$, nearly half of the variation in shipping time is explained by shipping distance.

d. $$s_{y \cdot x} = \sqrt{\frac{1550 - (-7.126)(168) - (0.0214)(125,051)}{20 - 2}} = 1.987$$

48. a. The correlation between assets and profits is 0.901

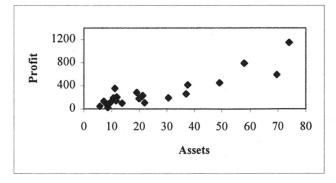

H_o: $\rho \leq 0$ $\qquad$ H_1: $\rho > 0$ $\qquad$ Reject H_o if $t > 1.711$

$$t = \frac{0.901\sqrt{26-2}}{\sqrt{1-(0.901)^2}} = 10.174$$

H_o is rejected. There is a positive correlation between assets and profits. There is a possible problem. The assets and the profits of the four largest credit unions are quite a bit larger than for the other 22. These four could have too much impact on the association.

b.　　H_o: $\rho \geq 0$　　H_1: $\rho < 0$　　Reject H_o if $t < -1.711$

$$t = \frac{-0.166\sqrt{26-2}}{\sqrt{1-(-0.166)^2}} = -0.825$$

H_o is not rejected. There is not a negative correlation between the 1997 profits and the capital ratio.

49.　　a.　　$Y' = 0.546 + 0.0227X$ Each additional employee cleans 0.0227 square feet. This is in millions of square feet, so it is actually 22,7000 square feet.

　　　b.　　The coefficient is 0.924

H_o: $\rho \leq 0$　　H_1: $\rho > 0$　　Reject H_o if $t > 1.729$

$$t = \frac{0.924\sqrt{21-2}}{\sqrt{1-(0.924)^2}} = 10.532$$

H_o is rejected. There is a positive correlation between the number of employees and the area cleaned.

50.　　The correlation between age and salary is 0.128

H_o: $\rho \leq 0$　　H_1: $\rho > 0$　　Reject H_o if $t > 1.68$

$$t = \frac{0.128\sqrt{55-2}}{\sqrt{1-(0.128)^2}} = 0.94$$

Do not reject H_o. We cannot conclude that there is a positive correlation between age and salary.

51.　　a.　　Answers will vary as the number of cottages available and their prices change. At this time there are 14 cottages that meet the criteria. The correlation between the number of baths and rental price is 0.668.

H_o: $\rho \leq 0$　　H_1: $\rho > 0$　　Reject H_o if $t > 1.782$

$$t = \frac{0.668\sqrt{14-2}}{\sqrt{1-(0.668)^2}} = 2.84$$

Reject H_o. There is a positive correlation between baths and cottage price.

　　　b.　　The regression equation is $Y' = 758 + 347X$. The weekly price increases almost $350 for each bathroom.

　　　c.　　H_o: $\rho \leq 0$　　H_1: $\rho > 0$　　Reject H_o if $t > 1.782$

$$t = \frac{0.085\sqrt{14-2}}{\sqrt{1-(0.085)^2}} = 0.269$$

Do not reject H_o. We cannot conclude that there is an association between people and price.

52. a. Using a statistical software package, the regression equation is $Y' = 60.85 + 0.0718X$, where size is the independent variable. The estimated selling price for a 2200 square foot home is 218.84 ($000), that is $218,840. The limits for a confidence interval are 210.30 and 227.39 ($000). For a prediction interval the limits are 131.57 and 306.12 ($000). The coefficient of determination is 14.4 percent, so this independent variable is not very effective.

   b. The regression equation is $Y' = 270.16 - 3.35X$. A home 20 miles from the center of the city is estimated to sell for 203.09 ($000). The 95 percent confidence interval is from 190.26 up to 215.91 and the 95 percent prediction interval is 114.09 up to 292.09. This interval is in ($000). Again, the coefficient of determination is quite low, 12.0 percent.

   c. For selling price and distance $r = -0.347$. n is 105, so there are 103 degrees of freedom. The null and the alternate hypotheses are:

   H_o: $\rho \geq 0$ H_1: $\rho < 0$ Reject H_o if $t < -1.66$

   $$t = \frac{-0.347\sqrt{105-2}}{\sqrt{1-(-0.347)^2}} = -3.755$$

   H_o is rejected. There is a negative correlation between selling price and distance.
   For selling price and area of the home, the correlation is 0.380. The hypotheses are:

   H_o: $\rho \leq 0$ H_1: $\rho > 0$ Reject H_o if $t > 1.66$

   $$t = \frac{0.380\sqrt{105-2}}{\sqrt{1-(0.380)^2}} = 4.169$$

   Reject H_o. There is a positive correlation between selling price and area of the home.

53. a. The correlation between wins and salary is 0.673 and $n = 28$

   H_o: $\rho \leq 0$ H_1: $\rho > 0$ Reject H_o if $t > 1.706$

   $$t = \frac{0.673\sqrt{28-2}}{\sqrt{1-(0.673)^2}} = 4.640$$

   Reject H_o. There is a positive correlation between wins and salary.
   The regression equation is $Y' = 62.766 + 0.471X$. An additional $5,000,000; would increase the number of wins by 2.355, found by 0.471(5).

   b. The correlation between wins and team batting average is 0.325 and the correlation between wins and ERA is -0.546. We conclude that the correlation is stronger between wins and ERA.

   For batting average: H_o: $\rho \leq 0$ H_1: $\rho > 0$ Reject H_o if $t > 1.706$

   $$t = \frac{0.325\sqrt{28-2}}{\sqrt{1-(0.325)^2}} = 1.752$$

   H_o is rejected. We conclude the two variables are positively correlated. The p-value is between 0.025 and 0.05.

   For ERA: H_o: $\rho \geq 0$ H_1: $\rho < 0$ Reject H_o if $t < -1.706$

   $$t = \frac{-0.546\sqrt{28-2}}{\sqrt{1-(-0.546)^2}} = -3.323$$

   Reject H_o. There is a negative correlation between variables. The p-value is less than 0.0005.

c. The correlation between wins and attendance is 0.590.

H_o: $\rho \le 0$ H_1: $\rho > 0$ Reject H_o if $t > 1.706$

$$t = \frac{0.590\sqrt{28-2}}{\sqrt{1-(0.590)^2}} = 3.726$$

Reject H_o. There is a positive correlation between wins and attendance. The p-value is less than 0.0005.

54. a. The correlation between circulation and Black and White cost is 0.872 and the correlation between circulation and color cost is 0.806. In both instances H_o is rejected if $t > 1.68$

For Color   *For Black and White*

H_o: $\rho \le 0$ H_o: $\rho \le 0$

H_1: $\rho > 0$ H_1: $\rho > 0$

$$t = \frac{0.806\sqrt{48-2}}{\sqrt{1-(0.806)^2}} = 9.235 \qquad t = \frac{0.872\sqrt{48-2}}{\sqrt{1-(0.872)^2}} = 12.082$$

In both cases H_o is rejected. The p-values are nearly 0.00.

b. The correlation between circulation and median income is -0.267.

H_o: $\rho \ge 0$ H_1: $\rho < 0$ Reject H_o if $t < -1.68$

$$t = \frac{-0.267\sqrt{48-2}}{\sqrt{1-(-0.267)^2}} = -1.879$$

H_o is rejected. The p-value is less than 0.05 but greater than 0.025.

55. a. The regression equation is $Y' = -699.2 + 391.71X$. Forty-three percent of the variation in the number of students in the system is explained by the variation percent of families on welfare. For an increase of one percent in the percent on welfare the number of students in the system can be expected to increase by about 392 students. The larger school systems have the higher percent of students on welfare. A system with ten percent of the students on welfare can expect to have 3218 students. The 95 percent confidence interval is from 2559 up to 3876. The 95 percent prediction interval is from -2691 students up to 9127 students. Logically, the end point of the prediction interval cannot be less than zero.

b. The independent variable regarding attendance rate explains 44.6 percent of the variation in the percent of students passing the comprehensive exam. The regression equation is $Y' = -718.7 + 8.235X$. An increase of one percent in the percent attending will result in an increase of 8.235 in the percent passing the exam. A school system with 90 percent attendance rate can be expected to have a passing rate of 22.45 percent. The 95 percent confidence interval is from 12.22 up to 32.68 percent and the 95 percent prediction interval is from -0.22 up to 45.12 percent.

c. H_o: $\rho \le 0$ H_1: $\rho > 0$ Reject H_o if $t > 2.326$

$$t = \frac{-0.668\sqrt{94-2}}{\sqrt{1-(-0.668)^2}} = -8.61$$

Reject H_o. There is a significant negative correlation between attendance and passing.

CHAPTER 13

MULTIPLE REGRESSION AND CORRELATION ANALYSIS

1.   a.   Multiple regression equation
         b.   the Y-intercept
         c.   \$374,748 found by $Y' = 64,100 + 0.39(796,000) + 9.6(6940) - 11,600(6.0)$

2.   a.   Multiple regression equation
         b.   One dependent, four independent
         c.   A regression coefficient
         d.   0.002
         e.   105.014, found by $Y' = 11.6 + 0.4(6) + 0.286(280) + 0.112(97) + 0.002(35)$

3.   a.   497.736, found by $Y' = 16.24 + 0.017(18) + 0.0028(26,500) + 42(3) + 0.0012(156,000) +$
            $0.19(141) + 26.8(2.5)$
         b.   Two more social activities. Income added only 28 to the index; social activities added
            53.6.

4.   a.   30.69 cubic feet
         b.   A decrease of 1.86 cubic feet, down to 28.83 cubic feet.
         c.   Yes, logically, as the amount of insulation increases and outdoor temperature increases,
            the consumption of natural gas decreases.

5.   a.   19
         b.   3
         c.   0.318 found by 21/66
         d.   1.732, found by $\sqrt{\dfrac{45}{(19-(3+1))}}$

6.   a.   26
         b.   5
         c.   0.3 found by 60/200
         d.   2.65 found by $\sqrt{\dfrac{140}{(26-(5+1))}}$

7.   a.

Source	DF	SS	MS	F
Regression	3	7,500	2500	18
Error	18	2,500	138.89	
Total	21	10,000		

      b. H_0: $\beta_1 = \beta_2 = \beta_3 = 0$ H_1: Not all β's are 0   Reject H_0 if $F > 3.16$
            Reject H_0. Not all net regression coefficients equal zero.
         c.   For X_1 for X_2 for X_3
            H_0: $\beta_1 = 0$ H_0: $\beta_2 = 0$ H_0: $\beta_3 = 0$
            H_1: $\beta_1 \neq 0$ H_1: $\beta_2 \neq 0$ H_1: $\beta_3 \neq 0$
            $t = -4.00$ $t = 1.50$ $t = -3.00$
            Reject H_0 if $t > 2.101$ or $t < -2.101$
            Delete variable 2, keep 1 and 3

8.   a.

Source	DF	SS	MS	F
Regression	5	1500	300	9.00
Error	15	50	33.33	
Total	20	2000		

    b. H_0: $\beta_1 = \beta_2 = \beta_3 = \beta_4 = \beta_5 = 0$ H_1: Not all β's are 0

Reject H_0 if $F > 2.90$

Reject H_0. Not all of the regression coefficients are zero.

    c.

For X_1	for X_2	for X_3	for X_4	for X_5
H_0: $\beta_1 = 0$	H_0: $\beta_2 = 0$	H_0: $\beta_3 = 0$	H_0: $\beta_4 = 0$	H_0: $\beta_5 = 0$
H_1: $\beta_1 \neq 0$	H_1: $\beta_2 \neq 0$	H_1: $\beta_3 \neq 0$	H_1: $\beta_4 \neq 0$	H_1: $\beta_5 \neq 0$
$t = 4.00$	$t = -0.833$	$t = 1.00$	$t = -3.00$	$t = 4.00$

Reject H_0 if $t > 2.131$ or $t < -2.131$

Delete variable 2 and 3 , keep 1, 4 and 5

9.   a. $n = 40$

    b.   4

    c. $R^2 = 750/1250 = 0.60$

    d. $S_{y \cdot 1234} = \sqrt{500/35} = 3.7796$

    e. H_0: $\beta_1 = \beta_2 = \beta_3 = \beta_4 = 0$ H_1: Not all β's equal 0

H_0 is rejected if $F > 2.65$

$$F = \frac{750/4}{500/35} = 13.125$$ H_0 is rejected. At least one β_i does not equal zero.

10. H_0: $\beta_1 = 0$ H_1: $\beta_2 = 0$

H_0: $\beta_1 \neq 0$ H_1: $\beta_2 \neq 0$

H_0 is rejected if $t < -2.074$ or $t > 2.074$

$$t = \frac{2.676}{0.56} = 4.779 \qquad t = \frac{-0.880}{0.710} = -1.239$$

The second variable can be deleted.

11.   a. $n = 26$

    b. $R^2 = 100/140 = 0.7143$

    c.   1.4142, found by $\sqrt{2}$

    d. H_0: $\beta_1 = \beta_2 = \beta_3 = \beta_4 = \beta_5 = 0$ H_1: Not all β's are 0   Reject H_0 if $F > 2.71$

Computed $F = 10.0$. Reject H_0. At least one regression coefficient if not zero.

    e. H_0 is rejected in each case if $t < -2.086$ or $t > 2.086$. X_1 and X_5 should be dropped.

12. H_0: $\beta_1 = \beta_2 = \beta_3 = \beta_4 = \beta_5 = 0$ H_1: Not all β's equal zero.

$df_1 = 5$ $df_2 = 20 - (5 + 1) = 14$, so H_0 is rejected if $F > 2.96$

Source	SS	df	MSE	F
Regression	448.28	5	89.656	17.58
Error	71.40	14	5.10	
Total	519.68	19		

So H_0 is rejected. Not all the regression coefficients equal zero.

13.   a. $28,000

b.   0.5809 found by $R^2 = \dfrac{SSR}{SStotal} = \dfrac{3050}{5250}$

c.   9.199 found by $\sqrt{84.62}$

d. H_o is rejected if $F > 2.97$ (approximately)   Computed $F = 762.50/84.62 = 9.01$
     H_o is rejected. At least one regression coefficient is not zero.

e.   If computed t is to the left of -2.056 or to the right of 2.056, the null hypothesis in each of these cases is rejected. Computed t for X_2 and X_3 exceed the critical value. Thus, "population" and "advertising expenses" should be retained and "number of competitors," X_1 dropped.

14.   a.   The strongest relationship is between sales and income (0.964). A problem could occur if both "cars" and "outlets" are part of the final solution. Also, outlets and income are strongly correlated (0.825). This is called multicollinearity.

b. $R^2 = \dfrac{1593.81}{1602.89} = 0.9943$

c. H_o is rejected. At least one regression coefficient is not zero. The computed value of F is 140.42.

d.   Delete "outlets" and "bosses" Critical values are -2.776 and 2.776

e. $R^2 = \dfrac{1593.66}{1602.89} = 0.9942$ There was little change in the coefficient of determination

f.   The normality assumption appears reasonable.

g.   There is nothing unusual about the plots.

15.   a.   The strongest correlation is between GPA and legal. No problem with multicollinearity.

b. $R^2 = \dfrac{4.3595}{5.0631} = 0.8610$

c. H_o is rejected if $F > 5.41$
     $F = 1.4532/0.1407 = 10.328$ At least one coefficient is not zero.

d.   Any H_o is rejected if $t < -2.571$ or $t > 2.571$. It appears that only GPA is significant. Verbal and math could be eliminated.

e. $R^2 = \dfrac{4.2061}{5.0631} = 0.8307$ R^2 has only been reduced 0.0303

f.   The residuals appear slightly skewed (positive), but acceptable.

g.   There does not seem to be a problem with the plot.

16.   a.   The correlation matrix is:

	Salary	Years	Rating
Years	0.868		
Rating	0.547	0.187	
Master	0.311	0.208	0.458

Years has the strongest correlation with salary. There does not appear to be a problem with multicollinearity.

b.   The regression equation is: $Y' = 9.92 + 0.899X_1 + 0.154X_2 - 0.67\,X_3$
     $Y' = 23.655$ or $23,655$

c. H_o is rejected if $F > 3.24$ Computed $F = 301.06/5.71 = 52.72$
     H_o is rejected. At least one regression coefficient is not zero.

d.   A regression coefficient is dropped if computed t is to the left of -2.120 or right of 2.120. Keep "years" and "rating"; drop "masters."

e. Dropping "masters", we have:
    Salary = 10.1157 + 0.8926(years) + 0.1464(rating)
f. The stem and leaf display and the histogram revealed no problem with the assumption of normality. Again using MINITAB:

```
Midpoint    Count
   -4         1  *
   -3         1  *
   -2         3  *  *  *
   -1         3  *  *  *
    0         4  *  *  *  *
    1         4  *  *  *  *
    2         0
    3         3  *  *  *
    4         0
    5         1  *
```

g. There does not appear to be a pattern to the residuals according to the following MINITAB plot.

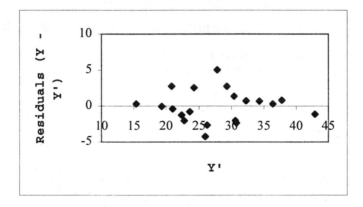

17. a. The correlation matrix is:

	Cars	Adv	Sales
Adv	0.808		
Sales	0.872	0.537	
City	0.639	0.713	0.389

Size of sales force (0.872) has strongest correlation with cars sold. Fairly strong relationship between location of dealership and advertising (0.713). Could be a problem.

b. The regression equation is: $Y' = 31.1328 + 2.1516adv + 5.0140sales + 5.6651city$
    $Y' = 31.1328 + 2.1516(15) + 5.0140(20) + 5.6651(1) = 169.352$

c. H_o: $\beta_1 = \beta_2 = \beta_3 = 0$ H_1: Not all β are 0
    Reject H_o if computed $F > 4.07$
    Analysis of Variance

Source	SS	DF	MS
Regression	5504.4	3	1834.8
Error	420.2	8	52.5
Total	5924.7	11	

$F = 1834.8/52.5 = 34.95$. Reject H_o. At least one regression coefficient is not 0.

d. H_o is rejected in all cases if $t < -2.306$ or if $t > 2.306$. Advertising and sales force should be retained, city dropped. (Note that dropping city removes the problem with multicollinearity.)

Predictor	Coef	Stdev	t-ratio	P
Constant	31.13	13.40	2.32	0.049
Adv	2.1516	0.8049	2.67	0.028
Sales	5.0140	0.9105	5.51	0.000
City	5.665	6.332	0.89	0.397

e. The new output is $Y' = 25.2925 + 2.6187\,\text{adv} + 5.0233\,\text{sales}$

Predictor	Coef	Stdev	t-ratio
Constant	25.30	11.57	2.19
Adv	2.6187	0.6057	4.32
Sales	5.0233	0.9003	5.58

Analysis of Variance

Source	SS	DF	MS
Regression	5462.4	2	2731.2
Error	462.3	9	51.4
Total	5924.7	11	

f. Stem and Leaf   Leaf Unit = 1.0

1	−1	6
1	−1	
2	−0	5
5	−0	110
(5)	0	01224
2	0	58

The normality assumption is reasonable.

g. The critical value could be a problem. However, with a small sample the residual plot is acceptable.

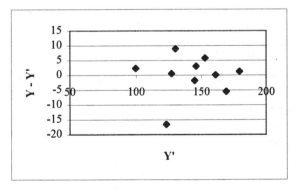

18. a. The regression equation is: $Y' = 1480.7 + 0.7315X_1 + 9.991X_2 - 2.308X_3$

b. $R^2 = 83.5\%$ or 0.835

c. $H_o: \beta_1 = \beta_2 = \beta_3 = 0$ H_1: Not all β_I's $= 0$ Reject H_o if $F > 3.59$

$$F = \frac{10{,}057.7/3}{1982.3/11} = 18.60$$

H_o is rejected. Some of the net regression coefficients do not equal zero.

d. $\beta_1 = 0$ $\beta_2 = 0$ $\beta_3 = 0$
    $\beta_1 \neq 0$ $\beta_2 \neq 0$ $\beta_3 \neq 0$
    Reject H_o if $t < -2.201$ or $t > 2.201$
    Reject H_o for area and spaces, do not reject for income. Delete income.

e. $R^2 = 0.804$, $Y' = 1342.49 + 0.7727X_1 + 11.634X_2$

19. a. The regression equation is: $Y' = 965.3 + 2.865X_1 + 6.75X_2 + 0.2873X_3$

b. Analysis of Variance

Source	DF	SS	MS
Regression	3	45510096	15170032
Error	12	12215892	1017991
Total	15	57725984	

$F = 15170032/1017991 = 14.902$

H_o is rejected because computed F of 14.9 is greater than the critical value of 3.49. At least one of the regression coefficients is not zero.

c. H_o: $\beta_1 = 0$ H_o: $\beta_2 = 0$ H_o: $\beta_3 = 0$
    H_1: $\beta_1 \neq 0$ H_1: $\beta_2 \neq 0$ H_1: $\beta_3 \neq 0$
    Reject H_o if $t < -2.179$ or $t > 2.179$

Both workers and dividends are not significant variables. Inventory is significant. Delete dividends and rerun analysis.

d. The regression equation (if we used X_1 and X_3) is: $Y' = 1134.8 + 3.258X_1 + 0.3099X_3$

Predictor	Coef	Stdev	t-ratio
Constant	1134.8	418.6	2.71
Workers	3.258	1.434	2.27
Inv	0.3099	0.1033	3.00

Analysis of Variance

Source	DF	SS	MS	F
Regression	2	45070624	22535312	23.15
Error	13	12655356	973489	
Total	15	57725968		

e. Histogram of C12   N = 16

Midpoint	Count	
−1500	1	*
−1000	3	***
−500	1	*
0	6	******
500	2	**
1000	2	**
1500	0	
2000	1	*

The normality assumption is reasonable.

f.

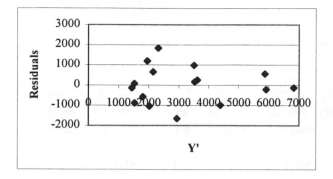

20.   a. $Y' = -5.7328 + 0.00754X_1 + 0.0509X_2 + 1.0974X_3$

b. H_0: $\beta_1 = \beta_2 = \beta_3 = 0$ H_1: Not all β_I's = 0   Reject H_0 if $F > 3.07$

$$F = \frac{11.3437 / 3}{2.2446 / 21} = 35.38$$

c.   All coefficients are significant. Do not delete any.

d.   The residuals appear to be random. No problem.

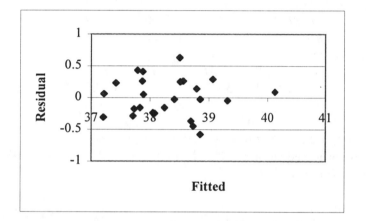

e.   The histogram appears to be normal. No problem.
Histogram of Residual $N = 25$

Midpoint	Count	
−0.6	1	*
−0.4	3	***
−0.2	6	******
−0.0	6	******
0.2	6	******
0.4	2	**
0.6	1	*

21. a. The correlation matrix is:

	Profit	Daily
Daily	0.997	
Sunday	0.995	0.984

The two independent variables are highly correlated.

b. The regression equation is:
$Y' = -0.643 + 0.401X_1 + 0.269X_2$
$Y' = -0.643 + 0.401(50) + 0.269(100) = 46.307$ or about $46.30 per week.

c. One hundred percent of the variation is accounted for by the two variables.

d. Each additional Sunday customer adds $0.269 profit per week and a daily customer adds $0.401 per week.

e. The large R-square is expected. There really are not other variables to be added.

22. a. $Y' = 28.2 + 0.0287X_1 + 0.650X_2 - 0.00040X_3 - 0.723X_5$

b. $R^2 = 0.750$

c & d.

Predictor	Coef	Stdev	t-ratio	P
Constant	28.242	2.986	9.46	0.000
Value	0.028669	0.004970	5.77	0.000
Years	0.6497	0.2412	2.69	0.014
Age	-0.04895	0.3126	-1.57	0.134
Mortgage	-0.000405	0.001269	-0.32	0.753
Sex	0.7227	0.2491	2.90	0.009

$s = 0.5911$ R-sq $= 75.0\%$ R-sq(adj) $= 68.4\%$

Analysis of Variance

Source	DF	SS	MS	F	p
Regression	5	19.8914	3.9783	11.39	0.000
Error	19	6.6390	0.3494		
Total	24	26.5304			

Consider dropping the variables age and mortgage.

e. The new regression equation is: $Y' = 29.81 + 0.0253X_1 + 0.41X_2 + 0.708X_5$
The R-square value is 0.7161

23. The computer output is:

Predictor	Coef	Stdev	t-ratio	P
Constant	651.9	345.3	1.89	0.071
Service	13.422	5.125	2.62	0.015
Age	-6.710	6.349	-1.06	0.301
Gender	205.65	90.27	2.28	0.032
Job	-33.45	89.55	-0.37	0.712

Analysis of Variance

Source	DF	SS	MS	F	p
Regression	4	1066830	266708	4.77	0.005
Error	25	1398651			
Total	29	2465481			

a. $Y' = 651.9 + 13.422X_1 - 6.710X_2 + 205.65X_3 - 33.45X_4$

b. $R^2 = 0.433$, which is somewhat low for this type of study.

c. H_o: $\beta_1 = \beta_2 = \beta_3 = \beta_4 = 0$ H_1: Not all β_I's $= 0$ Reject H_o if $F > 2.76$

$$F = \frac{1066830/4}{1398651/25} = 4.77$$ H_o is rejected. Not all the β_i's equal zero.

d. Using the 0.05 significance level, reject the hypothesis that the regression coefficient is 0 if $t < -2.060$ or $t > 2.060$. Service and gender should remain in the analyses, age and job should be dropped.

e. Following is the computer output using the independent variable service and gender.

Predictor	Coef	Stdev	t-ratio	P
Constant	784.2	316.8	2.48	0.020
Service	9.021	3.106	2.90	0.007
Gender	224.41	87.35	2.57	0.016

Analysis of Variance

Source	DF	SS	MS	F	p
Regression	2	998779	499389	9.19	0.001
Error	27	1466703			
Total	29	2465481			

A man earns $224 more per month than a woman. The difference between technical and clerical jobs in not significant.

24. The output is as follows:

Predictor	Coef	StDev	T	P
Constant	-28.88	19.74	-1.46	0.155
Acetic	0.328	4.460	0.07	0.942
H2s	0.003912	0.001248	3.13	0.004
Lactic	19.671	8.629	2.28	0.031

$s = 10.13 \qquad R\text{-sq} = 65.2\% \qquad R\text{-sq (adj)} = 61.2\%$

Analysis of Variance

Source	DF	SS	MS	F	P
Regression	3	4994.5	1664.8	16.22	0.000
Error	26	2668.4	102.6		
Total	29	7662.9			

1. To conduct the global test: H_0: $\beta_1 = \beta_2 = \beta_3 = 0$, H_1: Not all β_1's equal zero. Using the 0.05 significance level, H_0 is rejected if $F > 2.98$. The computed value of F is 16.22, so H_0 is rejected. Some of the regression coefficients do not equal zero.

2. For each independent variable the H_0 that the regression coefficient is 0 is rejected if $t < -2.056$ or $t > 2.056$. We should drop the variable acetic and keep H2s and Lactic.

3. If we rerun the analysis with two independent variables the equation is $Y' = -27.592 + 0.004X_2 + 19.887X_3$. The R-squared value is 0.652

25. The answers will vary. Here is one solution. The output is:

Predictor	Coef	StDev	T	P
Constant	1130.5	872.3	1.30	0.224
Bedrooms	138.5	126.8	1.09	0.300
Baths	295.1	104.3	2.83	0.018
People	-67.25	74.30	-0.91	0.387

$s = 306.4 \qquad R\text{-sq} = 51.0\% \qquad R\text{-sq (adj)} = 36.3\%$

Analysis of Variance

Source	DF	SS	MS	F	P
Regression	3	977839	325946	3.47	0.059
Error	10	938804	93880		
Total	13	1916643			

To conduct the global test: H_0: $\beta_1 = \beta_2 = \beta_3 = 0$, H_1: Some of the net regression coefficients do not equal zero. The null hypothesis is rejected if $F > 3.71$. The computed value of F is 3.47, so the null hypothesis cannot be rejected. We conclude that all the net regression coefficients could be equal to zero. The R-square value is 0.510

If we look at the p-value associated with each of the net regression coefficients, it seems that the number of bathrooms may be a useful predictor of price. The following output uses only the independent variable baths.

Predictor	Coef	StDev	T	P
Constant	879.3	347.7	2.53	0.026
Baths	304.95	97.73	3.12	0.009

$s = 296.9$ $\qquad$ R-sq = 44.8% $\qquad$ R-sq (adj) = 40.2%

Analysis of Variance

Source	DF	SS	MS	F	P
Regression	1	858548	858548	9.74	0.009
Error	12	1058095	88175		
Total	13	1916643			

The p-value is 0.009, so this variable is a useful estimator of the dependent variable price. The R-square value is 0.448.

26.　The computer output is as follows:

Predictor	Coef	StDev	T	P
Constant	39.49	39.06	1.01	0.314
Bedrooms	7.089	2.563	2.77	0.007
Size	0.03770	0.01472	2.56	0.012
Pool	18.466	6.996	2.64	0.010
Distance	−0.9018	0.7292	−1.24	0.219
Garage	35.861	7.644	4.69	0.000
Baths	22.922	9.014	2.54	0.013

$s = 33.24$ $\qquad$ R-sq = 53.5% $\qquad$ R-sq (adj) = 50.2%

Analysis of Variance

Source	DF	SS	MS	F	P
Regression	6	122561	20427	18.49	0.000
Error	98	108251	1105		
Total	104	230812			

a.　The regression equation is: $Y' = 39.5 + 7.09$ Bedrooms $+ 0.0377$ Size $+ 18.5$ Pool -0.902 Distance $+ 35.9$ Garage $+ 22.9$ Baths. Each additional bedroom adds about $7000 to the selling price, each additional square foot of space in the house adds $38 to the selling price, each additional mile the home is from the center of the city lowers the selling price about $900, a pool adds $18,500 to the selling price, an attached garage $35,900, and another bathroom $22,900.

b.　The R-square value is 0.531. The variation in the six independent variables explains somewhat more than half of the variation in the selling price.

c.   The correlation matrix is as follows:

	Price	Bedrooms	Size	Pool	Distance	Garage
Bedrooms	0.468					
Size	0.380	0.398				
Pool	0.294	0.005	0.197			
Distance	-0.347	-0.153	-0.134	-0.139		
Garage	0.526	0.234	0.090	0.114	-0.359	
Baths	0.382	0.329	0.044	0.055	-0.195	0.221

The independent variable Garage has the strongest correlation with price. Distance and price are inversely related, as expected. There does not seem to be any strong correlations among the independent variables.

d.   To conduct the global test: H_o: $\beta_1 = \beta_2 = \beta_3 = \beta_4 = \beta_5 = \beta_6 = 0$, H_1: Some of the net regression coefficients do not equal zero. The null hypothesis is rejected if $F > 2.25$. The computed value of F is 18.49, so the null hypothesis is rejected. We conclude that all the net coefficients are equal to zero.

e.   In reviewing the individual values, the only variable that appears not to be useful is distance. The p-value is greater than 0.05. We can drop this variable and rerun the analysis.

f.   The output is as follows:

Predictor	Coef	StDev	T	P
Constant	17.90	35.03	0.51	0.611
Bedrooms	7.117	2.570	2.77	0.007
Size	0.03913	0.01472	2.66	0.009
Pool	19.205	6.989	2.75	0.007
Garage	38.809	7.282	5.33	0.000
Baths	24.198	8.978	2.70	0.008

$s = 33.32$ R-sq = 52.4% R-sq (adj) = 50.0%

Analysis of Variance

Source	DF	SS	MS	F	P
Regression	5	120872	24174	21.77	0.000
Error	99	109940	1111		
Total	104	230812			

In this solution observe that the p-value for the Global test is less than 0.05 and the p-values for each of the independent variables are also all less than 0.05. The R-square value is 0.524, so it did not change much when the independent variable distance was dropped.

g.   The following histogram was developed using the residuals from part f. The normality assumption is reasonable.

Histogram of Residuals
```
-80    1     *
-60    7     *******
-40    13    *************
-20    20    ******************
  0    20    ******************
 20    26    **************************
 40    10    **********
 60    8     ********
```

h. The following scatter diagram is based on the residuals in part f. There does not seem to be any pattern to the plotted data.

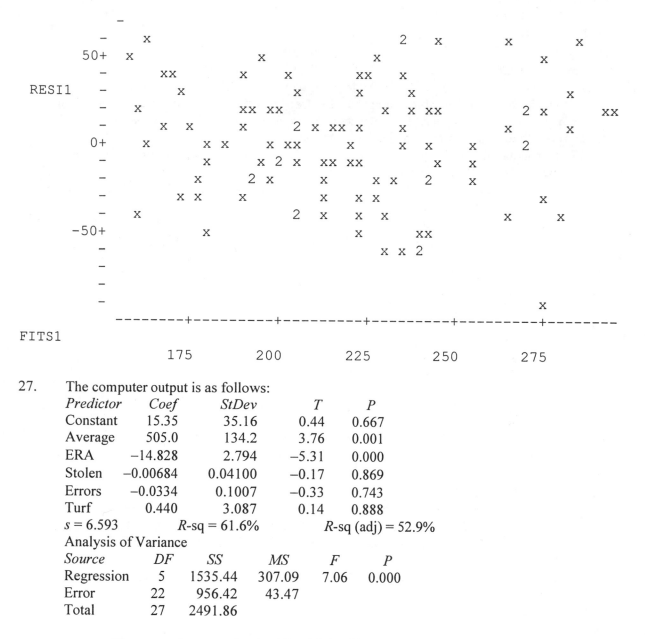

27. The computer output is as follows:

Predictor	Coef	StDev	T	P
Constant	15.35	35.16	0.44	0.667
Average	505.0	134.2	3.76	0.001
ERA	−14.828	2.794	−5.31	0.000
Stolen	−0.00684	0.04100	−0.17	0.869
Errors	−0.0334	0.1007	−0.33	0.743
Turf	0.440	3.087	0.14	0.888

$s = 6.593$ R-sq $= 61.6\%$ R-sq (adj) $= 52.9\%$

Analysis of Variance

Source	DF	SS	MS	F	P
Regression	5	1535.44	307.09	7.06	0.000
Error	22	956.42	43.47		
Total	27	2491.86			

a. The regression equation is: $Y' = 15.4 + 505$ Average $−0.0068$ Stolen $− 0.033$ Errors $+ 0.44$ Turf. For each additional point that the team batting average increases, the number of wins goes up by 5. That is, if a team had a batting average of 0.250 they would expect to win 126 games (505(0.250)), if the team average increased to 0.260 the number of wins would increase to 131. The variable ERA is negatively related to wins. If the team ERA increased by a point, say from 2.00 to 3.00 the number of wins would decrease by 14.8. An increase in the number of stolen bases decreases the number of wins. An increase of 100 stolen bases would result in losing about seven more games. Same with errors.

b. The coefficient of determination is 0.616. About 60 percent of the variation in the number of wins are accounted for in the variation in the five independent variables.

c. The correlation matrix is as follows:

	Wins	Average	ERA	Stolen	Errors
Average	0.325				
ERA	−0.546	0.363			
Stolen	−0.179	−0.334	−0.046		
Errors	0.047	0.154	0.009	−0.172	
Turf	−0.238	−0.365	0.037	0.279	0.026

The independent variable ERA has the strongest correlation with wins. The next strongest is between average and wins. There does not seem to be a problem with multicollinearity.

d. To conduct the global test: H_o: $\beta_1 = \beta_2 = \beta_3 = \beta_4 = \beta_5 = 0$, H_1: Some of the net regression coefficients do not equal zero. The null hypothesis is rejected if $F > 2.66$. The computed value of F is 7.06, so the null hypothesis is rejected. We conclude that not all the net coefficients are equal to zero.

e. In reviewing the individual net regression coefficients, the p-values, for ERA and average are less than 05, but the p-values for stolen bases, errors and turf are quite large. It seems reasonable that these three variables can be deleted from the analysis.

f. The output is as follows:

Predictor	Coef	StDev	T	P
Constant	12.25	27.43	0.45	0.659
Average	498.2	110.3	4.52	0.000
ERA	−14.742	2.569	−5.74	0.000

$s = 6.204$ $\qquad$ R-sq = 61.4% $\qquad$ R-sq (adj) = 58.3%

Analysis of Variance

Source	DF	SS	MS	F	P
Regression	2	1529.73	764.86	19.87	0.000
Error	25	962.13	38.49		
Total	27	2491.86			

Both of the independent variables are significant (p-values less than 0.05) and there was little change in the R-square value. R-square decreased from 0.616 to 0.614

g. The following histogram was developed using the residuals from part f. The normality assumption is reasonable.

Histogram of Residuals

−10	3	***
−8	2	**
−6	0	
−4	3	***
−2	4	****
0	3	***
2	6	******
4	2	**
6	1	*
8	2	**
10	1	*
12	0	
14	1	*

h. The following scatter diagram is based on the residuals in part f. There does not seem to be any pattern to the plotted data.

```
        -                 x
 RESI1  -
        -
        -                                          x
   8.0+                              x
        -                                 x
        -            x        x
        -            x              x    x
        -            x        x            x                          x
   0.0+   x                x       x
        -                          2
        -                          x              x              x
        -         x                                        x
        -
  -8.0+           x                          x
        -           x       x       x
        -
          --------+---------+---------+---------+---------+--------
FITS1
              72.0      78.0      84.0      90.0      96.0
```

28. The computer output is as follows:

Predictor	Coef	StDev	T	P
Constant	−21	1779	−0.01	0.991
Male	10.238	9.290	1.10	0.277
Age-med	−5.07	53.18	−0.10	0.924
College	−19.66	19.35	−1.02	0.316
B&Wcost	0.43666	0.07992	5.46	0.000
Color$	−0.21873	0.06398	−3.42	0.001

$s = 1617$ $R\text{-sq} = 83.4\%$ $R\text{-sq (adj)} = 81.5\%$

Analysis of Variance

Source	DF	SS	MS	F	P
Regression	5	553400788	110680158	42.33	0.000
Error	42	109809106	2614503		
Total	47	663209894			

a. The regression equation is: $Y' = −21 + 10.2$ Male $−5.1$ Age-med $−19.7$ College $+ 0.437$ B&W cost $−0.219$ Color$. The dependent variable circulation is in 000, so an increase of 1.0 percent in the percent of male readers would increase circulation by 10.2, which is 10,200. An increase in the mean age of the readership indicates a decline in the circulation. An increase of one year in the median age of the readership means a decrease of 5.1. Increases in both color advertising and the percent attending college will result in a decrease in circulation, where as an increase in the cost of black and white advertising cost will increase the circulation.

b. The five independent variables explain 0.834 of the variation in circulation.

c.   The correlation matrix is as follows:

	Circulat	Male	Age-med	College	B&Wcost
Male	−0.197				
Age-med	0.412	−0.022			
College	−0.260	0.231	0.103		
B&Wcost	0.872	−0.158	0.492	−0.111	
Color	0.806	−0.066	0.487	−0.028	0.981

There is a strong positive correlation between both black and white advertising cost and circulation and color advertising and circulation. The independent variables black and white advertising cost and color advertising cost are also strongly correlated. This could be a problem with multicollinearity.

d.   The global test of hypothesis is: H_0: $\beta_1 = \beta_2 = \beta_3 = \beta_4 = \beta_5 = 0$, H_1: Some of the net regression coefficients do not equal zero. The null hypothesis is rejected if $F > 2.44$. The computed value of F is 42.33, so the null hypothesis is rejected. We conclude that not all the net coefficients are equal to zero.

e.   In reviewing the calculated values of t and the p-values, the only two variables that are significant are black and white and color advertising costs

f.   The output is as follows:

Predictor	Coef	StDev	T	P
Constant	−548.9	475.2	−1.16	0.254
B&White	0.42846	0.06350	6.75	0.000
Color	−0.21321	0.05213	−4.09	0.000

$s = 1604$ R-sq $= 82.6\%$ R-sq (adj) $= 81.8\%$

Analysis of Variance

Source	DF	SS	MS	F	P
Regression	2	547499000	273749500	106.46	0.000
Error	45	115710894	2571353		
Total	47	663209894			

Both of the independent variables are significant, although there may be a problem with the correlation between the two variables. Often when the sign of the correlation coefficient between the dependent variable and an independent variable the sign of the net regression differ there is multicollinearity. That is the case in this instance with color advertising.

g.   The following histogram was developed using the residuals. It is reasonable to conclude that it is normal. There appears to be some outliers and the distribution is positively skewed.

Histogram of Residuals

−4000	1	*
−3000	0	
−2000	5	*****
−1000	4	****
0	31	*****************************
1000	3	***
2000	1	*
3000	1	*
4000	1	*
5000	0	
6000	0	
7000	1	*

h. Below is a plot of the fitted values and the residuals. There appear to be several values that are outliers. It seems that using the two advertising variables may be in violation of the regression assumptions.

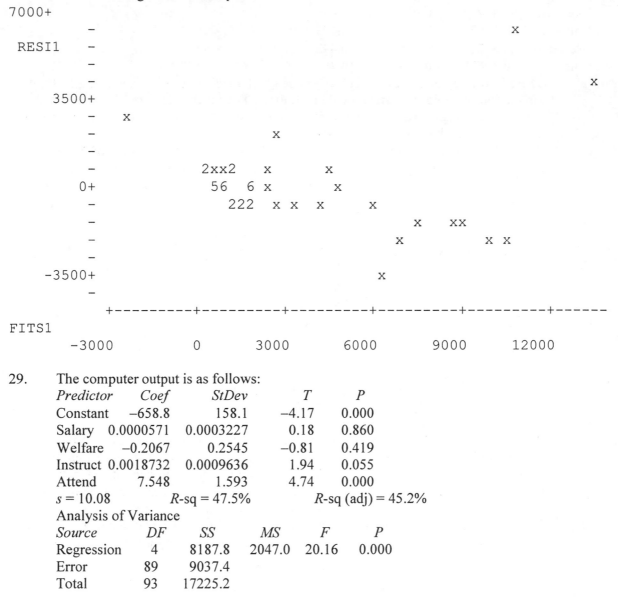

```
7000+
        -                                                                    x
 RESI1  -
        -
        -                                                                         x
 3500+
        -     x
        -                        x
        -
        -             2xx2     x          x
   0+                 56   6 x          x
        -               222   x  x   x        x
        -                                  x    xx
        -                              x            x  x
        -
-3500+                                      x
        -
        +---------+---------+---------+---------+---------+------
 FITS1
        -3000       0       3000      6000      9000     12000
```

29. The computer output is as follows:

Predictor	Coef	StDev	T	P
Constant	−658.8	158.1	−4.17	0.000
Salary	0.0000571	0.0003227	0.18	0.860
Welfare	−0.2067	0.2545	−0.81	0.419
Instruct	0.0018732	0.0009636	1.94	0.055
Attend	7.548	1.593	4.74	0.000

$s = 10.08$ $R\text{-sq} = 47.5\%$ $R\text{-sq (adj)} = 45.2\%$

Analysis of Variance

Source	DF	SS	MS	F	P
Regression	4	8187.8	2047.0	20.16	0.000
Error	89	9037.4			
Total	93	17225.2			

a. The regression equation is: $Y' = -659 + 0.000057$ Salary -0.207 Welfare $+ 0.00187$ Instruct $+ 7.55$ Attend. The percent of students passing in the district increases when the teacher salary is increased, when the instructional cost per student increases, and the percent attendance increases. The percent passing decreases when the percent on welfare in the district increases.

b. Less than half of the variation in percent passing is explained by the four independent variables. The R-square value is 0.475.

c.   The correlation matrix is as follows:

	Passing	Salary	Welfare	Instruct
Salary	−0.191			
Welfare	−0.560	0.091		
Instruct	0.093	0.033	0.006	
Attend	0.668	−0.329	−0.756	−0.095

There is a strong correlation between attendance and passing and between welfare and passing. There is also a strong correlation between these two independent variables. Salary and instructional cost do not show much correlation with the dependent variable.

d.   To conduct the global test: H_0: $\beta_1 = \beta_2 = \beta_3 = \beta_4 = \beta_5 = 0$, H_1: Not all the net regression coefficients equal zero. The null hypothesis is rejected if $F > 2.50$. The computed value of F is 20.16, so the null hypothesis is rejected. We conclude that not all the net coefficients are equal to zero.

e.   Comparing the p-values of the four independent variables, attendance is significant, salary and welfare are not significant, and instructions seems to be very close (p-value if 0.55). Rerunning the regression equation with attendance and instruction as independent variables, the output is as follows. Both independent variables are significant at the 0.05 significance level.

Predictor	Coef	StDev	T	P
Constant	−741.57	90.31	−8.21	0.000
Instruct	0.0019553	0.0009521	2.05	0.043
Attend	8.4191	0.9449	8.91	0.000

$s = 10.01$ R-sq $= 47.1\%$ R-sq (adj) $= 45.9\%$

Analysis of Variance

Source	DF	SS	MS	F	P
Regression	2	8104.7	4052.4	40.43	0.000
Error	91	9120.5	100.2		
Total	93	17225.2			

f.   The following is a histogram of the residuals. It seems reasonable to conclude that the distribution is normal.

Histogram of Residuals

```
−35    1     *
−30    0
−25    0
−20    3     ***
−15    2     **
−10   16     ****************
 −5   15     ***************
  0   19     *******************
  5   17     *****************
 10   13     *************
 15    5     *****
 20    1     *
 25    2     **
```

g. The following is a plot showing the relationship between the fitted values of Y and the residuals. There does not seem to be any unusual patterns. We conclude that instruction and attendance are reasonable independent variables, but the value of R-square is less than we would have hoped.

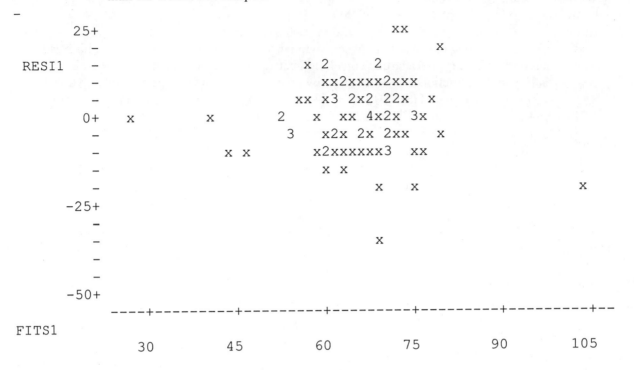

CHAPTER 14

NONPARAMETRIC METHODS: CHI-SQUARE APPLICATIONS

1.   a.   3
         b.   7.815

2.   a.   5
         b.   15.086

3.   a.   Reject H_o if $\chi^2 > 5.991$

         b. $\chi^2 = \dfrac{(10-20)^2}{20} + \dfrac{(20-20)^2}{20} + \dfrac{(30-20)^2}{20} = 10.0$

         c.   Reject H_o. The proportions are not equal.

4.   a.   Reject H_o if $\chi^2 > 7.815$

         b. $\chi^2 = \dfrac{(10-20)^2}{20} + \dfrac{(20-20)^2}{20} + \dfrac{(30-20)^2}{20} + \dfrac{(20-20)^2}{20} = 10.0$

         c.   Reject H_o. The categories are not equal.

5. H_o: The outcomes are the same H_1: The outcomes are not the same
   Reject H_o if $\chi^2 > 9.236$

   $$\chi^2 = \frac{(3-5)^2}{5} + ... + \frac{(7-5)^2}{5} = 7.60$$

   Do not reject H_o. Cannot reject H_o that outcomes are the same.

6. H_o: Absenteeism is the same for each day H_1: Absenteeism is not the same
   Reject H_o if $\chi^2 > 9.488$

   $$\chi^2 = \frac{(124-104)^2}{104} + ... + \frac{(120-104)^2}{104} = 15.308$$

   Reject H_o. The absence rate is not the same for each day.

7. H_o: There is no difference in the proportions H_1: There is a difference in the proportions
   Reject H_o if $\chi^2 > 15.086$

   $$\chi^2 = \frac{(47-40)^2}{40} + ... + \frac{(34-40)^2}{40} = 3.400$$

   Do not reject H_o. There is no difference in the proportions.

8. H_o: The proportions are the same H_1: The proportions are not the same
   Reject H_o if $\chi^2 > 18.475$

   $$\chi^2 = \frac{(6-10)^2}{10} + ... + \frac{(19-10)^2}{10} + \frac{(6-10)^2}{10} = 24.60$$

   Reject H_o. The accidents are not evenly distributed throughout the day.

9.   a.   Reject H_o if $\chi^2 > 9.210$

   b. $\chi^2 = \dfrac{(30-24)^2}{24} + \dfrac{(20-24)^2}{24} + \dfrac{(10-12)^2}{12} = 2.50$

   c.   Do not reject H_o

10. H_o: The proportions are as stated H_1: The proportions are not as stated
   Reject H_o if $\chi^2 > 7.824$

$$\chi^2 = \frac{(60-50)^2}{50} + \frac{(30-25)^2}{25} + \frac{(10-25)^2}{25} = 12.00$$

Reject H_o. Proportions are not as stated.

11. H_o: The proportions are as stated H_1: The proportions are not as stated
   Reject H_o if $\chi^2 > 11.345$

$$\chi^2 = \frac{(50-25)^2}{25} + \frac{(100-75)^2}{75} + \frac{(190-125)^2}{125} + \frac{(160-275)^2}{275} = 115.22$$

Reject H_o. Proportions are not as stated.

12. H_o: The proportions are as stated H_1: The proportions are not as stated
   Reject H_o if $\chi^2 > 7.185$

$$\chi^2 = \frac{(165-150)^2}{150} + \frac{(140-150)^2}{150} + \frac{(125-150)^2}{150} + \frac{(70-50)^2}{50} = 14.333$$

Reject H_o. Proportion of viewers is not as stated

13. H_o: Distribution is normally distributed H_1: It is not normally distributed
   Reject H_o if $\chi^2 > 11.070$

Time	z areas	f_0	f_e	$(f_0-f_e)^2/f_e$
Up to 4	0.0764	7	6.9	0.001
4 to 5	0.1625	14	14.6	0.025
5 to 6	0.2611	25	23.5	0.096
6 to 7	0.2611	22	23.5	0.096
7 to 8	0.1625	16	14.6	0.134
8 or more	0.0764	6	6.9	0.117
Total	1.000	90	90	0.469

Computed $\chi^2 = 0.469$ Do not reject H_o, the distribution is normal.

14. H_o: Distribution is normal H_1: The distribution is not normal
   Reject H_o if $\chi^2 > 15.086$ $df = 5$

Commission	Area	f_0	f_e	$(f_0-f_e)^2/f_e$
Less than $900	0.0228	9	11.40	0.51
900 to 1200	0.1359	63	67.95	0.36
1200 to 1500	0.3413	165	170.65	0.19
1500 to 1800	0.3413	180	170.65	0.51
1800 to 2100	0.1359	71	67.95	0.14
2100 or more	0.0228	12	11.40	0.03
Total	1.000	500	500	1.74

Do not reject H_o because $\chi^2 = 1.74$ conclude that the distribution is normal.

15. H_0: There is no relationship between size and section read $\qquad$ H_1: There is a relationship
Reject H_0 if $\chi^2 > 9.488$

$$\chi^2 = \frac{(170-157.50)^2}{157.50} + \ldots + \frac{(88-83.62)^2}{83.62} = 7.340$$

Do not reject H_0. There is no relationship between size and section read.

16. H_0: There is no relationship between quality and manufacturer
H_1: There is a relationship
Reject H_0 if $\chi^2 > 7.815$

$$\chi^2 = \frac{(12-9)^2}{9} + \frac{(8-9)^2}{9} + \ldots + \frac{(89-91)^2}{91} = 3.663$$

Do not reject H_0. There is no relationship between quality and manufacturer.

17. H_0: No relationship between error rates and item type
H_1: There is a relationship between error rates and item type
Reject H_0 if $\chi^2 > 9.21$

$$\chi^2 = \frac{(20-14.1)^2}{14.1} + \frac{(10-15.9)^2}{15.9} + \ldots + \frac{(200-199.75)^2}{199.75} + \frac{(225-225.25)^2}{225.25} = 8.033$$

Do not reject H_0. There is no relationship between error rates and item type.

18. H_0: No relationship between phone use and accidents
H_1: There is a relationship between phone use and accidents
Reject H_0 if $\chi^2 > 3.841$

$$\chi^2 = \frac{(25-31.45)^2}{31.45} + \frac{(300-293.55)^2}{293.55} + \frac{(50-43.55)^2}{43.55} + \frac{(400-406.45)^2}{406.45} = 2.523$$

Do not reject H_0. There is no relationship between phone use and accidents.

19. H_0: $\pi_s = 0.50$, $\pi_r = \pi_e = 0.25$ $\qquad$ H_1: Distribution is not as given above.
$df = 2$ $\qquad$ Reject H_0 if $\chi^2 > 4.605$.

Turn	f_o	f_e	$f_o - f_e$	$(f_o - f_e)^2/f_e$
Straight	112	100	12	1.44
Right	48	50	-2	0.08
Left	40	50	-10	2.00
Total	200	200		3.52

H_0 is not rejected. The proportions are as given in the null hypothesis.

20. H_0: $\pi_s = \pi_c = \pi_e$ $\qquad$ H_1: The proportions are not equal.
$df = 2$ $\qquad$ Reject H_0 if $\chi^2 > 5.991$.

Gift	f_o	f_e	$f_o - f_e$	$(f_o - f_e)^2/f_e$
Sweatshirt	183	166.67	16.33	1.6000
Coffee Cup	175	166.67	8.33	0.4163
Earrings	142	166.67	-24.67	3.6516
Total	500	500.00	0	5.6679

H_0 is not rejected. There is not a preference for the gifts.

21. H_o: There is no preference with respect to TV stations.
H_1: There is a preference with respect to TV stations.
$df = 3 - 1 = 2$ H_o is rejected if χ^2 is greater than 5.991

TV Station	f_o	f_e	$f_o - f_e$	$(f_o - f_e)^2$	$(f_o - f_e)^2/f_e$
WNAE	53	50	3	9	0.18
WRRN	64	50	14	196	3.92
WSPD	33	50	-17	289	5.78
Total	150	150			9.88

H_o is rejected. There is a preference for TV stations.

22. H_o: $\pi_1 = \pi_2 = \pi_3 = \pi_4$ H_1: The proportions are not equal.
$df = 3$ Reject H_o if $\chi^2 > 11.345$.

Entrance	f_o	f_e	$f_o - f_e$	$(f_o - f_e)^2/f_e$
Main	140	100	40	16.00
Broad	120	100	20	4.00
Cherry	90	100	-10	1.00
Walnut	50	100	-50	25.00
Total	400	400	0	46.00

H_o is rejected. The entrances are not equally likely.

23. H_o: $\pi_{ne} = 0.21$, $\pi_m = 0.24$, $\pi_s = 0.35$ and $\pi_w = 0.20$
H_1: The distribution is not as given.
Reject H_o if $\chi^2 > 11.345$.

Region	f_o	f_e	$f_o - f_e$	$(f_o - f_e)^2/f_e$
Northeast	68	84	-16	3.0476
Midwest	104	96	8	0.6667
South	155	140	15	1.6071
West	73	80	-7	0.6125
Total	400	400	0	5.9339

H_o is not rejected. The distribution of the destination of orders is reflective of the population.

24. H_o: Southern Medical Services distribution is same as national. H_1: There is a difference
Decision rule: If $\chi^2 > 7.815$ reject H_o.

No. Abortions	f_o	f_e	$f_o - f_e$	$(f_o - f_e)^2/f_e$
0	2441	2317.5	123.5	6.58
1	784	933.9	-149.9	24.06
2	184	173.0	11.0	0.70
3 or more	50	34.6	15.4	6.85
Total	3459			38.19

Reject H_o. The Southern Medical Services distribution is different.

25. H_o: The proportion of colors is as reported
H_1: The proportion are not as reported
Reject H_o if $\chi^2 > 11.070$

$$\chi^2 = \frac{(17 - 21.6)^2}{21.6} + \frac{(20 - 21.6)^2}{21.6} + \ldots + \frac{(7 - 7.2)^2}{7.2} = 6.426$$

Do not reject H_o. The actual breakdown of candies agrees with the expected distribution.

26. H_o: The distribution is normal H_1: The distribution is not normal
Reject H_o if $\chi^2 > 11.070$

Number of Set	f_o	Area	f_e	$(f_o - f_e)^2/f_e$
0	7	0.1112	11.12	1.526
1	27	0.1834	18.34	4.089
2	28	0.2611	26.11	0.137
3	18	0.2353	23.53	1.300
4	10	0.1409	14.09	1.187
5 or more	10	0.0681	6.81	1.494
Total	100			9.733

H_o cannot be rejected. Conclude that the distribution could be normal.

27. H_o: The distribution is normal H_1: The distribution is not normal
Reject if $\chi^2 > 4.605$

Wage	f	X	fX	fX^2
5.50 up to 6.50	20	6	120	720
6.50 up to 7.50	54	7	378	2646
7.50 up to 8.50	130	8	1040	8320
8.50 up to 9.50	68	9	612	5508
9.50 up to 10.50	28	10	280	2800
	300		2430	19,994

$$\overline{X} = \frac{2430}{300} = 8.10 \qquad s = \sqrt{\frac{19,994 - \frac{(2430)^2}{300}}{300 - 1}} = 1.02$$

Wage	f_o	Area	f_e	$(f_o - f_e)^2/f_e$
5.50 up to 6.50	20	0.0582	17.46	0.370
6.50 up to 7.50	54	0.2194	65.82	2.123
7.50 up to 8.50	130	0.3741	112.23	2.814
8.50 up to 9.50	68	0.2630	78.90	1.506
9.50 up to 10.50	28	0.0853	25.59	0.227
	300			7.04

Reject H_o. We cannot conclude that the distribution is normal.

28. H_o: Store size and advertising amount are not related
H_1: Store size and advertising amount are related
Reject H_o if $\chi^2 > 5.991$

$$\chi^2 = \frac{(40 - 56.97)^2}{56.97} + \ldots + \frac{(32 - 37.70)^2}{37.70} = 18.177$$

Reject H_o. Store size and advertising amount are related.

29. H_o: Level of management and concern regarding the environment are not related
H_1: Level of management and concern regarding the environment are related
Reject H_o if $\chi^2 > 16.812$

$$\chi^2 = \frac{(15 - 14)^2}{14} + \ldots + \frac{(31 - 28)^2}{28} = 1.550$$

Do not reject H_o. Levels of management and environmental concerns are not related.

30. H_o: Age and pressure are not related $\qquad$ H_1: Age and pressure are related
Reject H_o if $\chi^2 > 16.812$

$$\chi^2 = \frac{(20 - 19.44)^2}{19.44} + ... + \frac{(43 - 40.32)^2}{40.32} = 2.191$$

Do not reject H_o. Age and pressure are not related.

31. H_o: Whether a claim is filed and age is not related
H_1: Whether a claim is filed and age is related
Reject H_o if $\chi^2 > 7.815$

$$\chi^2 = \frac{(170 - 203.33)^2}{203.33} + \frac{(74 - 40.67)^2}{40.67} + ... + \frac{(24 - 35.67)^2}{35.67} = 53.639$$

Reject H_o. Age is related whether a claim is filed.

32. H_o: Pension plan preference and job class are not related
H_1: Pension plan preference and job class are related
Reject H_o if $\chi^2 > 13.277$

$$\chi^2 = \frac{(10 - 17.33)^2}{17.33} + ... + \frac{(22 - 33.94)^2}{33.94} = 84.04$$

Reject H_o. There is a relationship between pension plan preference and job class.

33. H_o: There is no relationship between finance and economic conditions
H_1: There is a relationship between financial and economic conditions
Reject H_o if $\chi^2 > 5.991$

Finance	Better	Not Better	Total
Worse	47	13	60
Same	41	21	62
Better	30	28	58
Total	118	62	180

$$\chi^2 = \frac{(47 - 39.33)^2}{39.33} + ... + \frac{(28 - 19.98)^2}{19.98} = 9.261$$

Reject H_o. There is a relationship between personal financial condition and view of the state of economic condition.

34. These answers will vary. Here is one solution.
H_o: The distribution is normal $\qquad$ H_1: The distribution is not normal
Reject H_o if $\chi^2 > 11.070$

Rental price	f_o	Area	f_e	$(f_o - f_e)^2/f_e$
2000 up to 2500	8	0.2877	17.262	4.970
2500 up to 3000	13	0.2123	12.738	0.005
3000 up to 3500	12	0.2123	12.738	0.042
3500 up to 4000	7	0.1542	9.252	0.548
4000 up to 4500	11	0.860	5.160	6.610
4500 up to 5000	9	0.475	2.850	13.271
	60			25.446

Reject H_o. Conclude this is not a normal distribution with a mean of $3000 and a standard deviation of $900.

35. a. H_o: There is no relationship between pool and township
    H_1: There is a relationship between pool and township
    Reject H_o if $\chi^2 > 9.488$

			Township			
Pool	1	2	3	4	5	Total
No	9	8	7	11	3	38
Yes	6	12	18	18	13	67
Total	15	20	25	29	16	105

$$\chi^2 = \frac{(9-5.43)^2}{5.43} + \ldots + \frac{(13-10.21)^2}{10.21} = 6.680$$

Do not reject H_o. There is no relationship between pool and township.

  b. H_o: There is no relationship between attached garage and township
    H_1: There is a relationship between attached garage and township
    Reject H_o if $\chi^2 > 9.488$

			Township			
Garage	1	2	3	4	5	Total
No	6	5	10	9	4	34
Yes	9	15	15	20	12	71
Total	15	20	25	29	16	105

$$\chi^2 = \frac{(6-4.86)^2}{4.86} + \ldots + \frac{(12-10.82)^2}{10.82} = 1.980$$

Do not reject H_o. There is no relationship between attached garage and township.

36. H_o: Salary and winning are not related H_1: Salary and winning are related
    Reject H_o if $\chi^2 > 3.84$

	Salary		
Winning	Lower half	Top half	Total
No	11	5	16
Yes	3	9	12
Total	14	14	28

$$\chi^2 = \frac{(11-8)^2}{8} + \ldots + \frac{(9-6)^2}{6} = 5.250$$

Reject H_o. Conclude that salary and winning are related.

37. a. H_o: The proportions are the same H_1: The proportions are not the same
Reject H_o if $\chi^2 > 9.488$

$$\chi^2 = \frac{(43-31.33)^2}{31.33} + \frac{(31-31.33)^2}{31.33} + \frac{(20-31.33)^2}{31.33} = 8.448$$

Reject H_o, the proportion on welfare are not the same.

b. H_o: Welfare and size are not related H_1: Welfare and size are related
Reject H_o if $\chi^2 > 5.991$

Welfare	Small	Size Medium	Large	Total
Low	22	17	4	43
Medium	8	18	5	31
High	6	7	7	20
Total	36	42	16	94

$$\chi^2 = \frac{(22-16.468)^2}{16.468} + ... + \frac{(7-3.404)^2}{3.404} = 10.716$$

Reject H_o; conclude that welfare and size are related.

1. a. If the number of pluses (successes) in the sample is 9 or more, reject H_o.
   b. Reject H_o because the cumulative probability associated with nine successes (0.073) does not exceed the significance level (0.10).

2. a. Reject H_o if number of + signs is either ≤ 1 or ≥ 8
   b. Do not reject H_o

3. a. H_o: $\pi \leq 0.50$ H_1: $\pi > 0.50$ $n = 10$
   b. H_o is rejected if there are nine or more plus sign. A "+" sign represents a loss.
   c. Reject H_o. It is an effective program, because there were nine people who lost weight.

4. a. H_o: $\pi \leq 0.50$ H_1: $\pi > 0.50$ $n = 13$
   b. Reject H_o if number of + signs ≥ 10
   c. Reject H_o. Twelve persons improved their self-confidence.

5. a. H_o: $\pi \leq 0.50$ (There is no change in weight)
      H_1: $\pi > 0.50$ (There is a loss of weight)
   b. Reject H_o if $z > 1.65$
   c. $z = \dfrac{(32 - 0.50) - (0.50)(45)}{0.50\sqrt{45}} = 2.68$
   d. Reject H_o. The weight loss program is effective.

6. a. H_o: $\pi \leq 0.50$ H_1: $\pi > 0.50$
   b. Reject H_o if $z > 1.65$
   c. $z = 2.97$, found by $(42 - 0.50 - 30)/3.87$
   d. Reject H_o. The program is effective.

7. H_o: $\pi \leq 0.50$ H_1: $\pi > 0.50$ Reject H_o if $z > 2.05$
   $z = \dfrac{42.5 - 40.5}{4.5} = 0.44$ Since $0.44 < 2.05$ do not reject H_o. No preference.

8. H_o: $\pi \leq 0.50$ H_1: $\pi > 0.50$ Reject H_o if $z > 1.65$
   $z = \dfrac{20 - 0.50 - 12.5}{2.5} = 2.80$ Reject H_o. Workers prefer to assemble entire computer.

9. a. H_o: Median $\leq \$40,000$ H_1: Median $> \$40,000$
   b. Reject H_o if $z > 1.65$
   c. $z = \dfrac{170 - 0.50 - 100}{7.07} = 9.83$
   H_o is rejected. The median income is higher than $40,000.

10. H_o: Median $\geq$ \$503 H_1: Median < \$503   Reject if $z < -1.65$

$$z = \frac{160.5 - 200}{10} = -3.95$$ Reject H_o. Median is less than \$503

11.

Couple	Difference	Rank
1	550	7
2	190	5
3	250	6
4	−120	3
5	−70	1
6	130	4
7	90	2

Sums: −4, +24. So $T = 4$ (the smaller of the two sums). From Appendix J, 0.05 level, one-tailed test, $n = 7$, the critical value is 3. Since the T of 4 > 3, do not reject H_o (one-tailed test). There is no difference in the square footage. Yuppies do not live in larger homes.

12. H_o: Mileage is the same H_1: Miles no the same
        H_o rejected if $T \leq 5$ Computed $T = 11$, do not reject H_o.

13.   a. H_o: The production is the same for the two systems
               H_1: Production using the Mump method is greater
        b. H_o is rejected if $T \leq 21$, $n = 13$
        c.   The calculations for the first three employees are:

Employee	Old	Mump	d	Rank	R^+	R^-
A	60	64	4	6	6	
B	40	52	12	12.5	12.5	
C	59	58	−1	2		2

        The sum of the negative ranks is 6.5. Since 6.5 is less than 21, H_o is rejected. Production using the Mump method is greater.

14.   a. H_o: Production has not changed
        b. H_1: Production has increased (one tail).
        c.   0.05, answers will vary
        d.   Reject H_o if $T \leq 21$
        e.   Computed $T = 34$, do not reject H_o

15. H_o: The distributions are the same. H_1: The distributions are not the same
        Reject H_o if $z < -1.96$ or $z > 1.96$

	A		B
Score	Rank	Score	Rank
38	4	26	1
45	6	31	2
56	9	35	3
57	10.5	42	5
61	12	51	7
69	14	52	8
70	15	57	10.5
79	16	62	13
	86.5		49.5

$$z = \dfrac{86.5 - \dfrac{8(8+8+1)}{2}}{\sqrt{\dfrac{(8)(8)(8+8+1)}{12}}} = 1.943 \quad H_o \text{ is not rejected. There is no difference in the two populations.}$$

16. H_o: The two populations are the same. H_1: The two populations are not the same

Reject H_o if $z < -1.96$ or $z > 1.96$

A		B	
Score	Rank	Score	Rank
12	1	13	2
14	3	16	5
15	4	19	6.5
19	6.5	21	8
23	10	22	9
29	11	33	12.5
33	12.5	35	14
40	15	43	<u>16</u>
51	<u>17</u>		73
	80		

$$z = \dfrac{80 - \dfrac{9(9+8+1)}{2}}{\sqrt{\dfrac{(9)(8)(9+8+1)}{12}}} = -0.096 \quad H_o \text{ is not rejected. There is no difference in the two populations.}$$

17. H_o: The distributions are the same. H_1: The distribution of Country is to the right.

Reject H_o if $z > 1.65$

Country		Rock	
Age	Rank	Age	Rank
26	6	28	8
42	16.5	16	1
65	22	42	16.5
38	13	29	9.5
29	9.5	31	11
32	12	22	3
59	21	50	20
42	16.5	42	16.5
27	7	23	4
41	14	25	<u>5</u>
46	19		94.5
18	<u>2</u>		
	158.5		

$$z = \dfrac{158.5 - \dfrac{12(12+10+1)}{2}}{\sqrt{\dfrac{(12)(10)(12+10+1)}{12}}} = 1.35$$

H_o is not rejected. There is no difference in the distributions.

18. H_o: The distributions are the same. $\qquad$ H_1: The experimental distribution is the to the left.
    Reject H_o if $z < -1.65$

Experimental		Current	
Time	Rank	Time	Rank
21	3.5	41	14
27	7	36	9
36	9	42	15
20	2	39	12.5
19	1	36	9
21	3.5	48	16
39	12.5	49	17
24	6	38	11
22	5		103.5
	49.5		

$$z = \frac{49.5 - \dfrac{9(9+8+1)}{2}}{\sqrt{\dfrac{(9)(8)(9+8+1)}{12}}} = -3.031$$

H_o is rejected. The distribution of experimental times is to the left. It takes less time to assemble with the experimental method.

19. ANOVA requires that we have two or more populations, the data are interval or ratio-level, the populations are normally distributed, and the population standard deviations are equal. Kruskal-Wallis requires only ordinal-level data, and no assumptions are made regarding the shape of the populations.

20. When there are more than two populations the Kruskal-Wallis test is used.

21. a. H_o: The three population distributions are equal
    b. Reject H_o if $H > 5.991$
    c.

Rank	Rank	Rank
8	5	1
11	6.5	2
14.5	6.5	3
14.5	10	4
16	12	9
64	13	19
	53	

$$H = \frac{12}{16(16+1)}\left[\frac{(64)^2}{5} + \frac{(53)^2}{6} + \frac{(19)^2}{5}\right] - 3(16+1) = 59.98 - 51 = 8.98$$

    d. Reject H_o because $8.98 > 5.991$. The three distributions are not equal.

22. a. H_o: The distributions are the same $\qquad$ H_1: The distributions are not the same
    b. Reject if $\chi^2 > 9.210$
    c. $H = 7.324$
    d. H_o is not rejected

23. H_o: The distributions of the lengths of life are the same.
        H_1: The distributions of the lengths of life are not the same
        H_o is rejected if $H > 9.210$

	Salt		Fresh		Others	
	Hours	Rank	Hours	Rank	Hours	Rank
	167.3	3	160.6	1	182.7	13
	189.6	15	177.6	11	165.4	2
	177.2	10	185.3	14	172.9	7
	169.4	6	168.6	4	169.2	5
	180.3	12	176.6	9	174.7	8
		46		39		35

$$H = \frac{12}{15(16)} \left[\frac{(46)^2}{5} + \frac{(39)^2}{5} + \frac{(35)^2}{5} \right] - 3(16) = 0.62$$

H_o is not rejected. There is no difference in the three distributions.

24. H_o: The distributions are the same H_1: They are not the same
        Reject H_o if $\chi^2 > 5.991$ Computed $H = 0.312$ Do not reject

25   a.

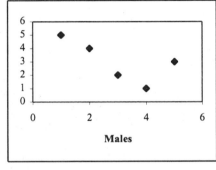

       b.

Rank males	Rank females	d	d^2
1	5	−4	16
4	1	3	9
3	2	1	1
2	4	−2	4
5	3	2	4
			34

$$r_s = \frac{6(34)}{5(5^2 - 1)} = -0.7$$

Fairly strong negative correlation among the ranks.

26.

Day Student rank	Evening Student rank	d	d^2
6	3	3	9
7	2	5	25
2	6	−4	16
5	4	1	1
1	7	−6	36
4	8	−4	16
3	5	−2	4
8	1	7	49
			156

$$r_s = 1 - \frac{6(156)}{8(8^2 - 1)} = -0.857$$

27.

Representative	Sales	Rank	Training	d	d^2
1	319	3	3	0	0
2	150	10	9	1	1
3	175	9	6	3	9
4	460	1	1	0	0
5	348	2	4	−2	4
6	300	4.5	10	−5.5	30.25
7	280	6	5	1	1
8	200	7	2	5	25
9	190	8	7	1	1
10	300	4.5	8	−3.5	12.25
					83.50

a. $r_s = 1 - \dfrac{6(83.5)}{10(10^2 - 1)} = 1 - 0.506 = 0.494$ A moderate positive correlation

b. H_o: No correlation among the ranks H_1: A positive correlation among the ranks
Reject H_o if $t > 1.860$

$$t = 0.494 \sqrt{\frac{10 - 2}{1 - (0.494)^2}} = 1.607$$

H_o is not rejected. We conclude that the correlation in population among the ranks could be 0.

28.

Player	Rank by Cann	Rank by Annelli	d	d^2
1	7	5	2	4
2	2	4	−2	4
3	10	10	0	0
4	i	3	−2	4
5	6	6	0	0
6	3	1	2	4
7	5	7	−2	4
8	4	2	2	4
9	8	9	−1	1
10	9	8	1	1
				26

a. $$r_s = 1 - \frac{6(26)}{10(10^2 - 1)} = 1 - 0.1576 = 0.8424$$

b. H_0: No correlation among the ranks $\qquad$ H_1: A positive correlation among the ranks
Reject H_0 if $t > 1.860$

$$t = 0.8424\sqrt{\frac{10-2}{1-(0.8424)^2}} = 4.422$$

H_0 is rejected. There is a positive association between the ratings of the two scouts.

29. H_0: $\pi = 0.50$ $\qquad$ H_1: $\pi \neq 0.50$ $\qquad$ $n = 19$
H_0 is rejected if there are either 5 or fewer "+" signs, or 14 or more. The total of 12 "+" signs falls in the acceptance region. H_0 is not rejected. There is no preference between the two shows.

30. a. H_0: The proportion preferring the pens is the same.
$\qquad$ H_1: More prefer Bic than Pilot $\qquad\qquad$ This is a one-tail test
b. $n = 17$ there are 3 ties
c. Reject H_0 if there are 13 or more "+" signs. A plus sign is recorded if a Bic is preferred.
d. Do not reject H_0, only 12 "+" signs

31. H_0: $\pi = 0.50$ $\qquad$ H_1: $\pi \neq 0.50$
H_0 is rejected if there are 12 or more or 3 or fewer "+" signs. Since there are only 8 plus signs, H_0 is not rejected. There is no preference with respect to the two brands of components.

32. a. H_0: Median $\leq \$1200$ $\qquad$ H_1: Median $> \$1200$
b. H_0 is rejected if $z > 1.65$
c. $z = 74.5 - 72 / 6 = 0.42$ $\qquad$ H_0 is not rejected. The median is not greater than $\$1200$

33. H_0: $\pi = 0.50$ $\qquad$ H_1: $\pi \neq 0.50$ $\qquad$ Reject if $z > 1.96$ or $z < -1.96$
$z = (159.5 - 100)/7.071 = 8.415$
Reject H_0. There is a difference in the preference for the two types of orange juice.

34. H_0: Community responsibility is the same before and after marriage
H_1: Community responsibility is not the same
H_0 is rejected if $T \leq 3$, $n = 8$
The calculations for the first four women are:

Name	Before	After	d	Rank	R^+	R^-
Beth	110	114	4	3	3	
Jean	157	159	2	2	2	
Sue	121	120	−1	1		1
Cathy	96	103	7	4.5	4.5	

The smaller sum of ranks is 13.5, which is the computed T. Do not reject H_0. There is no difference in community responsibility after marriage.

35. H_0: The rates are the same $\qquad$ H_1: The rates are not the same
H_0 is rejected if $H > 5.991$ $\qquad$ $H = 0.082$ $\qquad$ Do not reject H_0

36. H_0: Idle minutes are same H_1: Idle minutes are not the same
Reject H_0 if $z < -1.96$ or $z > 1.96$

| Day | | Night | |
Minutes	Ranks	Minutes	Rank
92	7	96	8
103	9	114	10
116	11	80	1
81	2	82	3
89	5	88	4
	34	91	6
			32

$$z = \frac{34 - \dfrac{5(5+6+1)}{2}}{\sqrt{\dfrac{5(6)(5+6+1)}{12}}} = 0.73$$

H_0 is not rejected. There is no difference in the distribution of idle minutes.

37. H_0: The populations are the same H_1: The populations are different
Reject H_0 if $H > 7.815$ $H = 14.30$ Reject H_0, accept H_1.

38. $\sum d^2 = 234$ $n = 14$

a. $r_s = 1 - \dfrac{6(234)}{14(14^2 - 1)} = -0.486$

b. H_0: The rank correlation is zero H_1: The rank correlation is greater than 0

Reject H_0 if $t > 1.782$ $t = 0.486\sqrt{\dfrac{14-2}{1-(0.486)^2}} = 1.926$

H_0 is rejected. The correlation among the ranks is greater than 0.

39. $r_s = 1 - \dfrac{6(78)}{12(12^2 - 1)} = 0.727$

H_0: There is no correlation between the rankings of the coaches and the rankings of the sports writers.
H_1: There is a positive correlation between the rankings of the coaches and the rankings of the sports writers.

Reject H_0 if $t > 1.812$ $t = 0.727\sqrt{\dfrac{12-2}{1-(0.727)^2}} = 3.348$

H_0 is rejected. There is a positive correlation between the sports writers and the coaches.

40. $r_s = 1 - \dfrac{6(60.50)}{12(12^2 - 1)} = 0.788$

H_0: There is no correlation between the order of completion and the rank of the scores
H_1: There is a positive correlation between the order of completion and the ranks of the scores.

Reject H_0 if $t > 1.812$ $t = 0.788\sqrt{\dfrac{12-2}{1-(0.788)^2}} = 4.047$

H_0 is rejected. There is a positive association between the order of finish and the rank of the scores.

41.   a.   Answers will vary. For the 1997 race, $r_s = 0.355$
      b. H_0: There is no correlation in the ranks
           H_1: There is a positive correlation in the ranks

           Reject if $t > 1.69$ $t = 0.355\sqrt{\dfrac{35-2}{1-(0.355)^2}} = 2.181$

      c.   There is a positive rank correlation between the starting position and the finishing position.

42. H_0: There is no difference in the distributions of spending in the regions.
      H_1: There is a difference in the distributions of spending in the regions.
      H_0 is rejected if χ^2 is greater than 5.991. The computed value of χ^2 is 6.29, so H_0 is rejected.
      There is a difference in the distributions of the expenditures per student.

43.   a. H_0: There is no difference in the distributions of the selling prices in the five townships.
           H_1: There is a difference in the distributions of the selling prices of the five townships.
           H_0 is rejected if H is greater than 9.448. The computed value of H is 4.70, so the null hypothesis is not rejected. The sample data does not suggest a difference in the distributions of selling prices.
      b. H_0: There is no difference in the distributions of the selling prices depending on the number of bedrooms.
           H_1: There is a difference in the distributions of the selling prices depending on the number of bedrooms.
           H_0 is rejected if H is greater than 9.448. The computed value of H is 16.34 so the null hypothesis is rejected. The sample data indicates there is a difference in the distributions of selling prices based on the number of bedrooms.
      c. H_0: There is no difference in the distributions of the distance from the center of the city depending on whether the home had a pool or not.
           H_1: There is a difference in the distributions of the distances from the center of the city depending on whether the home as a pool or not.
           H_0 is rejected if H is greater than 3.84. The computed value of H is 3.37, so the null hypothesis is not rejected. The sample data does not suggest a difference in the distributions of the distances.

44.   a.   The coefficient of rank correlation is 0.656.
           H_0: There is no correlation between the ranks of the wins and salary in the population.
           H_1: There is a positive correlation in the ranks of wins and salary.

           Reject H_0 if $t > 2.479$ $t = \dfrac{0.656\sqrt{28-2}}{\sqrt{1-(0.656)^2}} = 4.432$

           Reject H_0. There is a positive correlation between the rank of wins and the ranks of team's salary.

b. H_o: The two distributions are the same
   H_1: The two distributions are not the same   Reject H_o if $z > 1.65$
   The sum of the ranks for the National League is 217

$$z = \frac{217 - \frac{14(14+14+1)}{2}}{\sqrt{\frac{14(14)(14+14+1)}{12}}} = 0.643$$

Do not reject H_o. There is no difference in the distribution of the salaries in the two leagues.

45. a. The correlation between the ranks is 0.833
     H_o: There is no correlation between rank circulation and rank color of magazines.
     H_1: There is a correlation between rank circulation and rank color of magazines.
     Reject H_o if $t > 2.021$ or $t < -2.021$

$$t = 0.833\sqrt{\frac{48-2}{1-(0.833)^2}} = 10.211$$

Reject H_o. There is a correlation between rank circulation and rank color advertising cost.

b. H_o: The distributions are the same H_1: The distributions are not the same
    Reject H_o if $H > 3.841$ The computed value of $H = 4.09$
    Reject H_o there is a difference in magazine circulation between the two groups of male readers.

46. a. H_o: The distributions are the same H_1: The distributions are not the same
     Reject H_o if $H > 5.991$
     The computed value of H is 10.95, so H_o is rejected. We conclude that there is a different amount spent per students depending on the size of the district (number of students).

b. H_o: The distributions are the same H_1: The distributions are not the same
    Reject H_o if $H > 5.991$
    The computed value of H is 39.99, so H_o is rejected. We conclude that there is a difference in the distribution of the salaries, depending on the size of the district (number of students).

c. The coefficient of rank correlation is 0.72.
    H_o: There is no rank correlation between the number of students and teachers salary.
    H_1: There is a positive rank correlation between the number of students and teachers salary.

   Reject H_o if $t > 2.390$ $t = 0.72\sqrt{\frac{94-2}{1-(0.72)^2}} = 9.95$

Reject H_o. There is a positive correlation between students in the district and average teacher salary.

1.

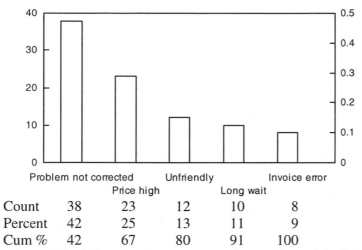

Count	38	23	12	10	8
Percent	42	25	13	11	9
Cum %	42	67	80	91	100

About 67% of the complaints concern the problem of not being corrected and the price being too high.

2.

Defect	Frequency	Percent
Oil Leak	52	47
Cracked block	30	27
Faulty cylinders	15	14
Leaky radiators	9	8
Ignition problem	4	4
	110	

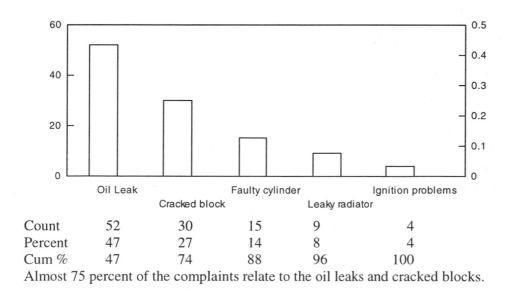

Count	52	30	15	9	4
Percent	47	27	14	8	4
Cum %	47	74	88	96	100

Almost 75 percent of the complaints relate to the oil leaks and cracked blocks.

3.   Chance variation is random in nature and because the cause is a variety of factors it cannot be entirely eliminated. Assignable variation is not random, it is usually due to a specific cause and can be eliminated.

4.   Variable control charts are concerned with actual measurements (weight, diameter, etc.). Attribute control charts are based on a classification of acceptable or not acceptable (door lock either works or it does not).

5.   a.   The A_2 factor is 0.729
      b.   The value for D_3 is 0, and for D_4 is 2.282

6.   0.215, found by $[(0.577)(0.50)(\sqrt{5})]/3$

7.   a.

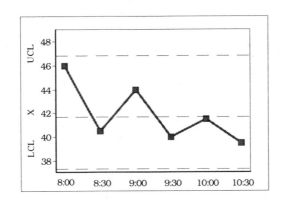

	$\overline{X}$ Arithmetic	R
Time	means	range
8:00 A.M.	46.0	16
8:30 A.M.	40.5	6
9:00 A.M.	44.0	6
9:30 A.M.	40.0	2
10:00 A.M.	41.5	9
10:30 A.M.	39.5	1
	251.5	40

$$\overline{\overline{X}} = \frac{251.5}{6} = 41.92 \qquad \overline{R} = \frac{40}{6} = 6.67$$

$$UCL = 41.92 + 0.729(6.67) = 46.78 \qquad LCL = 41.92 - 0.729(6.67) = 37.06$$

b.   Interpreting, the mean reading was 341.92 degrees Fahrenheit. If the oven continues operating as evidenced by the first six hourly readings, about 99.7 percent of the mean readings will lie between 337.06 degrees and 346.78 degrees.

8.　a.　$UCL = D_4\overline{R} = 2.282(6.67) = 15.22$　　　　　　$LCL = D_3\overline{R} = 0$

　　b.　Oven is operating within bounds except for the first range (8 A.M.) is outside the control limits.

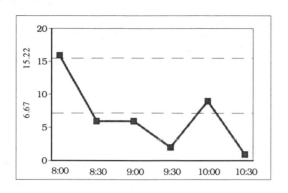

9.　$\overline{p} = \dfrac{37}{140} = 0.26$　　　　　　$0.26 \pm 3\sqrt{\dfrac{0.26(0.74)}{10}} = 0.26 \pm 0.42$

The control limits are from 0 to 0.68. The process is out of control on the seventh day.

10.　$\overline{c} = \dfrac{24}{15} = 1.6$　　　　　　$\overline{c} \pm 3\sqrt{\overline{c}} = 1.6 \pm 3\sqrt{1.6} = 1.6 \pm 3.79$

The control limits are from 0 to 5.39 tears. Each sample roll is within these limits.

11.　$\overline{c} = \dfrac{6}{11} = 0.545$　　　　　　$0.545 \pm 3\sqrt{0.545} = 0.545 \pm 2.215$

The control limits are from 0 to 2.760, so there are no receipts out of control.

12.　$\overline{c} = \dfrac{36}{10} = 3.6$　　　　　　$3.6 \pm 3\sqrt{3.6} = 3.6 \pm 5.69$

The control limits are from 0 to 9.29. There is no case where the number of voids is greater than 9, so the process is in control.

13.

Percent Defective	Probability of accepting lot
10	0.889
20	0.558
30	0.253
40	0.083

14.

Percent Defective	Probability of accepting lot
10	0.956
20	0.698
30	0.355
40	0.125

15. $P(X \le 1 \mid n = 10, \pi = 0.10) = 0.736$ $P(X \le 1 \mid n = 10, \pi = 0.20) = 0.375$
$P(X \le 1 \mid n = 10, \pi = 0.30) = 0.149$ $P(X \le 1 \mid n = 10, \pi = 0.40) = 0.046$

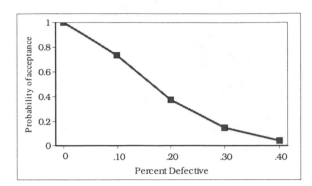

16. $P(X \le 3 \mid n = 25, \pi = 0.10) = 0.763$ $P(X \le 3 \mid n = 25, \pi = 0.20) = 0.235$
$P(X \le 3 \mid n = 25, \pi = 0.30) = 0.032$ $P(X \le 3 \mid n = 25, \pi = 0.40) = 0.002$

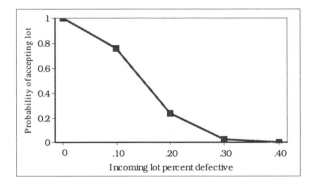

17.

Defect	Percent	Number of defects
Poor wiring	40.0	80
Short in coil	30.0	60
Defective plug	25.0	50
Other	5.0	10
	100.0	200

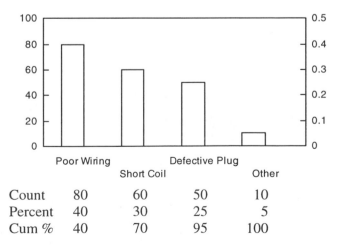

Count	80	60	50	10
Percent	40	30	25	5
Cum %	40	70	95	100

18.

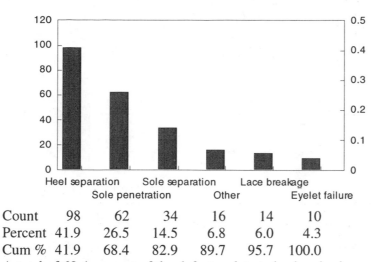

Count	98	62	34	16	14	10
Percent	41.9	26.5	14.5	6.8	6.0	4.3
Cum %	41.9	68.4	82.9	89.7	95.7	100.0

A total of 68.4 percent of the defects relate to heel and sole separation.

19.　a.　　$UCL = 10.0 + 0.577(0.25)$　　　　　　　$LCL = 10.0 - 0.577(0.25)$

　　　　　　$= 10.0 + 0.14425 = 10.14425$　　　　　$= 10.0 - 0.14425 = 9.85575$

　　　　$UCL = 2.115(0.25) = 0.52875$　　　　$LCL = 0(0.25) = 0$

　　b.　　The mean is 10.16 which is above the upper control limit and is out of control. There is too much cola in the soft drinks, an adjustment is needed. The process is in control for variation.

20.　a.　　$\overline{\overline{X}} = 87.36$　　$UCL = 88.11$　　$LCL = 86.61$

　　　　　$\overline{R} = 1.3$　　　$UCL = 2.75$　　$LCL = 0$

　　b.

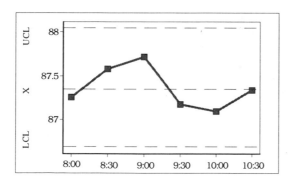

　c.

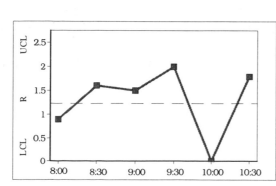

171　　　　　　　　　　　　　　　　　　　　Chapter 16

21.   a. $\bar{\bar{X}} = \dfrac{611.23}{20} = 30.5665$ $\bar{R} = \dfrac{312}{20} = 15.6$

               $UCL = 30.5665 + (1.023)(15.6) = 46.53$

               $LCL = 30.5665 - (1.023)(15.6) = 14.61$

               $UCL = 2.575(15.6) = 40.17$

  b.

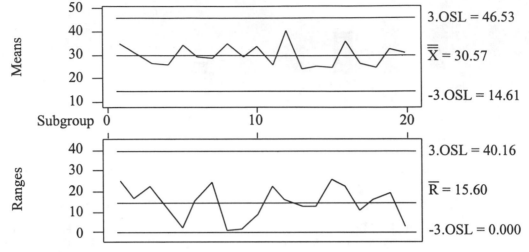

  c.   The points all seem to be within the control limits. No adjustments are necessary.

22. $\bar{\bar{X}} = \dfrac{551.4}{10} = 55.14$ $\bar{R} = \dfrac{355}{10} = 35.5$

      $UCL = 55.14 + (0.577)(35.5) = 75.62$

      $LCL = 55.14 - (0.577)(35.5) = 34.66$

      $UCL = 2.115(35.5) = 75.08$

      The last bank officer, Simonetti, is below the mean amount loaned for the group.

23. $\bar{\bar{X}} = \dfrac{4183}{10} = 418.3$ $\bar{R} = \dfrac{162}{10} = 16.2$

      $UCL = 418.3 + (0.577)(16.2) = 427.65$

      $LCL = 418.3 - (0.577)(16.2) = 408.95$

      $UCL = 2.115(16.2) = 34.26$

      All points are in control for both the mean and the range.

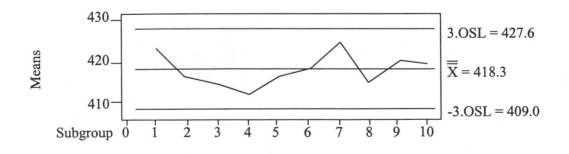

23.

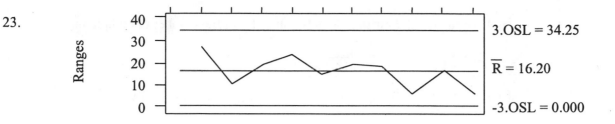

24. a. $\bar{p} = \dfrac{93}{15(200)} = 0.031$

b. $3\sqrt{\dfrac{0.031(1-0.031)}{200}} = 0.037$

$UCL = 0.031 + 0.037 = 0.068$ $LCL = 0.031 - 0.037 = 0$

c.   Ten packages mean $\bar{p} = 0.05$, which is well within the limits.

25. a. $\bar{p} = \dfrac{40}{10(50)} = 0.08$ $3\sqrt{\dfrac{0.08(1-0.08)}{50}} = 0.115$

$UCL = 0.08 + 0.115 = 0.195$ $LCL = 0.08 - 0.115 = 0$

b.

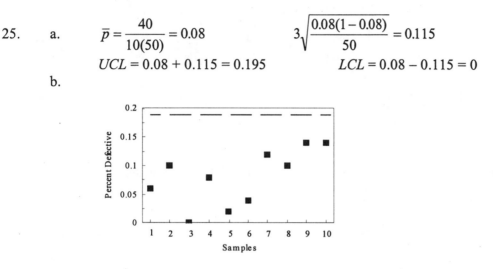

c.   There are no points that exceed the limits.

26. a. $\bar{p} = \dfrac{86}{12(50)} = 0.1433$ $3\sqrt{\dfrac{0.1433(1-0.1433)}{50}} = 0.15$

$UCL = 0.14 + 0.15 = 0.29$ $LCL = 0.14 - 0.15 = 0$

b.

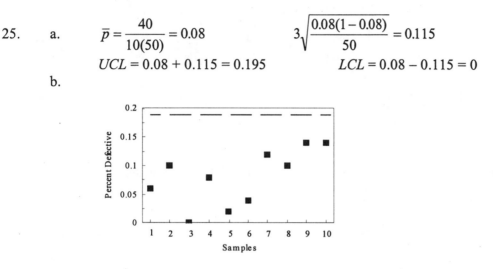

c.   None of the movies are out of control in terms of the number of complaints.

27.   a. $\bar{c} = \dfrac{213}{15} = 14.2$ $3\sqrt{14.2} = 11.30$

$UCL = 14.2 + 11.3 = 25.5$ $LCL = 14.2 - 11.3 = 2.9$

b.

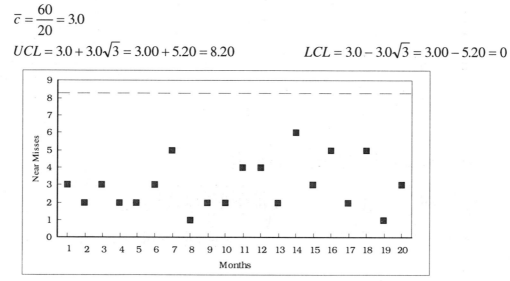

c.   All the points are in control.

28. $\bar{c} = \dfrac{60}{20} = 3.0$

$UCL = 3.0 + 3.0\sqrt{3} = 3.00 + 5.20 = 8.20$ $LCL = 3.0 - 3.0\sqrt{3} = 3.00 - 5.20 = 0$

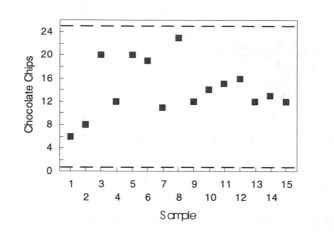

29. $\bar{c} = \dfrac{70}{10} = 7.0$

$UCL - 7.0 + 3.0\sqrt{7} = 7.00 + 7.9 = 14.9$ $\qquad LCL = 7.0 - 3.0\sqrt{7} = 3.00 - 7.9 = 0$

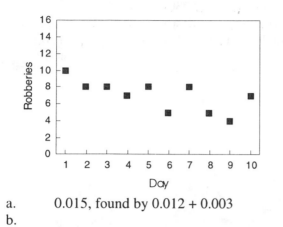

30.   a.   0.015, found by 0.012 + 0.003
      b.

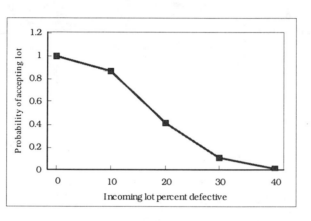

31. $P(X \le 3 \mid n = 20,\ \pi = 0.10) = 0.867$
      $P(X \le 3 \mid n = 20,\ \pi = 0.20) = 0.412$
      $P(X \le 3 \mid n = 20,\ \pi = 0.30) = 0.108$

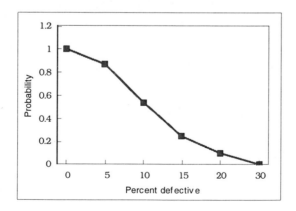

32.	a.	$P(X \le 2 | n = 25, \pi = 0.10) = 0.537$
		$P(X \le 2 | n = 25, \pi = 0.20) = 0.099$
		$P(X \le 2 | n = 25, \pi = 0.30) = 0.008$
	b.	$P(X \le 2 | n = 25, \pi = 0.15) = 0.0172 + 0.0759 + 0.1607 = 0.2538$
	c.	$P(X \le 2 | n = 25, \pi = 0.05) = 0.2774 + 0.3650 + 0.2305 = 0.8729$
		The probability (0.8729) is somewhat less than desired (0.90). (Note: A more extensive table, or some computer system such as MINITAB, is required for parts b.)

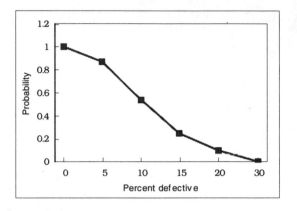

1. 164.5, found by ($2403/$1461)(100)
   197.6, found by ($2887/$1461)(100)

2. 1992: 72.4, found by ($21,885/$30,225)(100)
   1996: 104.7, found by ($31,645/$30,225)(100)
   Sales are 27.6 percent less in 1992 than in 1995. In 1996 sales were 4.7 percent more.

3. ($30,367 + $25,284)/2 = $27,825.50
   I = (($30,539)/27,825.50)100 = 109.75

4. 110.3 found by ($0.992/$0.899)(100) There was a 10.3 percent increase.

5. a. $P_t = \dfrac{2.69}{2.49}(100) = 108.3$ $\qquad$ $P_s = \dfrac{3.59}{3.29}(100) = 109.12$

   $P_c = \dfrac{1.79}{1.59}(100) = 112.58$ $\qquad$ $P_a = \dfrac{2.29}{1.79}(100) = 127.93$

   b. $P = \dfrac{10.36}{9.16}(100) = 113.1$

   c. $P = \dfrac{\$2.69(6) + 3.59(4) + 1.79(2) + 2.29(3)}{\$2.49(6) + 3.29(4) + 1.59(2) + 1.79(3)}(100) = 111.7$

   d. $P = \dfrac{\$2.69(6) + 3.59(5) + 1.79(3) + 2.29(4)}{\$2.49(6) + 3.29(5) + 1.59(3) + 1.79(4)}(100) = 112.2$

   e. $I = \sqrt{112.2(111.7)} = 111.95$

6. a. $P_B = \dfrac{0.35}{0.23}(100) = 152.17$ $\qquad$ $P_G = \dfrac{0.27}{0.29}(100) = 93.10$ $\qquad$ $P_A = \dfrac{0.35}{0.35}(100) = 100$

   $P_S = \dfrac{1.40}{1.02}(100) = 137.26$ $\qquad$ $P_O = \dfrac{0.99}{0.89}(100) = 111.24$

   b. $P = \dfrac{3.36}{2.78}(100) = 120.86$

   c. $P = \dfrac{0.35(100) + 0.27(50) + 0.35(85) + 1.40(8) + 0.99(6)}{0.23(100) + 0.29(50) + 0.35(85) + 1.02(8) + 0.89(6)}(100) = 118.1$

   d. $P = \dfrac{0.35(120) + 0.27(55) + 0.35(85) + 1.40(10) + 0.99(8)}{0.23(120) + 0.29(55) + 0.35(85) + 1.02(10) + 0.89(8)}(100) = 119.8$

   e. $P = \sqrt{119.8(118.1)} = 118.95$

7.   a. $P_W = \dfrac{0.10}{0.07}(100) = 142.9$ $P_C = \dfrac{0.03}{0.04}(100) = 75.0$

             $P_S = \dfrac{0.15}{0.15}(100) = 100$ $P_H = \dfrac{0.10}{0.08}(100) = 125.0$

     b. $P = \dfrac{0.38}{0.34}(100) = 111.8$

     c. $P = \dfrac{0.10(17{,}000) + 0.03(125{,}000) + 0.15(40{,}000) + 0.10(62{,}000)}{0.07(17{,}000) + 0.04(125{,}000) + 0.15(40{,}000) + 0.08(62{,}000)}(100) = 102.92$

     d. $P = \dfrac{0.10(20{,}000) + 0.03(130{,}000) + 0.15(42{,}000) + 0.10(65{,}000)}{0.07(20{,}000) + 0.04(130{,}000) + 0.15(42{,}000) + 0.08(65{,}000)}(100) = 103.32$

     e. $P = \sqrt{102.92(103.32)} = 103.12$

8.   a. $P_T = \dfrac{8.9}{8.1}(100) = 109.9$ $P_{Ad} = \dfrac{4.4}{4.0}(100) = 110.0$ $P_P = \dfrac{6.5}{6.0}(100) = 108.3$

             $P_{CP} = \dfrac{13}{12}(100) = 108.3$ $P_S = \dfrac{6.5}{6.1}(100) = 106.6$

     b. $P = \dfrac{39.3}{36.2}(100) = 108.6$

     c. $P = \dfrac{6.50(1500) + 8.90(10) + 4.40(250) + 6.50(1000) + 13(30)}{6.10(1500) + 8.10(10) + 4.00(250) + 6.00(1000) + 12(30)}(100) = 107.5$

     d. $P = \dfrac{6.50(2000) + 8.90(12) + 4.40(250) + 6.50(900) + 13(40)}{6.10(2000) + 8.10(12) + 4.00(250) + 6.00(900) + 12(40)}(100) = 107.3$

     e. $\sqrt{107.5(107.3)} = 107.4$

9. $V = \dfrac{1.87(214) + 2.05(489) + 1.48(203) + 3.29(106)}{1.52(200) + 2.10(565) + 1.48(291) + 3.05(87)}(100) = 93.8$

10. $V = \dfrac{28.80(4259) + 3.08(62{,}949) + 0.48(22{,}370)}{23.60(1760) + 2.96(86{,}450) + 0.40(9460)}(100) = 108.7$

11.   a. $I = \dfrac{6.8}{5.3}(0.20) + \dfrac{362.26}{265.88}(0.40) + \dfrac{125.0}{109.6}(0.25) + \dfrac{622{,}864}{529{,}917}(0.15) = 1.263$ so index is 126.3

     b.   Business activity increased 26.3 percent from 1989 to 1999.

12.   Answers will vary depending on weights selected. If the following weights were chosen:

	Chosen weight	
New businesses	0.15	16.02*
Business failures	0.10	8.29
Income tax	0.40	33.93
Enrollment	0.10	12.01
Sales tax	0.25	23.98
	100.00	94.23

                                                                    *(1162/1088)(100)(0.15) = 16.02

Economic activity has declined 5.77% between 1997 and the present year, found by 100.0 – 94.23.

13. $X = (\$32{,}000)/1.583 = \$20{,}214.78$ Salary increased $\$20{,}214.78 - \$19{,}800 = \$414.78$

14. $\text{Plumbers} = \dfrac{159.4}{133.8}(100) = 119.1$ $\text{Electrician} = \dfrac{158.7}{126.0}(100) = 126.0$

    Plumbers wages have increased 19.1 percent, where as electrician has increased 26.0 percent.

15.

Year	Tinora	Tinora	National Index
1990	$23,650	100.0	100
1995	$28,972	122.5	122.5
1999	$32,382	136.9	136.9

    The Tinora teachers received the same increase as the national average.

16.

Year	Index (Base 1990)	Index (Base 1995)	Wage	Real Increase
1995	148.3	100.0	125.0	125.0
1996	160.6	108.3	134.8	124.5
1997	173.6	117.1	145.2	124.0
1998	187.9	126.7	156.6	123.6
1999	203.3	137.1	168.8	123.1

    Sam's real wage in 1990 dollars declined from $125,000 to $123,100. A decline of $1900.

17.   The index for selected years is:

Year	1983	1988	1993	1994	1995	1996
Index	100.00	126.72	199.47	216.34	254.50	301.83

    The domestic sales increased by 201.83 percent from 1983 to 1996.

18.   The index for selected years is:

Year	1983	1988	1993	1994	1995	1996
Index	95.55	121.09	190.61	206.72	243.19	288.41

    The domestic sales increased by 188.41 percent from 1983 to 1996.

19.   The index for selected years is:

Year	1983	1988	1993	1994	1995	1996
Index	100.00	187.30	293.61	335.39	408.64	453.90

    International sales increased 353.90 percent from 1983 to 1996.

20.   The index for selected years is:

Year	1983	1988	1993	1994	1995	1996
Index	98.66	184.80	289.68	330.91	403.17	447.83

    International sales increased 347.83 percent from 1983 to 1996.

21.   The index for selected years is:

Year	1983	1988	1993	1994	1995	1996
Index	100.00	105.04	105.43	105.30	106.33	115.37

    The number of employees increased 15.37 percent during the period.

22.   The index for selected years is:

Year	1983	1988	1993	1994	1995	1996
Index	102.52	107.68	108.08	107.95	109.01	118.28

    The number of employees increased 18.28 percent during the period.

Chapter 17

23. The index for selected years is:

Year	1992	1993	1994	1995	1996
Index	100.00	231.70	227.84	105.15	255.67

Income increased 155.67 percent during the period.

24. The index for selected years is:

Year	1992	1993	1994	1995	1996
Index	60.30	139.70	137.37	63.40	154.16

Income increased 54.16 percent during the period.

25. The index for selected years is:

Year	1992	1993	1994	1995	1996
Index	100.00	108.80	121.30	129.63	131.48

The earnings per share increased 31.48 percent during the period.

26. The index for selected years is:

Year	1992	1993	1994	1995	1996
Index	95.79	104.21	116.19	124.17	125.94

The earnings per share increase 25.94 percent during the period.

27. $P_M = \dfrac{\$0.89}{\$0.81}(100) = 109.88 \qquad P_S = \dfrac{\$0.94}{\$0.84}(100) = 111.90$

$P_M = \dfrac{1.43}{1.44}(100) = 99.31 \qquad P_P = \dfrac{3.07}{2.91}(100) = 105.50$

28. $P = \dfrac{6.33}{6.00}(100) = 105.5$

29. $P = \dfrac{0.89(18) + 0.94(5) + 1.43(70) + 3.07(27)}{0.81(18) + 0.84(5) + 1.44(70) + 2.91(27)}(100) = 102.81$

30. $P = \dfrac{0.89(27) + 0.94(9) + 1.43(65) + 3.07(33)}{0.81(27) + 0.84(9) + 1.44(65) + 2.91(33)}(100) = 103.51$

31. $P = \sqrt{(102.81)(103.51)} = 103.16$

32. $V = \dfrac{0.89(27) + 0.94(9) + 1.43(65) + 3.07(33)}{0.81(18) + 0.84(5) + 1.44(70) + 2.91(27)}(100) = 114.43$

33. $P_R = \dfrac{0.60}{0.50}(100) = 120 \qquad P_S = \dfrac{0.90}{1.20}(100) = 75.0 \qquad P_W = \dfrac{1.00}{0.85}(100) = 117.65$

34. $P = \dfrac{2.50}{2.55}(100) = 98.04$

35. $P = \dfrac{0.60(320) + 0.90(110) + 1.00(230)}{0.50(320) + 1.20(110) + 0.85(230)}(100) = 106.87$

36. $$P = \frac{0.60(340) + 0.90(130) + 1.00(250)}{0.50(340) + 1.20(130) + 0.85(250)}(100) = 106.04$$

37. $$P = \sqrt{(106.87)(106.04)} = 106.45$$

38. $$V = \frac{0.60(340) + 0.90(130) + 1.00(250)}{0.50(320) + 1.20(110) + 0.85(230)}(100) = 117.13$$

39. $$P_C = \frac{0.05}{0.06}(100) = 83.33 \qquad P_C = \frac{0.12}{0.10}(100) = 120$$

    $$P_P = \frac{0.18}{0.20}(100) = 90 \qquad P_E = \frac{.015}{0.15}(100) = 100$$

40. $$P = \frac{0.50}{0.51}(100) = 98.04$$

41. $$P = \frac{0.05(2000) + 0.12(200) + 0.18(400) + 0.15(100)}{0.06(2000) + 0.10(200) + 0.20(400) + 0.15(100)}(100) = 89.79$$

42. $$P = \frac{0.05(1500) + 0.12(200) + 0.18(500) + 0.15(200)}{0.06(1500) + 0.10(200) + 0.20(500) + 0.15(200)}(100) = 91.25$$

43. $$P = \sqrt{(89.79)(91.25)} = 90.52$$

44. $$V = \frac{0.05(1500) + 0.12(200) + 0.18(500) + 0.15(200)}{0.06(2000) + 0.10(200) + 0.20(400) + 0.15(100)}(100) = 93.19$$

45. $$P_A = \frac{0.76}{0.287}(100) = 264.8 \qquad P_N = \frac{2.50}{0.17}(100) = 1470.59$$

    $$P_P = \frac{26.00}{3.18}(100) = 817.61 \qquad P_P = \frac{490}{133}(100) = 368.42$$

46. $$P = \frac{519.26}{136.637}(100) = 380.03$$

47. $$P = \frac{0.76(1000) + 2.50(5000) + 26(60,000) + 490(500)}{0.287(1000) + 0.17(5000) + 3.18(60,000) + 133(500)}(100) = 703.56$$

48. $$P = \frac{0.76(1200) + 2.50(4000) + 26(60,000) + 490(600)}{0.287(1200) + 0.17(4000) + 3.18(60,000) + 133(600)}(100) = 686.58$$

49. $$P = \sqrt{(703.56)(686.58)} = 695.02$$

Chapter 17

50. $$P = \frac{0.76(1200) + 2.50(4000) + 26(60,000) + 490(600)}{0.287(1000) + 0.17(5000) + 3.18(60,000) + 133(500)}(100) = 721.61$$

51. $$I = 100\left[\frac{1971.0}{1159.0}(0.20) + \frac{91}{87}(0.10) + \frac{114.7}{110.6}(0.40) + \frac{1501}{1214}(0.30)\right] = 123.05$$

The economy is up 23.05 percent from 1990 to 1999.

52. Using 1950 = 10; for 1980 indexes are:
   a.   Letting 1950 to 100.0 (base period)

Year	CPI	Labor Force	Productivity	GNP
1950	100.0	100.0	100.0	100.0
1967	138.7	126.6	154.1	275.9
1971	168.2	135.9	170.0	371.6
1975	223.6	148.4	177.0	529.8
1980	342.3	167.2	225.9	917.5

   b.   From 1950 to 1980 consumer prices increased 242.3 percent, the labor force 67.2 percent, productivity 125.9 percent, and the GNP 817.5 percent.

53. February: $$I = 100\left[\frac{6.8}{8.0}(0.40) + \frac{23}{20}(0.35) + \frac{303}{300}(0.25)\right] = 99.50$$

    March $$I = 100\left[\frac{6.4}{8.0}(0.40) + \frac{21}{20}(0.35) + \frac{297}{300}(0.25)\right] = 93.5$$

54. a. $$X = \frac{1}{131.8}(100) = 0.76$$
   b.   82 – 84 is $600
       1997 is $1517.45, found by $2000/1.318

55. For 1983 $2,000,000 found by $2,400,000/1.20
   For 1997   1,091,703 found by $3,500,000/3.206

56. In constant dollars sales at Master Chemical increase form 28.3 in January 1996 to 56.1542 in June 1997. The CPI for June 1997 is 160.3

1. $b = \dfrac{2469 - (721)(15)/5}{55 - (15)^2/5} = \dfrac{306}{10} = 30.6$ $\qquad a = \dfrac{721}{5} - 30.6\left(\dfrac{15}{5}\right) = 52.4$ for 2001, $t = 8$

$Y' = 52.4 + 30.6t = 52.4 + 30.6(8) = 297.2$

2. $b = \dfrac{912.6 - (252)(21)/6}{91 - (21)^2/6} = \dfrac{30.6}{17.5} = 1.7486$ $\qquad a = \dfrac{252}{6} - 1.7486\left(\dfrac{21}{6}\right) = 35.880$ for 2001, $t = 9$

$Y' = 35.880 + 1.7486t = 35.880 + 1.7486(9) = 51.6174$

3. $b = \dfrac{69 - (20)(15)/5}{55 - (15)^2/5} = \dfrac{9}{10} = 0.90$ $\qquad a = \dfrac{20}{5} - 0.90\left(\dfrac{15}{5}\right) = 1.30$

$Y' = 1.30 + 0.90t = 1.30 + 0.90(7) = 7.6 (\text{tons})$

4. $b = \dfrac{331.8 - (104.7)(15)/5}{55 - (15)^2/5} = \dfrac{17.7}{10} = 1.77$ $\qquad a = \dfrac{104.7}{5} - 1.77\left(\dfrac{15}{5}\right) = 15.63$

$Y' = 15.63 + 1.77(7) = 28.02$

5. a. $b = \dfrac{5.274318 - (1.390087)(15)/5}{55 - (15)^2/5} = \dfrac{1.104057}{10} = 0.1104057$

$a = \dfrac{1.390087}{5} - 0.1104057\left(\dfrac{15}{5}\right) = -0.0531997$ for 2001, $t = 8$

 b. 28.95%, found by $1.28945 - 1.0$

 c. $Y' = -0.0531997 + 0.1104057t =$

 $Y' = -0.0531997 + 0.1104057(8) = 0.8300459$ Antilog of $0.8300459 = 6.76$

6. a. $Y' = 1.9233 + 0.0415302t$, where 1987 is coded 1.

 b. 10.03%, found by taking the antilog of 0.0415302

 c. $Y' = 2.3801622$, the antilog is 239.97

7. Using the CBS system the final output is:

Quarter	Average SI Component	Seasonal Index
1	0.6859	0.6911
2	1.6557	1.6682
3	1.1616	1.1704
4	0.4732	0.4768

Chapter 18

8. Using the CBS system the final output is:

Quarter	Average SI Component	Seasonal Index
1	0.9122	0.9077
2	0.7647	0.7609
3	1.1318	1.1261
4	1.2159	1.2098

9.

t	estimated pairs (millions)	Seasonal index	Quarterly forecast (millions)
21	40.05	110.0	44.055
22	41.80	120.0	50.160
23	43.55	80.0	34.840
24	45.30	90.0	40.770

10. Sales for each quarter are 500, found by 2000/4. The estimated sales for the second quarter are 725, found by 500(1.45).

11. $Y' = 5.1658 + 0.37805t$. The following are the sales estimates.

Estimate	Index	Seasonally adjusted
10.080	0.6911	6.966
10.458	1.6682	17.446
10.837	1.1704	12.684
11.215	0.4768	5.343

12. $Y' = 5.48 - 0.0112t$. The following are the quarterly estimates.

Fitted	Index	Forecast
5.293	0.9077	4.8045
5.282	0.7609	4.0191
5.270	1.1261	5.9345
5.259	1.2089	6.3575

13. a. $Y' = 18,000 - 400t$, assuming the line starts at 18,000 in 1975 and goes down to 10,000 in 1995.
   b. 400
   c. 8000, found by $18,000 - 400(25)$

14. a. $Y' = 4000 + 933t$ assuming a straight line goes from 4000 to 18,000.
   b. $933

15. a.

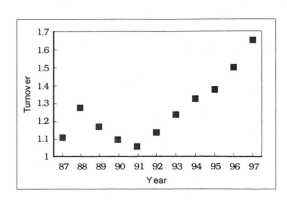

b. $Y' = 1.00455 + 0.04409t$, using $t = 1$ for 1987
c.   for 1990, $Y' = 1.18091$, and for 1995 $Y' = 1.40136$
d.   for 2002, $Y' = 1.70999$
e.   Each asset turned over 0.044 times

16.   a.

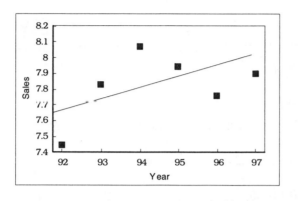

b. $Y' = 7.6340 + 0.05457t$, using $t = 1$ for 1992
c.   For 1994, $Y' = 7.79771$ and for 1996, $Y' = 7.90685$
d. $Y' = 8.12513$
e.   Sales increased 0.05457 billion dollars per year

17.   a.

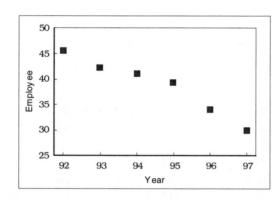

b. $Y' = 49.140 - 2.9829t$
c.   for 1994, $Y' = 40.1913$ and for 1996, $Y' = 34.2255$
d.   for 2000 $Y' = 22.2939$
e.   The number of employees decreases at a rate of 2983 per year.

18.　a.

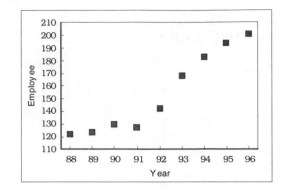

　　b.　　$Y' = 98.3083 + 11.2717t$
　　c.　　For 1990 $Y' = 132.12$, and for 1992 $Y' = 154.67$
　　d.　　$Y' = 244.84$
　　e.　　Trade increased at a rate of 11.27 billion per year.

19.　a.　　Log $Y' = 0.790231 + 0.113669t$
　　b.　　Log $Y' = 1.244907$, antilog is 17.575
　　　　　Log $Y' = 1.813252$, antilog is 65.05
　　c.　　29.92, which is the antilog of 0.113669 minus 1
　　d.　　Log $Y' = 2.154258$, antilog is 142.65

20.　a.　　Log $Y' = 1.92767 + 0.0272809t$
　　b.　　Log $Y' = 2.3096026$, antilog is 204.0
　　c.　　6.48 percent, which is the antilog of 0.0272809 minus 1

21.　a.　　Log $Y' = 0.2639 + 0.12195t$
　　b.　　Log $Y' = 2.82485$, antilog is 668.1
　　c.　　32.4 percent per year, which is the antilog of 0.12195 minus 1

22.　a.　　July 44.2, August 72.3, September 197.5
　　b.

Month	Total	Mean	Seasonal
Jan.	345.3	86.325	86.5
Feb.	424.3	106.075	106.3
March	697.8	174.450	174.8
April	483.9	120.975	121.2
May	239.2	59.800	59.9
June	190.3	47.575	47.7
July	180.6	45.150	45.2
August	295.6	73.900	74.0
Sept.	798.5	199.625	200.0
Oct.	351.9	87.975	88.1
Nov.	424.6	106.15	106.4
Dec.	358.6	<u>89.65</u>	89.8
		1197.65	

　　　　Correction = 1200/1197.65 = 1.001962
　　c.　　Sales for September and March are considerably above average and below average for May, June, and July.

23. a.   July 87.5, August 92.9, September 99.3, October 109.1

	Month	Total	Mean	Seasonal
b.	July	348.9	87.225	86.777
	Aug.	368.1	92.025	91.552
	Sept.	395.0	98.750	98.242
	Oct.	420.4	105.100	104.560
	Nov.	496.2	124.050	123.412
	Dec.	572.3	143.075	142.340
	Jan.	333.5	83.375	82.946
	Feb.	297.5	74.375	73.993
	March	347.3	86.825	86.379
	April	481.3	120.325	119.707
	May	396.2	99.050	98.541
	June	368.1	92.025	91.552
			1206.200	

Correction = 1200/1206.2 = 0.99486

c.   April, November, and December are periods of high sales, while February is low.

24. a.   *Seasonal Index by Quarter*

	Average SI	Seasonal
Quarter	Component	Index
1	0.7577	0.7558
2	0.9949	0.9924
3	1.4095	1.4060
4	0.8526	0.8505

b.   The third quarter is more than 40% above a typical quarter. The production activity is below average in the first and fourth quarters.

c. $Y' = 10.0989 + 0.14213t$

d.   The projections for 1998 are as follows:

Period	Production	Index	Forecast
21	13.084	0.7558	9.889
22	13.226	0.9924	13.125
23	13.368	1.4060	18.795
24	13.510	0.8505	11.490

25. a.   *Seasonal Index by Quarter*

	Average SI	Seasonal
Quarter	Component	Index
1	0.5014	0.5027
2	1.0909	1.0936
3	1.7709	1.7753
4	0.6354	0.6370

b.   The production is the largest in the third quarter. It is 77.5% above the average quarter. The second quarter is also above average. The first and fourth quarters are well below average, with the first quarter at about 50% of a typical quarter.

26. a. **Seasonal Index by Quarter**

Quarter	Average SI Component	Seasonal Index
1	1.1909	1.1939
2	1.1215	1.1243
3	0.4350	0.4361
4	1.2516	1.2548

b. $Y' = 163.208 + 4.1253t$

Period	Sales	Index	Forecast
29	282.8417	1.1939	337.6847
30	286.9670	1.1243	322.6370
31	291.0923	0.4361	126.9454
32	295.2176	1.2548	370.4390

27 a. **Seasonal Index by Quarter**

Quarter	Average SI Component	Seasonal Index
1	0.5549	0.5577
2	0.8254	0.8296
3	1.5102	1.5178
4	1.0973	1.1029

b. $Y' = 7.667 + 0.0023t$

c.

Period	Production	Index	Forecast
21	7.7153	0.5577	4.3028
22	7.7176	0.8296	6.4025
23	7.7199	1.5178	11.7173
24	7.7222	1.1029	8.5168

28. The linear trend equation is: $Y' = 13,616 + 367t$. The logarithmic trend equation is $\log Y = 4.14354 + 0.00863t$. In both cases the R^2 value is about 0.80. We recommend the linear because it is easier to understand. The estimated 1998 enrollment is 25,360 students, found by $13,616 + 367(32)$.

During the period there has been an increase in enrollment. In 1967 the enrollment was 12,755, and in 1997 it was 20,040. However, enrollment reached its peak in 1991 at 24,969 and has declined each year since.

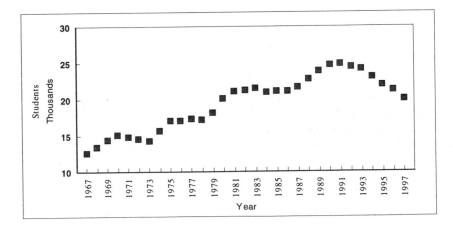

29.

Seasonal Index by Quarter

Quarter	Average SI Component	Seasonal Index
1	1.1962	1.2053
2	1.0135	1.0212
3	0.6253	0.6301
4	1.1371	1.1457

The regression equation is: $Y' = 43.611 + 7.21153t$

Period	Visitors	Index	Forecast
29	252.86	1.2053	304.77
30	260.07	1.0212	265.58
31	267.29	0.6301	168.42
32	274.50	1.1457	314.50

In 1997 there were a total of 928 visitors. A ten percent increase in 1998 means there will be 1021 visitors. The quarterly estimates are 1021/4 = 255.25 visitors per quarter.

Period	Visitors	Index	Forecast
Winter	255.25	1.2053	307.65
Spring	255.25	1.0212	260.66
Summer	255.25	0.6301	160.83
Fall	255.25	1.1457	292.44

The regression approach is probably superior because the trend is considered.

30. a.

Seasonal Index by Quarter

Quarter	Average SI Component	Seasonal Index
1	1.1900	1.1896
2	1.1044	1.1040
3	0.4449	0.4447
4	1.2621	1.2617

b. Fall quarter enrollment is the largest, about 26% above the average and the summer quarter is the lowest, about 44% of average enrollment.

c. $Y' = 1574 + 49.3t$

Period	Visitors	Index	Forecast
19	2510.7	1.1896	2987
20	2560.0	1.1040	2826
21	2609.3	0.4447	1160
22	2658.6	1.2617	3354

31. Purse: $Y' = 160 + 42.7t$ $\qquad R^2 = 0.955$
Purse: $Y' = 23.9 + 6.41t$ $\qquad R^2 = 0.955$
The total purse increased at a rate of \$42,700 per year. The regression equation is Log $Y = -50.118 + 0.0275421t$. The R-square value is 99.0, so the fit of the data is good. The forecast for the year 2000 is 92,512.4 found by $-50.118 + 0.0275421(2000) = 4.9662$, then taking the antilog of 4.9662. The winners share \$6410 per year. The winner's share is a constant 15 percent of the purse, so this ratio is not an effective estimator.

32. Develop a code for the years by subtracting 1879 from each year. This code is the dependent variable and the log of production is the dependent variable. The regression equation is $Y' = 1.63390 + 0.2754t$. The R^2 value is 0.990, so nearly all the variation is explained. The estimated production for 2000 is 92,521, found by $Y' = 1.63390 + 0.2754(121) = 4.96624$. The antilog of 4.96624 is 92521.

CHAPTER 19

1. $EMV(A_1) = 0.30(\$50) + 0.50(\$70) + 0.20(\$100) = \$70$

   $EMV(A_2) = 0.30(\$90) + 0.50(\$40) + 0.20(\$80) = \$63$

   $EMV(A_3) = 0.30(\$70) + 0.50(\$60) + 0.20(\$90) = \$69$

   Decision: Choose alternative 1

2. Choose returnables because EMV (returnables) is higher

   EMV (returnables)　　　 $= \$80(0.70) + \$40(0.30) = \$68$ thousand

   EMV (nonreturnables)　 $= \$25(0.70) + \$60(0.30) = \$35.5$ thousand

   Use returnable bottles

3.
   Opportunity loss

	S_1	S_2	S_3
A_1	$40	$ 0	$ 0
A_2	0	30	20
A_3	20	10	10

4.
   Opportunity loss ($000)

Type of bottle	Passed	Not passed
Returnable	0	$20
Nonreturnable	$55	0

5. Answers in $000

   $EOL(A_1) = 0.30(\$40) + 0.50(\$0) + 0.20(\$0) = \$12$

   $EOL(A_2) = 0.30(\$0) + 0.50(\$30) + 0.20(\$20) = \$19$

   $EOL(A_3) = 0.30(\$20) + 0.50(\$10) + 0.20(\$10) = \$13$

6. Answers in $000

   EOL (Returnables)　　　 $= \$0(0.70) + \$20(0.30) = \$6$ thousand

   EOL (Nonreturnables)　 $= \$55(0.70) + 0(0.30) = \$38.5$ thousand

7. Expected value under conditions of certainty is $82, found by $0.30(\$90) + 0.50(\$70) + 0.20(\$100)$　　 $EVPI = \$82 - \$70 = \$12$

8. Condition of Certainty　 $= \$80(0.70) + \$60(0.30) = \$74$ thousand

   Then $EVPI = \$74 - \$68 = \$6$ thousand

9. Yes, it changes the decision. Choose alternative 2 (answers in $000)

   $EMV(A_1) = 0.50(\$50) + 0.20(\$70) + 0.30(\$100) = \$69$

   $EMV(A_2) = 0.50(\$90) + 0.20(\$40) + 0.30(\$80) = \$77$

   $EMV(A_3) = 0.50(\$70) + 0.20(\$60) + 0.30(\$90) = \$74$

10. Choose returnables. Does not alter decision.

    EMV (returnables)　　　 $= \$80(0.30) + \$40(0.70) = \$52$ thousand

    EMV (nonreturnables)　 $= \$25(0.30) + \$60(0.70) = \$49.5$ thousand

11.   a.   Answers in ($000)

EMV (neither) $= 0.30(\$0) + 0.50(\$0) + 0.20(\$0) = \$0$
EMV (1) $= 0.30(\$125) + 0.50(\$65) + 0.20(\$30) = \$76$
EMV (2) $= 0.30(\$105) + 0.50(\$60) + 0.20(\$30) = \$67.50$
EMV (both) $= 0.30(\$220) + 0.50(\$110) + 0.20(\$40) = \$129$

b.   Choose both

c.

Opportunity loss

	S_1	S_2	S_3
Neither	$220	$110	$40
1	95	45	10
2	115	50	10
Both	0	0	0

d. EOL(neither) $= 0.30(\$220) + 0.50(\$110) + 0.20(\$40) - \$129.00$
EOL(1) $= 0.30(\$95) + 0.50(\$45) + 0.20(\$10) = \$53.00$
EOL(2) $= 0.30(\$115) + 0.50(\$50) + 0.20(\$10) = \$61.50$
EOL(both) $= 0.30(\$0) + 0.50(\$0) + 0.20(\$0) = \$0$

e. $EVPI = \$0$, found by $\$129 - \$129$
Certainty $= 0.30(\$220) + 0.50(\$110) + 0.20(\$40) = \$129$

12.

Weather

Transportation	Good	Bad
Plane	$115	$122.50
Train	80	110
Car	110	140

EMV(plane) $= \$115(0.40) + 122.50(0.60) = \$119.50$
EMV(train) $= \$80(0.40) + \$110(0.60) = \$98.00$
EMV(car) $= \$110(0.40) + \$140(0.60) = \$128$
Choose the train because $98 is the least cost.
Certainty $= \$80(0.40) + \$110(0.60) = \$98$ $EPVI = \$98 - \$98 = \$0$

13.   The payoff table is as follows in $000

	Recession S_1	No Recession S_2
Production	−$10.0	$15.0
Stock	−5.0	12.0
CD	6.0	6.0

a.   Purchase CD
b.   Increase production
c.   (Answers in $000)
EMV(Prod.) $= 0.20(-10) + 0.80(15.0) = 10.0$
EMV(Stock) $= 0.20(-5) + 0.80(12.0) = 8.6$
EMV(CD) $= 0.20(6) + 0.80(6) = 6.0$
Expand Production
d. $EVPI = [0.20(6) + 0.80(15)] - [10.0] = 13.2 - 10.0 = 3.2$

14. Payoff Table

   a.

	S_1	S_2	S_3
No Inspection	$7.2	$14.4	$21.60
Inspection	10.0	10.0	10.00

   b. EMV(No inspect) $= 0.70(7.2) + 0.20(14.4) + 0.1(21.60) = \$10.08$

   Inspect $= \$10.0$

   c. $EVPI = [0.70(7.2) + 0.20(10) + 0.10(10)] - 10.0 = -1.96$

15. a.

   Event

Act	10	11	12	13	14
10	$500	$500	$500	$500	$500
11	200	550	550	550	550
12	−100	250	600	600	600
13	−400	−50	300	650	650
14	−700	−350	0	350	700

   b.

Act	Expected profit
10	$500.00
11	504.50
12	421.50
13	233.50
14	−31.50

   Order 11 mobile homes because expected profit of $504.50 is the highest.

   c.

   Opportunity Loss

Supply	10	11	12	13	14
10	$0	$50	$100	$150	$200
11	300	0	50	100	150
12	600	300	0	50	100
13	900	600	300	0	50
14	1200	900	600	300	0

   d.

	Act				
	10	11	12	13	14
Expect. Opp. Loss	$95.50	$91	$174	$362	$627

   Decision: Order 11 homes because the opportunity loss of $91 is the smallest.

   e. $91, found by $595.50 − 504.50 = $91.00 value of perfect information

16. a.

   Event

Act	7	8	9	10
7	$35	$35	$35	$35
8	15	40	40	40
9	−5	20	45	45
10	−25	0	25	50

   b. Expected profits are:

Demand	Expected Payoff
7	$35.00
8	37.50
9	33.75
10	18.75

The computation for 9 snowmobiles is:

Event	Probability	Payoff	Expected Profit
X	P(X)	Y	P(X)Y
7	0.10	$-5	$-0.50
8	0.25	20	5.00
9	0.45	45	20.25
10	0.20	45	9.00
	Total		33.75

c. Lease 8 snowmobiles because the expected profit of $37.50 is the highest.

d. Opportunity loss table is:

	Act		Opportunity loss	
Number available	7	8	9	10
7	0	5	10	15
8	20	0	5	10
9	40	20	0	5
10	60	40	20	0

e. Computations for 8 snowmobiles:

Demand	Probability	Opp.Loss	Expected Loss
X	P(X)	OL	P(X)OL
7	0.10	$20	$2.00
8	0.25	0	0.00
9	0.45	5	2.25
10	0.20	10	2.00
Total			$6.25

The expected opportunity losses are:

	Number available			
	7	8	9	10
Expected Opp. Loss	$8.75	$6.25	$10.00	$25.00

f. Lease 8 snowmobiles

g. The expected value of perfect information is $6.25. Profit under certainty is $43.75, found by:

		Total		Expected
Event	Profit	Profit	Probability	Profit
7	$5	$35	0.10	$3.50
8	5	40	0.25	10.00
9	5	45	0.45	20.25
10	5	50	0.20	10.00
Total				$43.75

Then, $43.75 – $37.50 = $6.25

h. All evidence indicates that leasing 8 snowmobiles would be the most profitable.

17. a.

			Event			
Act	41	42	42	44	45	46
41	$410	$410	$410	$410	$410	$410
42	405	420	420	420	420	420
43	400	415	430	430	430	430
44	395	410	425	440	440	440
45	390	405	420	435	450	450
46	385	400	415	430	445	460

b. Expected profits are:

Act	Expected Payoff
41	$410.00
42	419.10
43	426.70
44	432.20
45	431.70
46	427.45

c. Order 44 because $432.20 is the largest expected profit.

d. Expected opportunity loss:

41	42	43	44	45	46
$28.30	$19.20	$11.60	$6.10	$6.60	$10.85

e. Order 44 because the opportunity loss of $6.10 is the smallest. Yes, it agrees.

f. $6.10, found by $438.30 − $432.20 = $6.10 value of perfect information
The maximum we should pay for perfect information is $6.10.

18. The cost per car is $4000, found by $6000 − $2000. If Kevin purchased 20 cars and he can rent 20 cars the payoff is $12,500. It is computed as follows:
(20 cars)(5 days)(50 weeks)($20 − $1.50) − (20 cars)($4000) = $92,500 − $80,000 = $12,500
The other payoffs are computed in a similar fashion.

Payoff (in$000)
States of Nature

		20	21	22	23	$EMV(A_1)$
A_1	20	12.5	12.500	12.500	12.500	12.5000
A_2	21	8.5	13.125	13.125	13.125	12.6625
A_3	22	4.5	9.125	13.750	13.750	11.9000
A_4	23	0.5	5.125	9.750	14.375	8.8250

$EMV(A_1) = 1(12.5) = 12.50$
$EMV(A_2) = 0.10(8.5) + 0.90(13.125) = 12.6625$
$EMV(A_3) = 0.10(0.45) + 0.20(9.125) + 0.70(13.75) = 11.90$
$EMV(A_4 = 0.10(0.5) + 0.20(5.125) + 0.50(9.75) + 0.20(14.375)) = 8.825$
$EVCP = 0.1(12.5) + 0.20(13.125) + 0.50(13.75) + 0.20(14.375) = 13.625$
$EVPI - 13.625 - 12.6625 = 0.9625$
$962.50

PART III

1. a. Sample
    b. Ratio
    c. $11.60, found by $58/5
    d. $11.70 Half the employees earn below $11.70 an hour and the other half earn above $11.70 per hour.

    e. $$s^2 = \frac{696.18 - \frac{(58)^2}{5}}{5-1} = 5.845$$

    f. $$sk = \frac{3(11.60 - 11.70)}{2.42} = -0.123$$
       A small amount of negative skewness

2. a. Population
    b. 5 hours, found by 30/6
    c. 4.5 Half the hours are above 4.5, half below it.
    d. No mode
    e. 2.67 hours, found by 16/6
    f. 3.56 hours, found by $\sqrt{12.6667}$
    g. 71 percent, found by (3.56/5)(100)

3 a.

Rolls	Frequency
3 up to 6	2
6 up to 9	6
9 up to 12	8
12 up to 15	3
15 up to 18	1

    b.

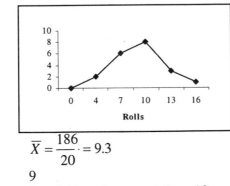

    c. $$\overline{X} = \frac{186}{20} = 9.3$$

    d. 9
    e. 9 and 10 each occur 4 times10

f.   14 using the frequency distribution, 13 using the actual data

g. $s^2 = \dfrac{1906 - \dfrac{(186)^2}{20}}{20-1} = 9.2736$

h. $s = \sqrt{9.2736} = 3.045$

i. $9.30 \pm 2(3.045)$ The limits are 3.21 up to 15.39

4.   a.   Ratio

   b.
Amount Spent	Frequency	CF	X	fX
5 up to 10	2	2	7.5	15.0
10 up to 15	4	6	12.5	50.0
15 up to 20	7	13	17.5	122.5
20 up to 25	10	23	22.5	225.0
25 up to 30	5	28	27.5	137.5
30 up to 35	2	30	32.5	65.0
Total	30			615.0

   c.

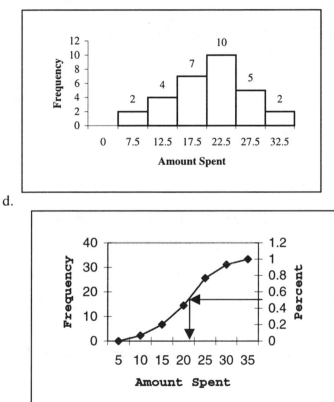

   d.

about 21 million

f. $\overline{X} = 615/30 = 205.0$ million

g.   24 – 18 = 8 (Answers will vary)
       QD = (24 – 18)/2 = 4.0

5.   a.   8.82%, found by 44.1/5

   b.   7.479%

   d.   Geometric mean since it is not highly influenced by the 19.5%

6.　　0.097 or 9.7% found by $\sqrt[10]{\dfrac{284}{113}} - 1$

7.

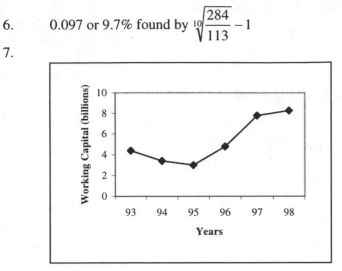

8.　　a.　　Box plot
　　　b.　　Median $= 48$　　$Q_1 = 24$　　　$Q_3 = 84$
　　　c.　　Positive, because the distance from the median to the third quartile is greater than the distance from the median to the first quartile.
　　　d.　　Yes, 168,204
　　　e.　　No

9.　　Ordinal

10.　　Statistic

11.　　Less-than-cumulative frequency polygon. About 45; about 35; 10, 35, found by $55 - 20$.

12.　　Frequency polygon. Positive skewness, mean would be larger than the median.

13.　　9.375%

14.　　1.5

15.　　Coefficient of variation

16.　　24. To explain, the range is about 6 times the standard deviation for a symmetrical distribution.

17.　　92 and 108, found by $100 \pm 2(4)$

18.　　Geometric mean

19 & 20
    a.   The following histogram is from MINITAB   Histogram of C1   N = 50

Midpoint	Count	
0	1	*
40	7	*******
80	3	***
120	8	********
160	15	***************
200	10	**********
240	3	***
280	3	***

20.   b & c

N	MEAN	MEDIAN	TRMEAN	STDEV	SEMEAN
50	147.90	148.50	146.11	69.24	9.79

MIN	MAX	Q1	Q3
14.00	299.00	106.00	186.25

The distribution is fairly symmetrical because the mean (147.90) and the median (148.50) are quite close. The mean is ±2s indicates that the middle 95% of the deposits are between $147.90 \pm 2(69.24) = 9.42$ and 286.38 Range = 299.00 – 14 = 285.00. There is a very slight negative skewness (because the mean is less than the median).

21.   a.   From MINITAB

	N	MEAN	MEDIAN	TRMEAN	STDEV	SEMEAN
C1	85	15.06	15.00	14.79	9.63	1.04

	MIN	MAX	Q1	Q3
C1	0.00	36.00	6.00	22.50

Typical length of service is about 15 years (mean or median)

    b.   Range is 36 years, found by 36 (max) – 0 (min)

    c.   Only slight positive skewness because the mean of 15.06 is slightly larger than the median (15.00)

    d.   Stem and Leaf of C1   N = 85

Leaf Unit = 1.0

12	0	011222333444
30	0	555555566677788999
42	1	000133334444
(16)	1	5555566666788899
27	2	00001233333
16	2	6667889
9	3	00123344
1	3	6

22.   a.

Per Capita Income	Number of States
$8.0 up to 10.0	1
10.0 up to 12.0	12
12.0 up to 14.0	17
14.0 up to 16.0	13
16.0 up to 18.0	5
18.0 up to 20.0	3
Total	51

b.   From MINITAB, either $13,767 (mean) or $13,600 (median)

	N	MEAN	MEDIAN	TRMEAN	STDEV	SEMEAN
C10	51	13.767	13.600	13.667	2.305	0.323

	MIN	MAX	Q1	Q3
C10	9.500	19.200	11.900	15.100

c.   Range = $9700, found by $19,200 - $9500

CV = 16.7%, found by $2.305/$13.767   AD = $1.827

d.   Positively skewed, $Sk = 0.243$, found by 3($13.787 - $13.600)/2.305

e.   State per capita incomes range from $9500 to $19,200. The mean income is $13,767 and half the states have per capital incomes above $13,600 and half below it. The distribution is somewhat symmetrical with the mean ($13,767) and median ($13,600) quite close. A stem and leaf chart verifies the approximate symmetrical shape.

Stem and Leaf of Years   N = 51   Leaf Unit = 0.10

```
   1     9    5
   4    10    566
  13    11    111113888
  20    12    1133688
 (10)   13    1111566888
  21    14    1335666
  14    15    11338
   8    16    67
   6    17    157
   3    18    28
   1    19    2
```

23.   The typical age is 55 years. The range is 27 years

	N	MEAN	MEDIAN	TRMEAN	STDEV	SEMEAN
Years	43	54.674	55.000	54.590	6.383	0.973

	MIN	MAX	Q1	Q3
Years	42.000	69.000	50.000	58.000

Stem and Leaf of years   N = 43   Leaf Unit = 1.0

```
   2     4    23
   2     4
   6     4    6677
   9     4    899
  15     5    001111
  17     5    22
  (8)    5    44445555
  18     5    6667777
  11     5    8
  10     6    0111
   6     6    2
   5     6    455
   2     6
   2     6    89
```

1. The following frequency distribution was developed.

Balance	f
0 up to 500	4
500 up to 1000	7
1000 up to 1500	15
1500 up to 2000	22
2000 up to 2500	11
2500 up to 3000	1
Total	60

A typical customer maintains a balance of about $1500. About twenty percent of the customers keep a balance of $2000 or more. The range of the balances is larger in cities 3 and 4, than 1 and 2.

The following MINITAB output is used to answer the remaining questions.

CITY	N	MEAN	MEDIAN	TRMEAN	STDEV	SEMEAN
1	16	1281	1397	1303	474	119
2	17	1879.6	1958.0	1894.7	350.9	85.1
3	14	1359	1505	1394	683	183
4	13	1423	1487	1435	709	197

CITY	MIN	MAX	Q1	Q3
1	343	1913	919	1679
2	1125.0	2409.0	1645.5	2140.5
3	32	2276	975	1833
4	167	2557	777	2094

2. The mean balance is $1499.90 and the median balance is $1604.50. Half the balances are larger than $1604.50 and half are less than $1604.50. The mean is smaller than the median, so the distribution is somewhat negatively skewed. The coefficient of skewness is –0.527, a small amount of negative skewness. The mean and median are much larger for city number 2. The mean balance in City 2 is $456.60 more than that of the next closest city. For reference, Cincinnati is City 1, Atlanta is City 2, Louisville is City 3, and Erie, Pennsylvania is City 4.

3. The data range from the smallest balance of $32 up to the largest, which is $2557. Fifty percent of the accounts balance range from $1121 up to $1947. The standard deviation is $596.90. There is more variation in the balance for cities 3 and 4, than for 1 and 2.

Review One

To begin, determine the cumulative and relative frequency distribution for the two distributions.

Salary ($000)	Women			Men		
	f	CF	Relative	f	CF	Relative
less than $30	2	2	0.04	0	0	0
30 up to 40	3	5	0.06	1	1	0.02
40 up to 50	17	22	0.34	4	5	0.07
50 up to 60	17	39	0.34	24	29	0.40
60 up to 70	8	47	0.16	21	50	0.35
70 up to 80	3	50	0.06	7	57	0.12
80 or more	0	50	0.00	3	60	0.05
Total	50		1.00	60		1.00

Summary of descriptive statistics

	Median	Q_1	Q_3
Women	51.76	44.41	59.12
Men	60.48	54.17	67.62

The salaries for the men are larger than for the women. The median salary for the men is $60.48(000) where as it is $51.76(000) for the women. The difference is $8.72. There are similar differences for the first and third quartile.

Comparing the relative frequency distributions, forty percent of the women earn less than $50.0(000), where as only nine percent of the men earn less than $50.00(000). It is reasonable to conclude that the men earn more than the women.

Listed below is a summary of the descriptive statistics from the MINITAB system.

Variable	N	Mean	Median	TrMean	StDev	SEMean
Athletic	40	822	527	737	830	131
Retail	30	1059.2	1074.5	1064.2	339.0	61.9

Variable	Min	Max	Q1	Q3
Athletic	4	3202	250	1182
Retail	12.0	1858.0	865.0	1291.8

The mean amount of commission earned by those selling to athletic departments is $822. The mean commission to retailers is $1059.20. The median commission is also larger for those selling to retailers. Note that for the retail commissions the mean and median are about $15 apart, whereas for the athletic commissions the difference is about $300. There is more variation in the sales to athletic departments. The standard deviation to athletic departments is $830 and to retailers it is $339. The quartile deviation for the athletic commissions is $932, found by $1182 – $250. The quartile deviation for the retail commissions is $426.80.

Below is the box plot of the athletic commissions. Note that there are two outliers, which have the effect of increasing both the mean and standard deviation. The distribution is positively skewed.

```
        ------------
      --|    +        |------------         **
        ------------

  +------+------+------+------+------+------
  0      600    1200   1800   2400   3000
```

Below is a box plot for the retail commissions. There is an outlier near $0, but this distribution seems more symmetrical and exhibits less variation.

```
                     --------
  *           ------|    +    |----------
                     --------

  +------+------+------+------+------+------
  0      350    700    1050   1400   1750
```

It is reasonable to conclude that those selling to retail customers earn larger commissions and there is less variability in the commissions earned.

1.   Subjective

2.   An experiment

3.   An outcome

4.   Mutually exclusive

5.   Complement rule: $1 - P(X) = 0.999$

6.   1.00

7.   Discrete

8.   1.   An outcome of an experiment is classified into mutually exclusive categories of a "success" or a "failure".
      2.   The resulting data result from counts.
      3.   The probability of a success and the probability of a failure stay the same from trial to trial.
      4.   The trials are independent.

9.   Discrete

10.   Only μ

11.   Bell-shaped, symmetrical, asymptotic

12.   Standard normal distribution

13.   a.   0.10, found by 20/200
      b.   0.725, found by 145/200
      c.   0.925, found by $1 - 15/200$

14.   a.   0.035 from Appendix A where $\pi = 0.8$ and $n = 15$
      b.   0.018, found by $0.001 + 0.003 + 0.014$
      c.   0.648, found by $0.250 + 0.231 + 0.132 + 0.035$

15.   a.   0.1353, found from Appendix C, where $\mu = 2.0$
      b.   398, found by $400 - 2$
      c.   0.3233, found by $1 - (0.1353 + 0.2707 + 0.2707)$

16. a. 0.0401, found by (13,500 – 10,000)/2000 = 1.75. The area is 0.4599. Then 0.5000 – 0.4599 = 0.0401
    b. 0.6147, found by (8000 – 10,000)/2000 = – 1.00. Area is 0.3413. (11,500 – 10,000)/2000 = 0.75. Area is 0.2734. Then 0.3413 + 0.2734 = 0.6147
    c. 7440, found by – 1.28 = (X – 10,000)/2000

17. a. 0.417, found by 223/535
    b. 0.407, found by 177/435
    c. 0.914, found by 489/535

18. 0.345 for a π of 20,   0.579 for a π of 0.30
    Use the binomial as an approximation. Let $n = 6$, $\pi = 0.20$, $P(X \geq 2) = 1 – P(X \leq 1) = 1 – (0.262 + 0.393) = 0.345$. If $\pi = 0.30$, then $P(X \geq 2) = 1 – P(X \leq 1) = 1 – (0.118 + 0.303) = 0.579$

19. a. $1.84 million found by 0 + 0.64 + 1.2
    b. 0.98
    c. 0.20
    d. Yes. The $2 million premium is greater than the expected loss of $1.84 million. Thus the expected profit is $0.16 million.

20. a. The mean number of children is 1.10 and the standard deviation is 1.18 children, found by:

Children	P(X)	XP(X)	$(X – \mu)^2 P(X)$
0	0.40	0.00	0.4840
1	0.30	0.30	0.0030
2	0.15	0.30	0.1215
3	0.10	0.30	0.3610
4	0.05	0.20	0.4205
	1.00	1.10	1.3900

    $\sigma = \sqrt{1.39} = 1.18$
    b. 550, found by 500(1.1) rounded up
    c. The probability distribution for those families with children is computed below:

Number of Children	Probability	Probability given children	
X		P(X)	XP(X)
1	0.30	0.500	0.500
2	0.15	0.250	0.500
3	0.10	0.167	0.501
4	0.05	0.083	0.332
	0.60	1.000	1.833

    Among those families with children, the mean number of children is 1.833.

The mean account balance is $1499.90 and the standard deviation is $596.90. There are actually 4 customers with a balance of less than $500. Using the normal distribution to approximate the numbers:

$$z = \frac{500 - 1499.90}{596.90} = -1.68$$

From the z table, the likelihood of a value less than -1.68 is $0.5000 - 0.4535 - 0.0465$. Multiplying the value by 60, the expected number is 2.79, or rounding we would report 3.

There are 12 customers with balances of more than $2000. The expected number is 12.03, found by

$$z = \frac{2000 - 1499.90}{596.90} = -0.84$$

Then $0.5000 - 0.2995 = 0.2005$ and $60(0.2005) = 12.03$.

The balance seems to follow the normal distribution. The following table was developed from the MINITAB system.

	City				
	1	2	3	4	Total
$0 up to $1200	6	1	5	5	17
1200 up to 1800	8	6	5	4	23
1800 or more	2	10	4	4	20
	16	17	14	13	60

It appears that city 2 is different from the others. One out of 17, or about 6 percent of the accounts are for less than $1200, and 59 percent are for $1800 or more. In city 1, only 12 percent of the accounts have a balance of $1800 or more. In the other 2 cities about one third of the frequencies fall in each cell.

The table below shows the fraction of invalid signatures, by district.

	Avondale	Midway	Kingston
Total defects	142	170	276
Total names validated	2800	1800	1400
Fraction invalid	0.05	0.094	0.197

Notice the number of invalid signatures is quite different in the three districts, that is about five percent of the signatures are invalid in Avondale, 9.4 percent in Midway, and 19.7 percent in Kingston.

Rounding these values to 0.05, 0.10, and 0.20 respectively, so we can use the binomial table, the probability of rejecting a page in each district for each district.

	Avondale	Midway	Kingston
Value of π	0.05	0.10	0.20
Sample of 5 ($X \geq 2$)	0.022	0.081	0.262
Sample of 10 ($X \geq 3$)	0.011	0.069	0.322

The results of the two plans are quite similar. For example, with either plan about two percent of the pages will be rejected in Avondale, about 7 percent in Midway and 28 to 30 percent in Kingston. Using a larger sample is not realistic, because there are only 20 names on a page. You would be sampling more than half the names on the page. Suggest using the same of $n = 5$.

Review Two

The number of successful sales calls per hour was organized into the following frequency distribution.

Successful Calls	Actual Frequency	Expected $\mu = 3.2$	Expected frequency
0	1	0.0408	1.4
1	4	0.1304	4.6
2	9	0.2087	7.3
3	5	0.2226	7.8
4	7	0.1781	6.2
5	8	0.1140	4.0
6 or more	1	0.1054	3.7
	35	1.0000	35.0

Assume a Poisson distribution with $\mu = 3.2$. The expected probability for two successful sales calls is 0.2087 found by: $P(2) = \dfrac{3.2^2 e^{-3.2}}{2!} = 0.2087$

The probability for 0 and 1 success is:

$P(0) = \dfrac{3.2^0 e^{-3.2}}{0!} = 0.0408$ $\qquad\qquad$ $P(1) = \dfrac{3.2^1 e^{-3.2}}{1!} = 0.1304$

The other probabilities shown in the above chart are computed similarly.

Because the actual and the theoretical distribution are similar, it is reasonable to use a Poisson distribution with a success rate of 3.2 per hour.

	Born	Points Earned Brendan	McLaughlin
Age	18	12	0
Time at address	20	0	20
Auto age	13	13	3
Monthly car payment	4	6	4
Housing cost	10	10	12
Checking/savings	<u>15</u>	<u>3</u>	<u>0</u>
Total	80	44	39
Profit probability	0.95	0.81	0.77

The probability that all three earn a profit for the bank is:
$$P(3) = P(A)P(B)P(C) = (0.95)(0.81)(0.77) = 0.5925$$

The probability of none earning a profit is:
$$P(0) = (1 - P(A))(1 - P(B))(1 - P(C)) = (0.05)(0.19)(0.23) = 0.0022$$

The probability of one earning a profit is:
$$P(1) = (0.95)(0.19)(0.23) + (0.05)(0.81)(0.23) + (0.05)(0.19)(0.77) = 0.0581$$

The probability of two earning a profit is:
$$P(2) = (0.95)(0.81)(0.23) + (0.95)(0.19)(0.77) + (0.05)(0.81)(0.77) = 0.3472$$

Summarizing, the probability distribution is as follows:

Number earning profit	P(X)
0	0.022
1	0.0581
2	0.3472
3	<u>0.5925</u>
	1.0000

1.	B	6.	E
2.	D	7.	E
3.	C	8.	B
4.	A	9.	A
5.	D	10.	B

11. H_o: $\mu \geq 36$ $\qquad$ H_1: $\mu < 36$ $\qquad$ Reject H_o if $z < -1.65$

$z = \dfrac{35.5 - 36.0}{0.9 / \sqrt{42}} = -3.60$ Reject H_o. The mean height is less than 36 inches.

12.   a. H_o: $\pi \leq 0.08$ H_1: $\pi > 0.08$

     b.   Alpha = 0.01

     c. $z = \dfrac{p - \pi}{\sqrt{\dfrac{\pi(1 - \pi)}{n}}}$

     d.   Reject H_o if $z > 2.33$

     e.   Computed $z = 0.737$, found by $z = \dfrac{0.10 - 0.08}{\sqrt{\dfrac{0.08(0.92)}{100}}} = 0.737$

     f.   Do not reject H_o. The difference can be attributed to sampling error.

13.   a.   457, found by $n = 0.05(1 - 0.05)\left(\dfrac{1.96}{0.02}\right)^2$

     b.   Change the level of confidence to 90 percent, or raise the allowable error.

14.   42, found by $n = \left(\dfrac{(2.58)(0.50)}{0.20}\right)^2$

15.   a. H_o: $\mu_b = \mu_v$ H_1: $\mu_b \neq \mu_v$

     b.   Two-tailed, no direction given

     c. $z = \dfrac{\overline{X}_b - \overline{X}_y}{\sqrt{\dfrac{s_b^2}{n_b} + \dfrac{s_v^2}{n_v}}}$

     d. -1.96 and 1.96

     e. $z = \dfrac{10.92 - 11.05}{\sqrt{\dfrac{(0.78)^2}{180} + \dfrac{(0.39)^2}{200}}} = -2.02$

       Reject H_o and accept H_1. The mean wages are not equal.

16. a. $H_0: \pi_1 = \pi_2$ $H_1: \pi_1 \neq \pi_2$ where π_1 is Chicago and π_2 is Dallas
     b. Two tailed, no direction given

     c. $$z = \frac{p_1 - p_2}{\sqrt{\dfrac{p_c(1 - p_c)}{n_1} + \dfrac{p_c(1 - p_c)}{n_2}}}$$

     d. Reject H_0 if computed z is > 1.96 or < -1.96

     e. $p_1 = 180/200 = 0.90$ $p_2 = 87/100 = 0.87$ $p_c = \dfrac{180 + 87}{300} = 0.89$

     $$z = \frac{0.90 - 0.87}{\sqrt{\dfrac{(0.89)(0.11)}{200} + \dfrac{(0.89)(0.11)}{100}}} = 0.783$$

     H_0 is not rejected. There is no difference in the proportion of records in Dallas and Chicago that have a discrepancy.

Twenty-six of the 60, or 0.4333 of the customers use a debit card. A 95 percent confidence interval is computed as follows:

$$0.4333 \pm 1.96 \sqrt{\frac{0.4333(1-0.4333)}{60}} = 0.4333 \pm 0.1254$$

The confidence limits are from 0.3079 up to 0.5587. The value of 0.50 is in the interval. Hence we cannot conclude that more than 0.50 of the customers use the card.

To find out if the mean account balance is now less than $1600, we conduct the following test of hypothesis:

H_o: $\mu \geq 1600$ H_1: $\mu < 1600$ H_o is rejected if $z < -1.65$

$$z = \frac{1499.90 - 1600}{596.7 / \sqrt{60}} = -1.299$$ H_o is not rejected. We cannot conclude that the mean is less than $1600.

To look at the mean number of ATM transactions, we conduct the following tests:

H_o: $\mu \leq 10$ H_1: $\mu > 10$ Using the 0.05 significance level, H_o is rejected if $z > 1.65$

$$z = \frac{10.30 - 10}{4.295 / \sqrt{60}} = 0.54$$ H_o is not rejected. We cannot conclude that the mean number of transactions is more than 10. The p-value is 0.2946

Can we conclude that it is more than 9?

H_o: $\mu \leq 9$ H_1: $\mu > 9$ Reject H_o if $z > 1.65$

$$z = \frac{10.30 - 9}{4.295 / \sqrt{60}} = 2.345$$ H_o is rejected. We can conclude that the mean number of ATM transactions is more than nine per month.

The mean cost for the 35 observations at the Marsh Store is $131.17 with a standard deviation of $4.89. The mean cost at Kazmaier's is $132.69, with a standard deviation of $4.99, for a sample of 38 observations. We conduct the following test of hypothesis:

H_o: $\mu_m = \mu_k$ H_1: $\mu_m \neq \mu_k$

$$z = \frac{131.17 - 132.69}{\sqrt{\frac{(4.89)^2}{35} + \frac{(4.99)^2}{38}}} = -1.31$$

For a two-tailed test the p-value is 0.1902, found by $2(0.5000 - 0.4049)$. We conclude that there is not a difference in the prices.

First conduct a test of hypothesis regarding the mean unpaid balance. The mean for the 50 customers is $1074 with a standard deviation of $968.

H_o: $\mu \geq 3900$ $\qquad$ H_1: $\mu < 3900$ $\qquad$ Reject H_o if $z < -1.65$, using $\alpha = 0.05$

$z = \dfrac{1074 - 3900}{968 / \sqrt{50}} = -20.6$ The mean balance for the Levenson customer is less than $3900.

Regarding the fraction who pay their balance at the end of the month.

H_o: $\pi \leq 0.33$ $\qquad$ H_1: $\pi > 0.33$ $\qquad$ Reject H_o if $z > 1.65$, using $\alpha = 0.05$

$z = \dfrac{0.36 - 0.33}{\sqrt{\dfrac{0.33(1 - 0.33)}{50}}} = 0.45$

Cannot reject H_o. Cannot conclude that the proportion who pays their balance is different from 0.33.

1.	B	7.	D	
2.	B	8.	D	
3.	A	9.	B	
4.	B	10.	D	
5.	D	11.	E	
6.	C	12.	A	

13. H_o: $\mu \le 20$ H_1: $\mu > 20$ Reject H_o if $t > 1.860$

$\bar{X} = 21$ $s = 6.185$ $t = \dfrac{21 - 20}{6.185/\sqrt{9}} = 0.485$

H_o is not rejected. The mean amount of break time is not more than 20 minutes.

14. H_o: $\mu_1 = \mu_2$ H_1: $\mu_1 \ne \mu_2$ Reject H_o if $t < -2.845$ or $t > 2.845$

$s_p^2 = \dfrac{(12-1)(5)^2 + (10-1)(8)^2}{12+10-2} = 42.55$ $t = \dfrac{250 - 252}{\sqrt{42.55\left(\dfrac{1}{12} + \dfrac{1}{10}\right)}} = -0.716$

H_o is not rejected. There is no difference in the mean strength of the two glues.

15. H_o: $\mu_d \le 0$ H_1: $\mu_d > 0$ Reject H_o if $t > 1.833$

$\bar{d} = 0.4$ $s_d = 6.11$ $t = \dfrac{0.4}{6.11/\sqrt{10}} = 0.21$

H_o is not rejected. There is no difference in the life of the paints.

16. H_o: $\mu_1 = \mu_2 = \mu_3 = \mu_4$ H_1: The means are not all the same H_o rejected if $F > 3.29$

Source	SS	df	MS	F
Treatments	20.736	3	6.91	1.04
Error	100.00	15	6.67	
Total	120.736	18		

H_o is not rejected. There is no difference in the mean sales.

17. H_o: $\mu_1 = \mu_2 = \mu_3 = \mu_4 = \mu_5$ H_1: Means not all equal   Reject if $F > 3.84$

H_o: $\mu_1 = \mu_2 = \mu_3$ H_1: Means not all equal   Reject if $F > 4.46$

Source	SS	df	MS	F
Treatments	165.73	4	41.43	11.098
Blocks	22.8	2	11.40	3.054
Error	29.87	8	3.73	
Total	218.40	14		

There is a difference in fertilizer types, but not soil conditions.

18. H_o: $\sigma_N^2 \le \sigma_E^2$ H_1: $\sigma_N^2 > \sigma_E^2$ H_o is rejected if $F > 1.95$(estimated)

$F = \dfrac{(3.9)^2}{(2.85)^2} = 1.87$

H_o is not rejected. There is no difference in the variation of the two groups.

ANOVA is used to compare the mean checking account balances in the four cities.

H_o: H_o: $\mu_c = \mu_a = \mu_l = \mu_e$, $\qquad$ H_1: The means are not all the same $\qquad$ Reject H_o if the computed value of $F > 2.76$

Source	DF	SS	MS	F
City	3	3568073	1189358	3.82
Error	56	17453360	311667	
Total	59	21021432		

Level	N	Mean	StDev
1	16	1281.4	474.3
2	17	1879.6	350.9
3	14	1359.4	683.5
4	13	1423.5	709.2

H_o is rejected. The mean account balances in the four cities are not the same.

A 95 percent confidence interval for the difference in mean account balance in Cincinnati and Atlanta is:

$$(1281.4 - 1879.6) \pm 1.96 \sqrt{311{,}667\left(\frac{1}{16} + \frac{1}{17}\right)} = (-598.2) \pm 381$$

So the interval ranges from –$979.20 up to –$217.2, and the pair of means differs. Comparing the next largest difference, Atlanta and Louisville we find:

$$(1876.6 - 1359.4) \pm 1.96 \sqrt{311{,}667\left(\frac{1}{17} + \frac{1}{14}\right)} = 520.20 \pm 395$$

So this interval ranges from $125.20 up to $915.20, and the pair of means differ.
Comparing Atlanta to Erie:

$$(1879.6 - 1423.5) \pm 1.96 \sqrt{311{,}667\left(\frac{1}{17} + \frac{1}{13}\right)} = 456.1 \pm 403$$

The interval ranges from $53.1 up to $859.1, so this pair of means differ.

The ANOVA output for comparing ATM use is as follows:

Source	DF	SS	MS	F
City	3	32.1	10.7	0.57
Error	56	1056.5	18.9	
Total	59	1088.6		

H_o is not rejected. There is no difference in ATM use among the four branches.

To answer the question regarding debit cards and the mean number of times the ATM was used. The hypotheses are: H_o: $\mu_{ND} = \mu_D$ $\qquad$ H_1: $\mu_{ND} \neq \mu_D$

Debit Card	n	$\overline{X}$	s
Yes	34	10.35	4.32
No	26	10.23	4.35

$$s_p^2 = \frac{(34-1)(4.32)^2 + (26-1)(4.35)^2}{34+26-2} = 18.77 \qquad t = \frac{10.35 - 10.23}{\sqrt{18.77\left(\dfrac{1}{34} + \dfrac{1}{20}\right)}} = 0.098$$

Do not reject H_o. There is no difference in the mean ATM use for those using the debit card and not using the debit card.

Comparing accounts that do not pay interest with those that pay interest.

Interest	n	$\overline{X}$	s
Yes	16	10.94	3.40
No	44	10.07	4.59

$$s_p^2 = \frac{(16-1)(3.40)^2 + (44-1)(4.59)^2}{16+44-2} = 18.6091 \qquad t = \frac{10.94 - 10.07}{\sqrt{18.6091\left(\dfrac{1}{16} + \dfrac{1}{44}\right)}} = 0.691$$

Do not reject H_o. There is no difference in the ATM use in the two groups.

SOLUTION TO CASE II

BELL GROVE MEDICAL CENTER

Using ANOVA, the hypothesis are: H_o: $\mu_m = \mu_t = \mu_w = \mu_{t,} = \mu_f$ and H_1: The means are not the same. Reject H_o if $F > 3.06$. The ANOVA table is as follows:

Source	DF	SS	MS	F
Factor	4	411.30	102.82	15.54
Error	15	99.25	6.62	
Total	19	510.55		

H_o is rejected. The mean number of patients is not the same on each day.

From the following chart, we conclude that the number of patients is greater on Monday and Friday.

Level	N	Mean	StDev
Mon	4	36.750	1.258
Tues	4	27.000	1.826
Wed	4	26.250	2.872
Thurs	4	25.500	4.203
Fri	4	33.750	1.500

Pooled StDev = 2.572

Individual 95% CIs For Mean Based on Pooled StDev

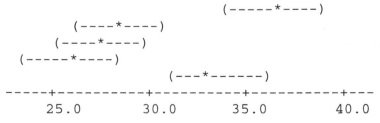

1. Coefficient of correlation or the coefficient of determination

2. Strong negative association

3. H_o: $\rho \leq 0$ H_1: $\rho > 0$ Critical value of t is 1.671 computed $t = 3.324$
   H_o is rejected, there is positive correlation.

4. X explains a total of 38 percent of the variation in Y.

5. The square of the coefficient of correlation is the coefficient of determination.

6. Net profit

7. $Y' = a + b_1 X_1 + b_2 X_2 + b_3 X_3 + b_4 X_4$

8. $163,200

9. About 86% of the variation in net profit is explained by the four variables.

10. About 68 percent of the net profits would be within 1($3000) of the estimates, about 95 percent would be within 2($3000) or $6000, of the estimates and, virtually all would be within 3($3000) of the estimates.

11. a.

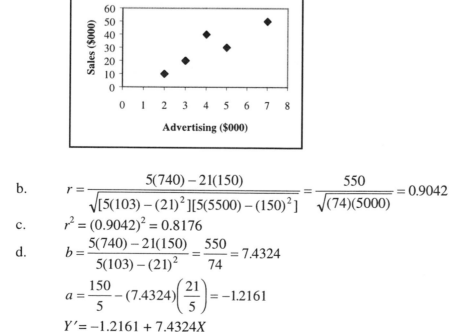

b. $r = \dfrac{5(740) - 21(150)}{\sqrt{[5(103) - (21)^2][5(5500) - (150)^2]}} = \dfrac{550}{\sqrt{(74)(5000)}} = 0.9042$

c. $r^2 = (0.9042)^2 = 0.8176$

d. $b = \dfrac{5(740) - 21(150)}{5(103) - (21)^2} = \dfrac{550}{74} = 7.4324$

      $a = \dfrac{150}{5} - (7.4324)\left(\dfrac{21}{5}\right) = -1.2161$

      $Y' = -1.2161 + 7.4324X$

e. $Y' = -1.2161 + 7.4324(4.5) = \$32.23$ in thousands

f.   Strong positive association between amount spent on advertising and monthly sales. For each additional \$1000 spent on advertising, sales increase \$7432.40.

12.   a.   0.9261

         b.   2.0469, found by $\sqrt{83.8/20}$

         c. H_0: $\beta_1 = \beta_2 = \beta_3 = \beta_4 = 0$ H_1: not all coefficients are zero

               Reject if $F > 2.87$, computed $F = 62.697$, found by 162.70/4.19.

         d.   Could delete X_2 because t-ratio (1.29) is less than the critical t value of 2.086. Otherwise reject H_0 for X_1, X_3, and X_4 because all of those t-ratios are greater than 2.086.

Below is a correlation matrix, showing all possible simple coefficients of correlation. The independent variable ATM, indicating the number of ATM transactions per month, has the strongest correlation with the dependent variable balance. There are not any strong correlations among any of the independent variables.

	Balance	ATM	Services	Debt
ATM	0.709			
Services	0.374	0.227		
Debit	0.124	−0.014	0.174	
Interest	0.197	0.090	0.026	−0.0223

Following output shows the relationship between the dependent variable, balance, and the four independent variables. The multiple coefficient of determination is 0.585. This indicates that 58.5 percent of the variation in the account balance is accounted for by the four independent variables.

The global test of hypothesis is as follows:

H_o: $\beta_1 = \beta_2 = \beta_3 = \beta_4 = 0$ H_1: Not all β_i's equal 0.

The decision rule is to reject the null hypothesis if the computed value of F is greater than 2.55. The computed value of F is 19.36, so the null hypothesis is rejected. We conclude that not all the regression coefficients equal 0.

Source	DF	SS	MS	F	p
Regression	4	12292186	3073047	19.36	0.000
Error	55	8729247	158714		
Total	59	21021432			

$s = 398.4$ $R\text{-sq} = 58.5\%$ $R\text{-sq(adj)} = 55.5\%$

Next, we can test the net regression coefficients individually to find which should remain in the regression equation and which should be dropped. The critical values of t are −2.00 and 2.00. From the column headed "t-ratio", the computed value for ATM and Services exceed the critical values and those of Debit and Interest do not. This suggests that the two independent variables debit and interest can be dropped from the analysis.

The regression equation is:

Balance = 1.75 + 90.5 ATM + 60.0 Services + 161 Debit + 219 Interest

Predictor	Coef	Stdev	t-ratio	p
Constant	174.9	167.1	1.05	0.300
ATM	90.47	12.45	7.27	0.000
Services	59.99	27.43	2.19	0.033
Debit	161.0	108.4	1.49	0.143
Interest	218.8	119.9	1.82	0.073

The computer output is a follows.

Predictor	Coef	Stdev	t-ratio	p
Constant	13.3863	0.4683	28.58	0.000
Prep	−0.01408	0.03883	−0.36	0.719
Delivery	0.00241	0.01415	0.17	0.866
Distance	0.88586	0.05162	17.16	0.000

$s = 0.7729$ R-sq = 95.7%   R-sq(adj) = 95.4%

The three independent variables explain more than 95 percent of the variation in cost. The estimated delivery cost is $0.75, found by $13.4 - 0.141(10) + 0.0024(30) + 0.866(14)$.

The compute value of F and the p-values indicate that not all the net regression coefficients equal 0. Looking at the individual regression coefficients, Distance is the only one that is significant. The others can be dropped. With only Distance as an independent the regression output is as follows.

Predictor	Coef	Stdev	t-ratio	p
Constant	13.2559	0.3158	41.98	0.000
Distance	0.89385	0.02755	32.44	0.000

$s = 0.7579$ R-sq = 95.6%   R-sq(adj) = 95.5%

Analysis of Variance

Source	DF	SS	MS	F	p
Regression	1	604.48	604.48	1052.35	0.000
Error	48	27.57	0.57		
Total	49	632.05			

The value of R-square is virtually the same and the independent variable Distance is significant. So we conclude that the only variable that is related to Cost is the Distance. The cost increases about $0.90 for each additional mile.

1.   Frequency observed and frequency expected.

2.   Contingency table

3.   Chi-square distribution

4.   6, found by $(4-1)(3-1)$

5.   Not rejected because 11.248 is less than 12.592.

6. H_o is rejected.

7.   There is no difference between the observed and the expected set of frequencies.

8.   At least interval

9.   Nominal level

10. Ordinal

11. To determine if two independent populations are the same.

12. No assumptions are necessary.

13. To determine if three or more populations are the same.

14. To determine if the distribution of differences in paired observations has a median of 0.

15. Kruskal-Wallis

16. Sign test and the Wilcoxon signed-rank test.

17. Yes

18. One-tailed

19. No, it is positively skewed.

20. The number of categories minus one.

21. H_o: Median = \$27,000 H_1: Median $\neq$ \$27,000
     Use the 0.05 significance level and the sign test. The critical values are $z < -1.96$ and $z > 1.96$.
     Count the number of values above the median, compute z, assuming a large sample, and make a
     decision.

H_o: There is no relationship between branch and whether the customer has a debit card.
H_1: There is a relationship between branch and whether a customer has a debit card.
Reject if $\chi^2 > 7.815$

Debit	1	2	3	4	Total
No	9	9	8	8	34
Yes	7	8	6	5	26
	16	17	14	13	60

The computed value of χ^2 is 0.224, so H_o is not rejected. We cannot conclude that there is a relationship between branch and whether a customer has a debit card.

CASE II

THOMAS TESTING LABS

Using the sign test: H_o: $\pi \leq 0.50$ $\quad$ H_1: $\pi > 0.50$
Reject H_o if z value is greater than 1.65. There is one tie, so n is reduced from 25 to 24.
$\mu = 24(0.5) = 12$ $\qquad$ $\sigma = \sqrt{24(0.5)(0.5)} = 2.4495$
There are 16 cases where the number of errors increased
$z = \dfrac{15.5 - 12}{2.4495} = 1.43$ $\qquad$ Do not reject H_o. The number of driving errors has not increased.

Using the Wilcoxon test:
H_o: There is no difference in the number of errors.
H_1: There are more errors with alcohol
With $n = 24$ and using the 0.05 significance level, H_o is rejected if $T \leq 91$.
The sum of the negative differences is 70.5, so H_o is rejected. We conclude that there are more errors with alcohol.

STUDY GUIDE ASSIGNMENT ANSWERS

CHAPTER 1

WHAT IS STATISTICS?

Part I Part II Part III

1. Quantitative	**6.** Discrete	**11.** Nominal	**16.** Ratio
2. Qualitative	**7.** Continuous	**12.** Interval	**17.** Ordinal
3. Quantitative	**8.** Discrete	**13.** Nominal	**18.** Ratio
4. Quantitative	**9.** Continuous	**14.** Ratio	**19.** Interval
5. Qualitative	**10.** Continuous	**15.** Ordinal	**20.** Nominal

Part IV

21. C   **22.** D   **23.** A   **24.** B   **25.** B

CHAPTER 2

DESCRIBING DATA: FREQUENCY DISTRIBUTIONS AND GRAPHIC PRESENTATION

Part I

1. B   **2.** A   **3.** B   **4.** B   **5.** C
6. C   **7.** B   **8.** C   **9.** A   **10.** D

Part II

11. Line graph for J. M. Smucker Company.

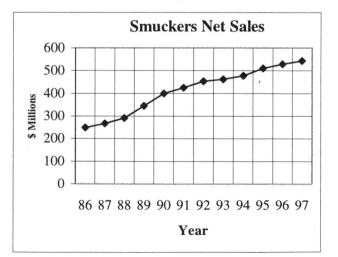

12. Pie chart

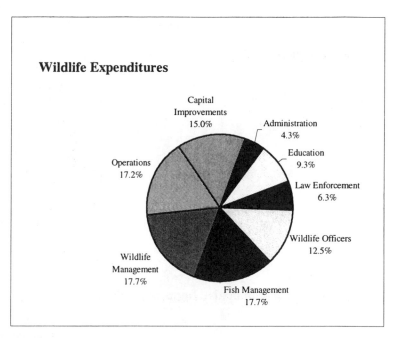

Wildlife Expenditures

13. **a. & b.** Frequency distribution and cumulative frequency distribution:

Class Limits	Frequency	Cumulative Frequency
180 up to 210	7	7
210 up to 240	6	13
240 up to 270	4	17
270 up to 300	2	19
300 up to 330	4	23
330 up to 360	1	24

c. Histogram:

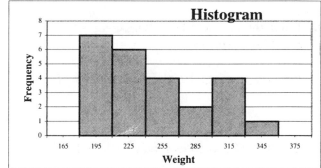

d. Frequency Polygon

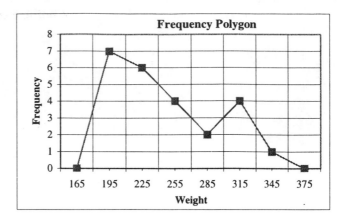

e. Less-than-cumulative frequency polygon:

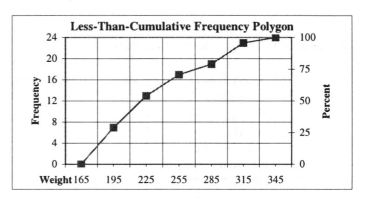

14. Using the stem and leaf plot:
    a. 23 took the test

    b. highest score = 100, lowest score = 56

    c. 16 scored 70 or higher

    d. 30.43% scored less than 70, found by: (23 −16) / 23 = 7 / 23 = 0.3043 = 30.43%

DESCRIBING DATA: MEASURES OF LOCATION

Part I

1. A	**2.** C	**3.** C	**4.** A	**5.** B
6. B	**7.** C	**8.** B	**9.** A	**10.** B

Part II

11. a. Mean: $\overline{X} = \dfrac{\Sigma X}{n} = \dfrac{6+12+7+12+8+4+5}{7} = \dfrac{54}{7} = 7.71$

    b Median is 7

    c. Mode is 12

    d. Positively skewed, mean is greater than median.

12. Average weight = 8 pounds found by:
(10 x 7.4) + (12 x 8.2) + (6 x 8.7) = 224.6/ 28 = 8.0

13. 94.3% found by $\sqrt[8]{(.957)(.953)(.955)(.95)(.947)(.937)(.938)(.907)} = \sqrt[8]{0.6246} = 0.9428$

14. Percent increase: $GM = \sqrt[16]{\dfrac{543}{157}} - 1 = \sqrt[16]{3.458598} - 1 = (1.0806 - 1) = 0.806 = 8.06\%$

15. a. Mean:

Hours	Frequency f	Class Midpoint X	fX
0 up to 10	3	5	15
10 up to 20	7	15	105
20 up to 30	15	25	375
30 up to 40	10	35	350
40 up to 50	5	45	225
Total	40		1070

$\overline{X} = \dfrac{\Sigma fX}{n} = \dfrac{1070}{40} = 26.75$

    b. Median :

$Median = L + \dfrac{\frac{n}{2} - CF}{f}(i) = 20 + \dfrac{\frac{40}{2} - 10}{15}(10) = 20 + \dfrac{10}{15}(10) = 20 + 6.67 = 26.67$

    c. Mode is 25 hours

CHAPTER 4

DESCRIBING DATA: MEASURES OF DISPERSION

Part I

1. D   2. B   3. B   4. B   5. D
6. D   7. B   8. D   9. D   10. D

Part II

11. **a.** Range: $102 - 15 = 87$
    b. Mean deviation:

$$\overline{X} = \frac{\Sigma X}{n} = \frac{\$594}{11} = \$54$$

$$MD = \frac{\Sigma\left|X - \overline{X}\right|}{n} = \frac{\$362}{11} = \$32.91$$

Revenue X	$X - \overline{X}$		Absolute Deviations
$15	| −39 |	=	$39
17	| −37 |	=	37
23	| −31 |	=	31
26	| −28 |	=	28
27	| −27 |	=	27
35	| −19 |	=	19
72	| +18 |	=	18
88	| +34 |	=	34
91	| +37 |	=	37
98	| +44 |	=	44
102	| +48 |	=	48
$594			$362

   c. Standard deviation:

X	$X - \overline{X}$	$\left|X - \overline{X}\right|$	$(X - \overline{X})^2$	X^2
15	15 − 54	39	1,521	225
17	17 − 54	37	1,369	289
23	23 − 54	31	961	529
26	26 − 54	28	784	676
27	27 − 54	27	729	729
35	35 − 54	19	361	1,225
72	72 − 54	18	324	5,184
88	88 − 54	34	1,156	7,744
91	91 − 54	37	1,369	8,281
98	98 − 54	44	1,936	9,604
102	102 − 54	48	2,304	10,404
594		362	12,814	44,890

$$s^2 = \frac{\Sigma X^2 - \frac{(\Sigma X)^2}{n-1}}{n-1} = \frac{44,890 - \frac{(594)^2}{11}}{11-1} = 1,281.40$$

d. Quartiles and median:

To locate the first quartile, let P = 25 and $L_p = (n+1)\dfrac{P}{100} = (11+1)\dfrac{25}{100} = 3$

Then locate the 3rd observation in the array which is 23. Thus Q1 = 23.

To locate the third quartile, let $P = 75$ and $L_p = (n+1)\dfrac{P}{100} = (11+1)\dfrac{75}{100} = 9$

Then locate the 9th observation in the array, which is 91. Thus Q3 = 91.

To locate the median, let P = 50 and $L_p = (n+1)\dfrac{P}{100} = (11+1)\dfrac{50}{100} = 6$

Then locate the 6th observation in the array, which is 35. Thus Q2 = the median =35

e. Box Plot:

Minimum value = 15, $Q_3 = 23$, $Q_2 = 35$ $Q_3 = 91$,   Maximum value = 102

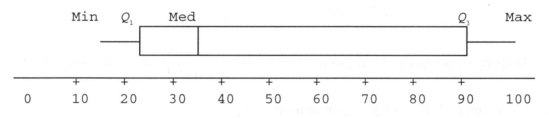

f. Positive skew since mean (54) larger than median (35)

12. a. Range = 45 – 15 = 30

# of Passengers	f	X	fX	fx²	CF
15 up to 20	3	17.5	52.5	918.8	3
20 up to 25	8	22.5	180.0	4050.0	11
25 up to 30	12	27.5	330.0	9075.0	23
30 up to 35	15	32.5	487.5	15843.8	38
35 up to 40	7	37.5	262.5	9843.8	45
40 up to 45	5	42.5	212.5	9031.3	50
Total	50		1525.0	48,762.5	

b. Standard Deviation:

$$s = \sqrt{\frac{\Sigma fX^2 - \frac{(\Sigma fX)^2}{n}}{n-1}} = \sqrt{\frac{48{,}762.50 - \frac{(1525)^2}{50}}{50-1}} = 6.776$$

c. First and Third Quartile:

$$Q_1 = L + \frac{\frac{n}{4} - CF}{f}(i) \qquad\qquad Q_3 = L + \frac{\frac{3n}{4} - CF}{f}(i)$$

$$= 25 + \frac{\frac{50}{4} - 11}{12}(5) \qquad\qquad = 30 + \frac{\frac{3(50)}{4} - 23}{15}(5)$$

$$= 25.625 \qquad\qquad\qquad = 34.833$$

d. Quartile Deviation:

$$Q.D. = \frac{Q_3 - Q_1}{2} = \frac{34.833 - 25.625}{2} = \frac{9.208}{2} = 4.604$$

13. a.
$$k = \frac{X - \overline{X}}{s} = \frac{3.3 - 6.5}{2} = -1.6 \qquad\qquad k = \frac{X - \overline{X}}{s} = \frac{9.7 - 6.5}{2} = 1.6$$

Applying Chebyshev's Theorem: $Cheb\,Th = 1 - \frac{1}{k^2} = \left(1 - \frac{1}{1.6^2}\right) = (1 - 0.39) = 0.61 = 61\%$

b. Plus or minus 2 standard deviations or about 95%.

c. Coefficient of Variation for the gallons and time spent:

For the gallons: **For the length of time spent:**

$$CV = \frac{0.75}{9.5}(100) \qquad\qquad CV = \frac{2}{6.5}(100)$$
$$= 7.9\% \qquad\qquad\qquad = 30.8\%$$

There is more relative dispersion in the time spent.

d. Coefficient of skewness for the gallons pumped:

$$sk = \frac{3(\overline{X} - \text{median})}{s} = \frac{3(9.5 - 10.0)}{0.75} = -2.0$$

The distribution is negatively skewed.

CHAPTER 5

A SURVEY OF PROBABILITY CONCEPTS

Part I

1. D	**2.** A	**3.** D	**4.** A	**5.** A
6. C	**7.** B	**8.** B	**9.** D	**10.** A

Part II

11. 38%, found by $0.30 + 0.20 - 0.12$

12. **a.** 0.78, found by $0.92 \times 0.92 \times 0.92$
  b. 0.22, found by $(1 - 0.78)$

13. Likelihood both increased = 0.2368, found by: $\dfrac{10}{20} \times \dfrac{9}{19} = 0.2368$

14. Put ratings into an array: 0.46   0.59   0.64   0.72   0.76   0.81

     a. $\dfrac{2}{6} = \dfrac{1}{3}$ **b.** $\dfrac{3}{6} = \dfrac{1}{2}$ **c.** $\overline{X} = 0.66,\ \dfrac{3}{6} = \dfrac{1}{2}$ **d.** $\dfrac{0}{6} = 0$

15. Possible outfits: $(4)(6)(10) = 240$

16. Different lists: $\quad {}_nC_r = \dfrac{n!}{r!(n-r)!} = {}_{15}C_8 = \dfrac{15!}{8!(15-8)!} = \dfrac{15!}{8!(7!)} = 6435$

17. Probability he took the bus:

$$P(NB|D) = \frac{P(NB)\,P(D|NB)}{P(B)\,P(D|B) + P(NB)\,P(D|NB)}$$

$$P(Bus|\,Late) = \frac{(0.4)(0.2)}{(0.4)(0.2) + (0.6)(0.05)} = 0.727$$

18. **a.** $P(\sim W) = 0.27$ or 27%
  b. $P(A) = 0.38$ or 38%
  c. $P(A \text{ and } W) = 0.3$ or 30%
  d. $P(A \text{ or } \sim W) = 0.57$ found by $0.38 + 0.27 - 0.08$
  e. $P(A \text{ given } W) = 0.41$ found by $0.30/0.73$

Part I:

1. D	2. A	3. B	4. C	5. A	6. C
7. B	8. D	9. D	10. C		

Part II:

11. a. Mean: $\mu = \Sigma[xP(x)] = 2.4$

Number of Connections per Two Minutes X	Probability P(X)	xP(x)	$(x-\mu)$	$(x-\mu)^2 P(X)$
0	0.1	0	0 – 2.4	(5.76)(0.1) = 0.576
1	0.2	0.2	1 – 2.4	(1.96)(0.2) = 0.392
2	0.1	0.2	2 – 2.4	(0.16)(0.1) = 0.016
3	0.4	1.2	3 – 2.4	(0.36)(0.4) = 0.144
4	0.2	0.8	4 – 2.4	(2.56)(0.2) = 0.512
Σ	1.0	2.4		$\Sigma = 1.64$

b. Standard deviation: $\sigma = \sqrt{\Sigma[(x-\mu)^2 P(x)]} = \sqrt{1.64} = 1.28$

$$P(x) = \frac{n!}{x!(n-x)!}(\pi)^x (1-\pi)^{n-x}$$

12. a. Exactly five:

$$P(5) = \frac{8!}{5!(8-5)!}(0.75)^5 (0.25)^3 = 0.208$$

b. All eight:

$$P(8) = \frac{8!}{8!(8-8)!}(0.75)^8 (0.25)^0 = 0.1$$

c. At least seven: $P(7) + P(8) = 0.267 + 0.100 = 0.367$,

$$P(7) = \frac{8!}{7!(8-7)!}(0.75)^7 (0.25)^1 = 0.267$$

d. At least one: $[1 - P(0)] = [1 - 0.000015] = 0.999985$,

$$P(0) = \frac{8!}{0!(8-0)!}(0.75)^0 (0.25)^8 = 0.000015$$

e. Expected return: $\mu = np = 8(0.75) = 6$

13. a. Ten survive: $P(10) = \dfrac{12!}{10!(12-10)!}(0.8)^{10}(0.2)^2 = 0.283$

b. At least ten: $P(\text{at least } 10) = P(10) + P(11) + P(12)$

$$= 0.283 + 0.206 + 0.069 = 0.558$$

$$P(11) = \dfrac{12!}{11!(12-11)!}(0.8)^{11}(0.2)^1 = 0.206$$

$$P(12) = \dfrac{12!}{12!(12-12)!}(0.8)^{12}(0.2)^0 = 0.069$$

14. Exactly 12:

$$P(x) = \dfrac{\mu^x e^{-\mu}}{x!}$$

$$P(12) = \dfrac{15^{12} e^{-15}}{12!} = 0.083$$

15. a. No new accounts:

$$P(x) = \dfrac{\mu^x e^{-\mu}}{x!}$$

$$P(0) = \dfrac{2^0 e^{-2}}{0!} = e^{-2} = 0.1353$$

b. At least one: $P(x = 1) = [1 - P(0)] = [1 - 0.1353] = 0.8647$

16. Two of each: $P(2sm,2fl) = \dfrac{(_6C_2)(_4C_2)}{(_{10}C_4)} = \dfrac{\left(\dfrac{6!}{2!4!}\right)\left(\dfrac{4!}{2!2!}\right)}{\left(\dfrac{10!}{4!6!}\right)} = \dfrac{3}{7} = 0.42857$

17. a. Three females and two males: $P(3f,2m) = \dfrac{(_{13}C_3)(_{15}C_2)}{(_{28}C_5)} = 0.305$

b. Five males: $P(5m) = \dfrac{(_{13}C_0)(_{15}C_5)}{(_{28}C_5)} = 0.031$

c. Five females: $P(5f) = \dfrac{(_{13}C_5)(_{15}C_5)}{(_{28}C_5)} = 0.013$

d. At least one male: $P(\text{at least } 1m) = [1 - P(0m)] = (1 - 0.013) = 0.987$

CHAPTER 7

Part I

1. A	2. D	3. D	4. C	5. C
6. B	7. B	8. A	9. D	10. B

Part II

11. **a.** 28.81%, found by $z = \dfrac{X - \mu}{\sigma} = \dfrac{120 - 100}{25} = 0.8$ from Appendix D: 0.2881

    b. 78.81%, found by (0.50 + 0.2881)

    c. 5.48%, found by (0.50 − 0.4452), $z = \dfrac{X - \mu}{\sigma} = \dfrac{60 - 100}{25} = -1.60$, Appendix D: 0.4452

    d. 18.91%, found by (0.4772 − 0.2881), Appendix D: 0.4772 for $z = \dfrac{150 - 100}{25} = 2.00$

    e. 73.33%, found by (0.2881 + 0.4452) from parts a and c

    f. 121 minutes, found by (0.50 − 0.2), $z = 0.84$, solve $0.84 = \dfrac{X - 100}{25}$

12. **a.** $P(t < 60) = 0.0018$, found by (0.50 − 0.4982), $z = \dfrac{60 - 92}{11} = -2.91$, Appendix D: 0.4982

    b. $P(t > 100) = 0.2327$, found by (0.50 − 0.2673) $z = \dfrac{100 - 92}{11} = 0.73$, Appendix D: 0.2673

    c. $P(70 < t < 90) = 0.4058$, found by (0.4772 − 0.0714)

    $z = \dfrac{70 - 92}{11} = -2.00$, Appendix D: 0.4772 $z = \dfrac{90 - 92}{11} = -0.18$, Appendix D: 0.0714

    d. $P(60 < t < 120) = 0.9928$, found by (0.4982 + 0.4946)

    $z = \dfrac{60 - 92}{11} = -2.91$, Appendix D: 0.4982 $z = \dfrac{120 - 92}{11} = 2.55$, Appendix D: 0.4946

    e. 103.44 minutes found by, (0.50 − 0.15) = 0.35, $z = 1.04$, solve $1.04 = \dfrac{X - 92}{11}$

13. 501.5 minutes or about 8 • hours, found by $(0.50 - 0.04) = 0.46$,

$z = -1.75$ (negative because z is left of the mean) solve $-1.75 = \dfrac{X - 540}{22}$

14. **a.** Mean $\mu = (0.05)(40) = 2$ Standard deviation $\sigma = \sqrt{(0.05)(40)(0.95)} = 1.3784$

b. $P(3 \text{ or more defective}) = 0.3594$, found by $(0.50 - 0.1406)$ $z = \dfrac{2.5 - 2}{1.3784} = 0.36$, Appendix D: 0.1406

c. $P(3 \text{ defective}) = 0.2215$, found by $(0.3594 - 0.1379)$

$z = \dfrac{3.5 - 2}{1.3784} = 1.09$, Appendix D: 0.3621, then $(0.50 - 0.3621) = 0.1379$

d. $P(\text{more than 4}) = 0.0351$, found by $(0.50 - 0.4649)$, $z = \dfrac{4.5 - 2}{1.3784} = 1.81$, Appendix D: 0.4649

15. **a.** Mean: $\mu = (0.60)(35) = 21$ Standard deviation $\sigma = \sqrt{(0.60)(35)(0.40)} = 2.8983$

b. $P(18 \text{ or more}) = 0.8869$, found by $(0.50 + 0.3869)$, $z = \dfrac{17.5 - 21}{2.8983} = -1.21$, Appendix D: 0.3869

c. $P(30 \text{ or more}) = 0.0017$, found by $(0.50 - 0.4983)$, , $z = \dfrac{29.5 - 21}{2.8983} = 2.93$, Appendix D: 0.4983

d. $P(<12) = 0.0005$, found by $(0.5 - 0.4995)$, $z = \dfrac{11.5 - 21}{2.8983} = -3.28$, Appendix D: 0.4995

e. $P(12 \text{ to } 30) = 0.999$, found by $(0.4995 + 0.4995)$, $z = \dfrac{30.5 - 21}{2.8983} = 3.28$, Appendix D: 0.4995 and solution from part d.

16. **a.** Mean: $\mu = (0.20)(50) = 10$ Standard deviation $\sigma = \sqrt{(0.20)(50)(0.80)} = 2.8284$.

b. $P(16 \text{ or more}) = 0.0107$, found by $(0.50 - 0.4893)$, $z = \dfrac{16.5 - 10}{2.8284} = 2.30$, Appendix D: 0.4893

c. $P(\text{Exactly } 14) = 0.0516$, found by $(0.4441 - 0.3925)$,

$z = \dfrac{14.5 - 10}{2.8284} = 1.59$, Appendix D: 0.4441 $z = \dfrac{13.5 - 10}{2.8284} = 1.24$, Appendix D: 0.3925

d. $P(7 \text{ to } 15) = 0.3211$, found by $(0.3925 - 0.0714)$

$z = \dfrac{6.5 - 10}{2.8284} = -1.24$, Appendix D: 0.3925 $z = \dfrac{9.5 - 10}{2.8284} = -0.18$, Appendix D: 0.0714

e. $P(7 \text{ to } 9) = 0.8663$, found by $(0.3925 + 0.4738)$

from d and $z = \dfrac{15.5 - 10}{2.8284} = 1.94$, Appendix D: 0.4738

Chapter 8

Sampling Methods and Sampling Distributions

Part I

1. D	**2.** A	**3.** B	**4.** A	**5.** A
6. C	**7.** B	**8.** B	**9.** A	**10.** D

Part II

11. a.   10, found by $_5C_2 = \dfrac{5!}{2!3!} = \dfrac{5 \times 4}{2} = 10$

b.

Sample Number	Bundle	Total Pencils	Mean Number of Pencils
1	1,2	16	8.0
2	1,3	20	10.0
3	1,4	21	10.5
4	1,5	22	11.0
5	2,3	16	8.0
6	2,4	17	8.5
7	2,5	18	9.0
8	3,4	21	10.5
9	3,5	22	11.0
10	4,5	23	11.5
			98.0

c.   Population mean = 9.8 found by $\dfrac{10 + 6 + 10 + 11 + 12}{5} = \dfrac{49}{5} = 9.8$

Sample mean = 9.8 found by $\dfrac{98}{10} = 9.8$

The population mean is exactly equal to the mean of the samples.

12. 31.422 up to 32.578 found by $\quad 32 \pm 2.33\left(\dfrac{2}{\sqrt{65}}\right) = 32 \pm 0.578$

13. 5.019 to 5.141 found by $\quad = 5.08 \pm 2.05\left(\dfrac{1.89}{\sqrt{4000}}\right) = 5.08 \pm 0.061$

14. 5.033 to 5.127 found by $\quad 5.08 \pm 2.05\left(\dfrac{1.89}{\sqrt{4000}}\right)\sqrt{\dfrac{10,000-4,000}{10,000-1}} = 5.08 \pm 0.047$

15. 0.4698 to 0.6421 found by $\quad 0.556 \pm 1.645\sqrt{\dfrac{0.556(1-0.556)}{90}} = 0.556 \pm 0.086 = 0.470$ to 0.642

16. 0.741 to 0.859 found by $\quad 0.8 \pm 2.575\sqrt{\dfrac{0.8 \times 0.2}{305}} = 0.8 \pm 0.059$

17. 62 days found by $\quad n = \left(\dfrac{1.96 \times 400}{100}\right)^2$

18. 193 found by $\quad n = \left(\dfrac{2.17 \times 16,000}{2500}\right)^2$

19. 1068 found by $\quad n = 0.5(1-0.5)\left(\dfrac{1.96}{0.03}\right)^2$

20. 849 people found by $\quad n = 0.5(1-0.5)\left(\dfrac{2.33}{0.04}\right)^2$

CHAPTER 9

TESTS OF HYPOTHESIS: LARGE SAMPLES

Part I

1. D	2. B	3. C	4. A	5. C
6. B	7. A	8. D	9. C	10. C

Part II

11. **a** $H_0\colon \mu = 90$ **b.** $H_0\colon \mu \geq 162{,}500$ **c.** $H_0\colon \mu \leq 100$ **d.** $H_0\colon \mu \geq 32{,}000$
$\phantom{11. \textbf{a} }H_1\colon \mu \neq 90$ $\phantom{\textbf{b.} }H_1\colon \mu < 162{,}500$ $\phantom{\textbf{c.} }H_1\colon \mu > 100$ $\phantom{\textbf{d.} }H_1\colon \mu < 32{,}000$

12. **a.** I. Reject claim that mean pulse is 90 when it is 90.

II. Accept claim that mean pulse is 90 when it is not 90.

b. I. Reject claim that mean salary is greater than or equal to $162,500 when it is greater than or equal to $162,500.

II. Accept claim that the mean salary is greater than or equal to $162,500 when it is not greater than or equal to $162,500.

c. I. Reject claim that the mean IQ is less than or equal to 100 when it is less than or equal to 100.

II. Accept claim that the mean IQ is less than or equal to 100 when it is not less than or equal to 100.

d. I. Reject claim that the mean annual income of sales associates is greater than or equal to $32,000 when it is greater than or equal to $32,000.

II. Accept claim that the mean annual income of sales associates is greater than or equal to $32,000 when it is not greater than or equal to $32,000.

13. a. $H_0: \mu \geq 40 \qquad H_1: \mu < 40$

b. Critical value is 1.645, found by $(0.50 - 0.05) = 0.45$, If $z < -1.645$, reject H_0.

c. $z = \dfrac{39 - 40}{8 / \sqrt{100}} = -1.25$

d. p-value $= P(z < -1.25) = (0.5000 - 0.3944) = 0.1056$ The p-value of $0.1056 \geq 0.05$, do not reject H_0

e. H_0 is not rejected. We do not reject the claim that it takes 40 hours to learn the statistics program.

14. $\begin{array}{l} H_0: \mu \leq 20 \\ H_1: \mu > 20 \end{array}$ Reject H_0 if $z > 1.645$ $z = \dfrac{20.8 - 20}{3.7 / \sqrt{40}} = 1.37$, therefore H_0 is not rejected.

A claim cannot be made that the mean time to side a house is more than 20 hours.

15. $\begin{array}{l} H_0: \mu_i = \mu_g \\ H_1: \mu_i \neq \mu_g \end{array}$ Reject H_0 if $z < -2.58$ or $z > 2.58$ $z = \dfrac{1100 - 1090}{\sqrt{\dfrac{(45)^2}{35} + \dfrac{(55)^2}{40}}} = 0.87$

p-value $= 2(0.5000 - 0.3078) = 0.3844$

H_0 is not rejected. There is no difference in the mean amount of increase.

16. $H_0: \mu \leq 0.20$
$H_1: \mu > 0.20$
Reject H_0 if $z > 1.645$
$$z = \frac{\frac{94}{400} - 0.200}{\sqrt{\frac{(0.20)(1-0.20)}{400}}} = 1.75$$

p-value $= (0.5000 - 0.4599) = 0.0401$, H_0 is rejected. The percent of viewers has increased.

17. $H_0: \mu \leq 0.15$
$H_1: \mu > 0.15$
Reject H_0 if $z > 1.28$
$$z = \frac{0.17 - 0.15}{\sqrt{\frac{(0.15)(1-0.15)}{1000}}} = 1.77$$

H_0 is rejected. The ad campaign is effective in increasing product identity of CherryBerry Soda.

18. $H_0: p_a \leq p_d$
$H_1: p_a > p_d$
Reject H_0 if $z > 2.33$

$$\rho_c = \frac{18 + 15}{80 + 120} = 0.165$$

$$z = \frac{\frac{18}{80} - \frac{15}{120}}{\sqrt{\frac{(0.165)(1-0.165)}{80} + \frac{(0.165)(1-0.165)}{120}}} = \frac{0.225 - 0.125}{\sqrt{\frac{(0.165)(0.835)}{80} + \frac{(0.165)(0.835)}{120}}} = 1.87$$

p-value $= (0.5000 - 0.4693) = 0.0307$, H_0 is not rejected

There is no difference in the proportion of absences on the two shifts.

19. $H_0: p_w \leq p_m$
$H_1: p_w > p_m$
Reject H_0 if $z > 1.645$

$$\rho_c = \frac{95 + 64}{300 + 180} = \frac{159}{480} = 0.33125 = 0.3313$$

$$z = \frac{\frac{64}{180} - \frac{95}{300}}{\sqrt{\frac{(0.3313)(1-0.3313)}{180} + \frac{(0.3313)(1-0.3313)}{300}}} = \frac{0.36 - 0.32}{\sqrt{\frac{(0.3313)(0.6687)}{180} + \frac{(0.3313)(0.6687)}{300}}} = 0.9014$$

Do not reject H_0 the difference can be attributed to chance.

Study Guide Assignment Answers

CHAPTER 10

TESTS OF HYPOTHESIS: SMALL SAMPLES

Part I

1. D   2. B   3. D   4. C   5. C

6. B   7. A   8. B   9. C   10. A

Part II

11. **a.**
$$H_0 : \mu \le 1750$$
$$H_1 : \mu > 1750$$
b. Reject H_0 if $t > 2.093$

c. $t = \dfrac{2017 - 1750}{867 / \sqrt{20}} = 1.377$ **d.** p-value is between 0.1 and 0.05

e. Do not reject H_0. The large sample mean is due to chance.

12. **a.** $H_0: \mu \ge 1.80$ $H_1: \mu < 1.80$ **b.** Reject H_0 if $t < -2.998$

c. $\overline{X} = \dfrac{13.7}{8} = 1.7125$ $t = \dfrac{1.7125 - 1.80}{0.21 / \sqrt{8}} = -1.179$ $s = \sqrt{\dfrac{23.77 - \dfrac{(13.7)^2}{8}}{8 - 1}} = 0.21$

d. p-value is greater than 0.10

e. Do not reject H_0. The mean time in the mall is not less than 1.8 hours.

13. **a.** $H_0 : \mu_p \le \mu_{np}$ $H_1 : \mu_p > \mu_{np}$ **b.** Reject H_0 if $t > 1.708$

c. $s_p^2 = \dfrac{(15-1)(5,500)^2 + (12-1)(6,500)^2}{25} = 35,530,000$ $t = \dfrac{62,000 - 58,000}{\sqrt{35,530,000\left(\dfrac{1}{15} + \dfrac{1}{12}\right)}} = 1.733$

d. . p-value between 0.025 and 0.05

e. H_0 is rejected. Accountants at partnership level do earn larger salaries.

14. **a** $H_0 : \mu_m \le \mu_{nm}$ $H_1 : \mu_m > \mu_{nm}$ **b.** Reject H_0 if $t > 2.492$

c. $s_p^2 = \dfrac{(14-1)(5,800)^2 + (12-1)(7,400)^2}{24} = 43,320,000$ $\quad t = \dfrac{32,741-27,839}{\sqrt{43,320,000\left(\dfrac{1}{14}+\dfrac{1}{12}\right)}} = 1.893$

d. p-value between 0.025 and 0.05

e. Do not reject H_0. The higher salary of the sample of teachers with a Master Degree is due to chance.

15. a. $H_0: \mu_d \leq 0$ $\qquad H_1: \mu_d > 0$ $\qquad$ **b.** $\qquad$ Reject H_0 if $z > 3.143$

Pilot	Before	After	d	d^2
1	255	210	45	2,025
2	230	225	5	25
3	290	215	75	5,625
4	242	215	27	729
5	300	240	60	3,600
6	250	235	15	225
7	215	190	25	625
			252	12,854

c. $t = \dfrac{36}{25.1064/\sqrt{7}} = 3.794$ $\qquad \bar{d} = \dfrac{252}{7} = 36$ $\qquad s_d = \sqrt{\dfrac{12854 - \dfrac{252^2}{7}}{7-1}} = 25.1064$

d. p-value is between 0.005 and 0.0005

e. H_0 is rejected. The diet is effective in lowering cholesterol levels

16. a. $H_0: \mu_d \leq 0$ $\qquad H_1: \mu_d > 0$ $\qquad$ **b.** $\qquad$ Reject H_0 if $t > 2.132$

c. $t = \dfrac{6.6}{4.037/\sqrt{5}} = 3.656$ $\qquad \bar{d} = \dfrac{33}{5} = 6.6$ $\qquad s_d = \sqrt{\dfrac{283 - \dfrac{(33)^2}{5}}{5-1}} = 4.037$

d. p-value is between 0.025 and 0.01

e. H_0 is rejected. The intervention plan is effective in improving scores.

Part I

1. A	**2.** C	**3.** B	**4.** D	**5.** D
6. A	**7.** A	**8.** A	**9.** C	**10.** C

Part II

11. a. $H_0: \sigma_1^2 \le \sigma_2^2$ $H_1: \sigma_1^2 > \sigma_2^2$ **b.**   Reject H_0 if $F > 2.59$

c. $F = \dfrac{1.25^2}{0.45^2} = 7.716$

d. H_0 is rejected. There is more variation in the shipments by Brown Truck.

12. a. $H_0: \sigma_1^2 \le \sigma_2^2$ $H_1: \sigma_1^2 > \sigma_2^2$ **b.** Reject H_0 if $F > 2.08$, df num $= 24$, df den $= 20$

c. $F = \dfrac{7.35^2}{5.75^2} = 1.63$

d. H_0 is not rejected. There is no difference in the variation in his golf scores when the temperature is below 65 degree or above 65 degrees.

13. a. $H_0: \mu_1 = \mu_2 = \mu_3$ H_1: Treatment means are not equal.

b. H_0 is rejected if F is greater than 3.81.

	Youngsville		Northeast		Corry		
	X	X^2	X	X^2	X	X^2	Total
	2.20	4.84	2.3	5.29	0.9	0.81	
	1.20	1.44	1.5	2.25	0.8	0.64	
	1.90	3.61	1.2	1.44	1.1	1.21	
	3.10	9.61	1.4	1.96	1.2	1.44	
	1.80	3.24	2.2	4.84	0.7	0.49	
	1.50	2.25					
T_c	11.70		8.6		4.7		25
$\sum X^2$		24.99		15.78		4.59	45.36
n_c	6		5		5		16

$$SS\,\text{Total} = \Sigma X^2 - \frac{(\Sigma X)^2}{n}$$

$$= 45.36 - \frac{25^2}{16}$$

$$= 45.36 - 39.06 = 6.30$$

$$SST = \Sigma\left(\frac{T_c^2}{n_c}\right) - \frac{(\Sigma X)^2}{n}$$

$$= \left[\frac{11.7^2}{6} + \frac{8.6^2}{5} + \frac{4.7^2}{5}\right] - \frac{25^2}{16}$$

$$= [22.82 + 14.79 + 4.42] - 39.06$$

$$= 42.03 - 39.06 = 2.97$$

$$SSE = SS\,total - SST$$

$$= 6.30 - 2.97$$

$$= 3.33$$

c. $\quad F = \dfrac{\dfrac{2.97}{2}}{\dfrac{3.33}{13}} = 5.79$

d. H_0 is rejected. The mean response time is not the same for the three companies.

14. a. $\quad H_0: \mu_A = \mu_B = \mu_C$

$\quad\quad H_1$: not all means are equal

b. H_0 is rejected if F is greater than 3.89. $\quad\quad$ **c.** $\quad F = 5.64$

d. H_0 is rejected, F is greater than 3.89. The mean length of time the toothbrushes lasted is different between brands.

```
One-Way Analysis of Variance
Analysis of Variance
Source    DF     SS       MS      F       p
Factor     2   16.93     8.47    5.64    0.019
Error     12   18.00     1.50
Total     14   34.93
                              Individual 95% CIs For Mean
                              Based on Pooled StDev
Level     N      Mean    StDev  ---------+---------+---------+------
Brand A    5    4.000    1.225            (-------*-------)
Brand B    5    2.800    1.304   (-------*-------)
Brand C    5    5.400    1.140                    (-------*-------)
                              ---------+---------+---------+------
Pooled StDev =    1.225          3.0       4.5       6.0
MTB >.
```

d. The Minitab output indicates that the means do not differ between brand A and brand B and between brand A and brand C, but do differ between brand B and brand C.

Part I

1. C	**2.** D	**3.** B	**4.** A	**5.** B
6. A	**7.** D	**8.** B	**9.** C	**10.** D

Part II

11. a. $H_0: \rho \le 0$
$H_1: \rho > 0$

b. Reject H_0 if $t > 1.771$

c. $t = \dfrac{0.45\sqrt{15-2}}{\sqrt{1-(0.45)^2}} = 1.817$

d. H_0 is rejected. The number of crimes and the number of police have a positive association.

12.

X	Y	XY	X^2	Y^2
45	22	990	2025	484
52	26	1352	2704	676
49	21	1029	2401	441
60	28	1680	3600	784
67	33	2211	4489	1089
61	32	1952	3721	1024
334	162	9214	18940	4498

a. $r = \dfrac{6(9,214)-(334)(162)}{\sqrt{(6(18,940)-334^2)(6(4,498)-162^2)}} = \dfrac{1,176.00}{1,245.19} = 0.944$

b. $H_0: \rho \le 0$ Reject H_0 if $t > 2.132$
$H_1: \rho > 0$

$t = \dfrac{0.944\sqrt{4}}{\sqrt{1-0.944^2}} = 5.72$ H_0 is rejected.

There is a positive correlation between the fuel consumption and automobile speed.

13.

X	Y	XY	X^2	Y^2
5	53	265	25	2809
5	47	235	25	2209
7	48	336	49	2304
4	50	200	16	2500
10	58	580	100	3364
12	62	744	144	3844
3	45	135	9	2025
11	60	660	121	3600
57	423	3155	489	22655

a. $r = \dfrac{8(3,155)-(57)(423)}{\sqrt{\left(8(489)-57^2\right)\left(8(22,655)-423^2\right)}} = \dfrac{1,129.00}{1,237.82} = 0.912$

b. 0.83 found by $r^2 = 0.912^2 = 0.8317$. There is a strong positive correlation between the two variables. About 83 percent of the variation between the number of cars sold is accounted for by the size of the sales staff.

c. $b = \dfrac{8(3,155)-(57)(423)}{\sqrt{8(489)-57^2}} = \dfrac{25,240-24,111}{\sqrt{3912-3249}} = \dfrac{1,129}{633} = 1.703$

$a = \dfrac{423}{8} - 1.703\left(\dfrac{57}{8}\right) = 40.741$

$Y' = 40.741 + 1.703X$

d. The equation crosses the Y-axis at 40.741. For each additional sales person, the number of cars sold will increase by about 1.7 cars.

e. $s_{yx} = \sqrt{\dfrac{22,655 - 40.741(423) - 1.703(3,155)}{8-2}} = 2.846$

f. $57.771 \pm 2.447(2.846)\sqrt{\dfrac{1}{8} + \dfrac{(10-7.125)^2}{489 - \dfrac{57^2}{8}}}$ so 57.771 plus or minus 3.301, 54.47 to 61.07

g. $57.771 \pm 2.447(2.846)\sqrt{1 + \dfrac{1}{8} + \dfrac{(10-7.125)^2}{489 - \dfrac{57^2}{8}}}$ so 57.771 plus or minus 7.707, 50.06 to 65.48

CHAPTER 13

MULTIPLE REGRESSION AND CORRELATION

Part I

1. A	2. B	3. D	4. B	5. C
6. B	7. A	8. D	9. A	10. C

Part II

11. a. The independent variable "years with firm" has the strongest correlation with the dependent variable salary.

b. None of the correlations among the independent variables are strong, so there is not a problem with mutlicollinearity.

12. a
$$H_0: \beta_1 = \beta_2 = \beta_3 = 0$$
$$H_1: \text{Not all the } \beta_i = 0$$

b. Reject H_0 if $F > 3.59$

c.
$$F = \frac{\frac{641.10}{3}}{\frac{168.94}{11}} = \frac{213.7}{15.36} = 13.91$$

Because the computed value of 13.91 is greater than the critical value of 3.59, the null hypothesis is rejected. Not all β_i equal 0.

d.
$$R^2 = \frac{641.10}{810.04} = 0.791$$

Nearly 80 percent of the variation in salary is accounted for by the set of independent variables.

13. a.

$H_0: \beta_1 = 0$	$H_0: \beta_2 = 0$	$H_0: \beta_3 = 0$
$H_1: \beta_1 \bullet 0$	$H_1: \beta_2 \bullet 0$	$H_1: \beta_3 \bullet 0$

b. Reject H_0 if $t < -2.201$ or $t > 2.201$.

c. The null hypothesis is rejected for the independent variables years and perform (t is 4.38 and 2.25, respectively). These variables should remain in the analysis. The null hypothesis is not rejected for absent, therefore this variable should be deleted.

CHAPTER 14

NONPARAMETRIC METHODS: CHI-SQUARE APPLICATIONS

Part I

1. B	2. A	3. D	4. C	5. D
6. A	7. C	8. A	9. D	10. B

Part II

11. **a.** H_0 : The proportions are all the same.
    H_1 : The proportions are not all the same.

    b. Reject H_0 if $\chi^2 > 12.592$

c.

Day of week	f_0	f_e	$(f_0 - f_e)$	$(f_0 - f_e)^2 / f_e$
Monday	20	60	−40	26.67
Tuesday	30	60	−30	15.00
Wednesday	20	60	−40	26.67
Thursday	60	60	0	0.00
Friday	80	60	20	6.67
Saturday	130	60	70	81.67
Sunday	80	60	20	6.67
Total	420			163.35

d. The null hypothesis is rejected. There is a preference for shopping on certain days of the week.

12. **a.** H_0: There is no difference between the sample data and the expected set of frequencies.
    H_1: There is a difference between the sample data and the expected set of frequencies.

b. Reject H_0 if $\chi^2 > 4.605$

c.

Category	f_0	f_e	$(f_0 - f_e)$	$(f_0 - f_e)^2 / f_e$
Refuse	140	120	20	3.33
More info.	50	60	−10	1.67
Donate	10	20	−10	5.00
Total	200	200		10.00

d. The null hypothesis is rejected. The donation pattern was different last week.

13. **a.** H_0: There is not a relationship between loan decision and the bank officer.

    H_1: There is a relationship between loan decision and the bank officer.

Study Guide Assignment Answers

b. Reject the null hypothesis if chi-square is greater than 5.991

c.

	Felix f_0	Felix f_e	Otis f_0	Otis f_e	Foxburrow f_0	Foxburrow f_e	Total
Approved	50	52.50	70	70	55	52.50	175
Not approved	10	7.50	10	10	5	7.50	25
Total	60	60.00	80	80	60	60.00	200

$$\chi^2 = \frac{(50-52.5)^2}{52.5} + \frac{(70-70)^2}{70} + \ldots + \frac{(5-7.5)^2}{7.5} = 1.904$$

d. The null hypothesis is not rejected. There is not a relationship between the loan decision and the bank officer.

14. a. H_0: The distribution is normal.

   H_1: The distribution is not normal.

b. Reject H_0 if the computed value of χ^2 is greater than 12.592.

c.

Months	Area	f_e	f_o	$f_o - f_e$	$(f_o - f_e)^2$	$f_o - f_e)^2/f_e$
below 1	0.0548	8.220	15	6.780	45.9684	5.5923
1 to 2	0.1214	18.210	18	−0.210	0.0441	0.0024
2 to 3	0.2174	32.610	42	9.390	88.1721	2.7038
3 to 4	0.2618	39.270	36	−3.270	10.6929	0.2723
4 to 5	0.2023	30.345	21	−9.345	87.3290	2.8779
5 to 6	0.1005	15.075	13	−2.075	4.3056	0.2856
6 or more	0.0418	6.270	5	−1.270	1.6129	0.2572
Total	1.0000	150.000	150			11.9915

d. The computed value of χ^2 is 11.9915, which is less than the critical value of 12.592. Hence, the null hypotheses is not rejected. We conclude that the sample could have been obtained from a normal population.

CHAPTER 15

NONPARAMETRIC METHODS: ANALYSIS OF RANKED DATA

Part I

1.	D	2.	C	3.	D	4.	D	5.	C
6.	A	7.	A	8.	B	9.	C	10.	D

Part II

11. **a.** H_0: There is no difference in the tax liability between the two firms ($\pi = 0.50$)
   H_1: There is a difference in the tax liability of the two firms. ($\pi \neq 0.50$)

   b. Reject H_0 if there are 0, 1, 2, 10, 11, or 12 + signs

   c. See Table for problem 12, for number of plus (+) signs.

   d. There are 4 plus signs so the null hypothesis is not rejected. There is no difference in the tax liability between the two accounting firms.

12. **a.** H_0: There is no difference in the tax liability between the two firms.
   H_1: There is a difference in the tax liability of the two firms.

   b. Reject H_0 if the smaller of the two rank sums is 17 or less.

   c.

Taxpayer	Sheets	Square	Differ	Absolute	Rank	R^+	R^-
Scwind	18.9	28.0	−9.1	9.1	11.0		11
Gankowski	33.1	24.8	8.3	8.3	9.5	9.5	
Virost	38.2	28.0	10.2	10.2	12.0	12.0	
Williamson	30.2	38.0	−7.8	7.8	8.0		8.0
Govito	30.7	31.7	−1.0	1.0	2.0		2.0
Trares	30.9	25.7	5.2	5.2	6.0	6.0	
Willbond	28.1	30.7	−2.6	2.6	4.0		4.0
Fowler	27.2	29.9	−2.7	2.7	5.0		5.0
Hawley	30.2	31.0	−0.8	0.8	1.0		1.0
Hall	26.2	34.5	−8.3	8.3	9.5		9.5
Sanchez	33.4	35.3	−1.9	1.9	3.0		3.0
Naymik	33.6	28.2	5.4	5.4	7.0	7.0	
Total						34.5	43.5

   d. Because the smaller rank sum is 34.5, the null hypothesis is not rejected. There is not a difference in the tax liability.

13. **a.** H_0: The two distributions are the same. H_1: The distributions are not the same.
   b. The null hypothesis is rejected if z is less than -1.65 or z is greater than 1.65.

c.

Copier A	Rank	Copier B	Rank
12,965	11	4,462	1
13,145	12	4,990	2
13,504	14	5,106	3
13,603	15	5,844	4
13,727	16	7,470	5
13,833	17	7,740	6
13,925	18	8,429	7
14,438	19	9,954	8
14,948	21	10,957	9
15,202	22	12,532	10
		13,338	13
		14,828	20
		21,641	23
		23,045	24
		28,110	25
Total	165		160

$$z = \frac{165 - \dfrac{10(10+15+1)}{2}}{\sqrt{\dfrac{10(15)(10+15+1)}{12}}} = 1.941$$

d. H_0 is rejected. $1.941 > 1.65$ **e.** There is a difference between the two distributions.

14. a.

Husband	Rank	Wife	Rank	d	d²
1	1	3	2	−1	1
20	10	18	9	1	1
3	2.5	2	1	1.5	2.25
5	5	7	6	−1	1
4	4	5	5	−1	1
16	9	19	10	−1	1
10	8	11	8	0	0
3	2.5	4	3.5	−1	1
9	7	9	7	0	0
6	6	4	3.5	2.5	
				−6.25	
					14.5

b. $r_s = 1 - \dfrac{6(14.5)}{10(99)} = 0.912$ There is a strong correlation between the ranks by the husband and the

wife.

CHAPTER 16

STATISTICAL QUALITY CONTROL

Part I

1.	B	**2.**	A	**3.**	A	**4.**	C	**5.**	D
6.	C	**7.**	D	**8.**	B	**9.**	D	**10.**	A

Part II

11.

Month	Total	Mean	Range
Jan	6.0	1.20	0.6
Feb	5.7	1.14	0.9
March	3.5	0.70	0.7
April	6.6	1.32	1.0
May	3.9	<u>0.78</u>	<u>0.9</u>
TOTAL		5.14	4.1

a. $\text{Mean} = \dfrac{5.14}{5} = 1.028$ $\qquad$ $\text{Average range} = \dfrac{4.1}{5} = 0.82$

$1.028 \pm 0.577(0.82) = 1.028 \pm 0.473$

Limits are LCL = 0.555 and UCL = 1.501

b. For range: UCL = 2.115(0.82) = 1.734 $\qquad$ LCL = 0(0.82) = 0

12. $\bar{p} = \dfrac{51}{300} = 0.17$, so $0.17 \pm 3\sqrt{\dfrac{0.17(0.83)}{30}} = 0.170 \pm 0.206$

The LCL = 0 and the UCL = 0.376

13. $\bar{c} = \dfrac{65}{15} = 4.333$ $\qquad$ $\bar{c} \pm c\sqrt{\bar{c}} = 4.333 \pm 3\sqrt{4.333} = 4.333 \pm 6.245$

The LCL = 0 and the UCL = 10.578

14. a. $P(X \le 2 | \pi = 0.10, n = 20) = 0.677$ found by, $(0.122 + 0.270 + 0.285)$

$\quad$ **b.** $P(X \le 2 | \pi = 0.20, n = 20) = 0.207$ found by $(0.012 + 0.058 + 0.137)$

15. **a.** $\bar{p} = \dfrac{39}{700} = 0.056$ so $0.056 \pm 3\sqrt{\dfrac{0.056(0.944)}{100}} = 0.056 \pm 0.069$ so

The LCL = 0 and the UCL = 0.125

b. 13 rods found by 0.125 x 100

16. **a.**

	Mean	Ran.
9:00	1.2775	0.04
11:00	1.2700	0.03
1:00	1.2800	0.04
3:00	1.2725	0.03
5:00	1.2825	0.03
TOTAL	6.3825	0.17

Average mean $= \dfrac{6.3825}{5} = 1.2765$

Average range $= \dfrac{0.17}{5} = 0.034$

$1.2765 \pm 0.729(0.034)$

The LCL = 1.252 and the UCL = 1.301

b. For range: UCL = 2.282(.034) = 0.0776

LCL = 0(0.034) = 0

Part I

1. B	**2.** A	**3.** B	**4.** D	**5.** A
6. B	**7.** C	**8.** C	**9.** A	**10.** D

Part II

11.

Year	Index
1993	100
1994	123.7
1995	100.0
1996	110.2
1997	130.5

found by $\dfrac{2.19}{1.77}(100) = 123.728$

12. \$38,452   found by $\dfrac{\$61,100}{158.9}(100)$

13. **a.** 120.04 found by $\dfrac{\$5.99}{\$4.99}(100)$ **b.** 123.50 found by $\dfrac{\$11.56}{\$9.36}(100)$

c. 123.92 found by $\dfrac{\$808.25}{\$652.25}(100)$ **d.** 124.84 found by $\dfrac{\$854.30}{\$684.30}(100)$

e. 130.98 found by $\dfrac{\$854.30}{\$652.25}(100)$

14. **a.** 125 found by $\dfrac{150}{120}(100)$ Thus the % increase is 25%

b. 125 found by $\dfrac{150}{120}(100)$

c. Net profit has increased by \$6,648 from 1990 to 1998, found by (\$52,028 − \$45,380). \$52,028 is found by (\$65,035/ 125)100

Part I

1.	B	**2.**	C	**3.**	A	**4.**	C	**5.**	B
6.	D	**7.**	B	**8.**	D	**9.**	D	**10.**	A

Part II

11. **a.**

Year	Y	t	Yt	t^2
1993	$3.19	1	3.19	1
1994	2.10	2	4.20	4
1995	2.80	3	8.40	9
1996	2.08	4	8.32	16
1997	3.15	5	15.75	25
1998	3.47	6	20.82	36
Total	16.79	21	60.68	91

$$b = \frac{\Sigma tY - (\Sigma Y)(\Sigma t)/n}{\Sigma t^2 - (\Sigma t)^2/n} = \frac{60.68 - 16.79(21)/6}{91 - (21)^2/6} = \frac{1.915}{17.5} = 0.1094$$

$$a = \frac{\Sigma Y}{n} - b\left(\frac{\Sigma t}{n}\right) = \frac{16.79}{6} - 0.1094\left(\frac{21}{6}\right) = (2.798 - 0.3829) = 2.4151$$

$$Y' = 2.4151 + 0.1094\ t$$

b.   Estimate for 1999 is $3.18, found by letting $t = 7$ in the trend equation:

$$Y' = 2.4151 + 0.1094\ t$$
$$= 2.4151 + 0.1094(7) = 2.4151 + 0.7658 = 3.1809 = \$3.18$$

	Qt	Homes	Moving Total	Moving Average	Centered Moving Average	Specific Seasonal
1992	I	5				
	II	9				
			30	7.50		
	III	8			7.625	104.918
			31	7.75		
	IV	8			7.750	103.226
			31	7.75		
1993	I	6			7.875	76.190
			32	8.00		
	II	9			8.000	112.500
			32	8.00		
	III	9			8.000	112.500
			32	8.00		
	IV	8			8.125	98.462
			33	8.25		
1994	I	6			8.375	71.642
			34	8.50		
	II	10			8.375	119.403
			33	8.25		
	III	10			8.250	121.212
			33	8.25		
	IV	7			8.250	84.848
			33	8.25		
1995	I	6			8.125	73.846
			32	8.00		
	II	10			8.125	123.077
			33	8.25		
	III	9				
			27			
	IV	8				

12.

Year	I	II	III	IV	
1992			104.918	103.226	
1993	76.190	112.500	112.500	98.462	
1994	71.642	119.403	121.212	84.848	
1995	73.846	123.077			
Total	221.678	354.980	338.630	286.536	Total
Mean	73.893	118.327	112.877	95.512	400.608
Typical Index	73.781	118.147	112.705	95.367	400.0000

CHAPTER 19

AN INTRODUCTION TO DECISION MAKING

Part I

1. C	2. D	3. B	4. A	5. A
6. B	7. C	8. C	9. A	10. B

Part II

11. a.

Acts	Improves	Recession
Build new	$100,000	−$40,000
Expand	25,000	−5,000
Do nothing	0	0

    b. $E(A_1) = 0.25\ (\$100{,}000) + 0.75\ (-\$40{,}000) = -\$5{,}000$

       $E(A_2) = 0.25\ (\$25{,}000) + 0.75\ (-\$5{,}000) = \$2{,}500$

       $E(A_3) = 0.25\ (0) + 0.75\ (0) = 0$

    c. $EMV = 0.25\ (\$100{,}000) + 0.75\ (0) = \$25{,}000$

       $EVPI = (\ \$25{,}000 - \$2{,}500\ ) = \$22{,}500$

    d. Opportunity loss table

Acts	Improves	Recession
Build new	0	$40,000
Expand	$75,000	5,000
Do nothing	100,000	0

    e. The decision alternative with the largest expected value is to expand the current facility. The cost of the uncertainty is $22,500. This is the expected value of perfect information.

Irwin/McGraw-Hill

Instructor's Manual to accompany STATISTICAL TECHNIQUES IN BUSINESS AND ECONOMICS 10/E by Mason, Lind, and Marchal.

We hope this manual and the text are error free and easy for you to use. Invariably, however, there are errors. We would appreciate knowing about such errors as soon as possible so that we can correct them in subsequent printings and future editions. Please help us by using this postage-paid form to report any that you find. Thank you.

Attention: R. Hercher

Name_____ School_____

Office Phone _____

Please fold and seal so that our address is visible, and mail.

(fold)

(fold)

Irwin/McGraw-Hill

Instructor's Manual to accompany STATISTICAL TECHNIQUES IN BUSINESS AND ECONOMICS 10/E by Mason, Lind, and Marchal.

We hope this manual and the text are error free and easy for you to use. Invariably, however, there are errors. We would appreciate knowing about such errors as soon as possible so that we can correct them in subsequent printings and future editions. Please help us by using this postage-paid form to report any that you find. Thank you.

Attention: R. Hercher

Name_____ School_____

Office Phone _____

Please fold and seal so that our address is visible, and mail.

(fold)

(fold)

Irwin/McGraw-Hill

Instructor's Manual to accompany STATISTICAL TECHNIQUES IN BUSINESS AND ECONOMICS 10/E by Mason, Lind, and Marchal.

We hope this manual and the text are error free and easy for you to use. Invariably, however, there are errors. We would appreciate knowing about such errors as soon as possible so that we can correct them in subsequent printings and future editions. Please help us by using this postage-paid form to report any that you find. Thank you.

Attention: R. Hercher

Name_____ School_____
Office Phone _____

Please fold and seal so that our address is visible, and mail.

Irwin/McGraw-Hill
Instructor's Manual to accompany STATISTICAL TECHNIQUES IN BUSINESS AND ECONOMICS 10/E by Mason, Lind, and Marchal.

We hope this manual and the text are error free and easy for you to use. Invariably, however, there are errors. We would appreciate knowing about such errors as soon as possible so that we can correct them in subsequent printings and future editions. Please help us by using this postage-paid form to report any that you find. Thank you.

Attention: R. Hercher

Name_____ School_____
Office Phone _____

Please fold and seal so that our address is visible, and mail.

BUSINESS REPLY MAIL
FIRST-CLASS MAIL   PERMIT NO. 204   OAKBROOK, IL

POSTAGE WILL BE PAID BY ADDRESSEE

ATTENTION: R. T. Hercher

THE McGRAW-HILL COMPANIES
RICHARD D. IRWIN
1333 BURR RIDGE PKY.
BURR RIDGE, IL 60521-0085

(fold)

(fold)

Irwin/McGraw-Hill
Instructor's Manual to accompany STATISTICAL TECHNIQUES IN BUSINESS AND ECONOMICS 10/E by Mason, Lind, and Marchal.

We hope this manual and the text are error free and easy for you to use. Invariably, however, there are errors. We would appreciate knowing about such errors as soon as possible so that we can correct them in subsequent printings and future editions. Please help us by using this postage-paid form to report any that you find. Thank you.

Attention: R. Hercher

Name_____ School_____
Office Phone _____

(fold)

(fold)